This Book is Dedicated to
A.T. (Tom) Turnbull

As you will soon see, this isn't your ordinary font book. That's only appropriate, because Tom Turnbull wasn't your ordinary teacher.

When I was a junior at the University of Kentucky School of Journalism, I had a Typography class; the text was Graphics of Communication, by Tom Turnbull and Russell N. Baird.

I loved that class. I think it was because the book was easy to read and explained things so well. (As we have all discovered, not every college text is like that.) Well, that textbook is in its 8th edition now, and it is still the definitive book on the topic. Many thousands of college students over the past 35+ years have used Turnbull & Baird's book for their classes.

For most students, their exposure to the wisdom of Turnbull & Baird ended with that one class.

I was one of the lucky few. After graduating from the University of Kentucky, I worked for a year, then went back to school. I received a graduate assistantship at the Ohio University School of Journalism. By the luck of the draw, I was assigned to work with Prof. Turnbull.

The first time I met him, I discovered a lot about this special man. When I addressed him as "Professor Turnbull," he immediately smiled and said, "Call me Tom."

That was how my year of working side by side with a legend began.

Tom soon discovered my love for advertising and graphics, and by the second week of school, on a Thursday afternoon, he said, "How about coming to the house for hamburgers tonight? I called Avanelle and told her to put another one on the stove."

That began my weekly visits to Tom's family for their Thursday hamburger dinner. That was the beginning of a relationship that was more like father-son than teacher-student.

In class, I discovered someone with a great talent for teaching, and outside of class, I discovered a mentor who would literally teach me something new every day.

And when I did all the "grunt work" for a research project that he had published in a scholarly journal, I was stunned to see that he had given me equal billing as the author. I never knew another teacher who did that for his graduate assistant.

For one magical year, Tom was my teacher, my mentor, my hero, my role model. And when the year ended, I was never far away from him. I would visit him as often as possible, and when I married and had children, my family was welcomed for Thursday hamburgers at the Turnbulls. Even though miles separated us, the phone kept us connected. For many years, I kept in touch with him on a regular basis. We had developed a special bond, and he loved to hear what new things "his boy" had been doing. Unfortunately, Tom died all too young.

Tom was not only a great teacher, but he was a person who changed the lives of many of his students. I happened to be one of the lucky ones.

Thanks, Tom. You were one of a kind.

Back in the 1950s, when I was first exposed to a typography class in college, I learned that there were five basic type categories:

ROMAN
GOTHIC
SCRIPT
CURSIVE
ORNAMENTAL

At the time, those five categories seemed adequate. After all, "type" then was most often the result of hot metal, not film, and most type books were essentially specimen books from a single type source. They acted as catalogs for their type products. A type book with 200 font families was big. Then, as now, most type books look something like this:

Qwerty is the meaning of life.
Qwerty is the meaning of life.
Qwerty is the meaning of life.
Qwerty is the meaning of life.

This was what font books looked like 35 years ago, and it's pretty much what most of them look like now. (By the way, one of the best font reference books of all time is Ben Rosen's *Type and Typography*, which is still available at used book websites such as **bibliofind.com** and others.)

However, typography has undergone a revolution in recent years. The Macintosh has changed all the rules about type (Even if you work on a PC). Metal type is now "antique", and unusual fonts are no longer something available only from "type houses". The digital revolution has changed everything, and now it's time for a change in type books.

As I work with type on a regular basis, I have come to realize there is a need for a font book that is a useful tool for people in the graphics world. Specifically, I wanted to see a font book that would:

1. Show thousands of fonts, from all the best sources, not just from one company.

2. List the source, so I can buy the fonts I want. (Many of the fonts shown here are available immediately via internet download.)

3. Have more than five broad categories of type. I wanted to be able to look for a "typewriter" look, or a "cartoon" look. (Previously, you could spend a lot of time going through every page of a font book, trying to find what you wanted. I wanted a book that would be as easy for you to use as possible.)

4. Finally, I wanted a font book that didn't have one mind-numbing sentence repeated time after time in the book.

This is the book I wanted.

To the type producers whose products are shown here, this will be a super catalog with perhaps 20,000 copies in worldwide distribution. But to the designer—the font user—this should be a very user-friendly single sourcebook for a huge variety of fonts from a large number of type firms.

One short note on how this book is organized: You *will* find sections with Serif and Sans Serif fonts (just like the old font books), but beyond that, I have tried to define many other categories with sections such as:

COMIC BOOK
RETRO
Calligraphic
Grunge

and a whole lot more. On each page, the fonts are all shown in 30 point size, to give you some feel for the effective proportion of each font.

This is the book I've wanted for a long time. I hope you find it very useful.

David E. Carter

The Big Book of 5,000 Fonts

(and where to get them)

David E. Carter

The Big Book of 5,000 Fonts

First published in 2001 by HBI,
an imprint of HarperCollins Publishers
10 East 53rd Street
New York, NY 10022-5299

Hardcover ISBN: 0-06-093803-X
Flexibinding ISBN: 0-8230-0489-9

Distributed in the U.S. and Canada by
Watson-Guptill Publications
770 Broadway
New York, NY 10003-9595
Tel: (800) 451-1741
          (732) 363-4511 in NJ, AK, HI
Fax: (732) 363-0338

Distributed throughout the rest of the world by
HarperCollins International
10 East 53rd Street
New York, NY 10022-5299
Fax: (212) 207-7654

First published in Germany by Nippan
Nippon Shuppan Hanbai
Deutschland GmbH
Krefelder Strasse 85
D-40549 Dusseldorf
Tel: (0211) 5048089
Fax: (0211) 5049326
nippan@t-online.de

ISBN: 3-931884-95-3

Printed in Hong Kong by Everbest Printing Company through Four Colour
Imports, Louisville, Kentucky.

LIKE MOST FIFTIES KIDS, I GREW UP READING COMIC BOOKS.

AbsolutelyFabulous—Regular • Comicraft

WE DIDN'T HAVE A LOT TO DO.

AchtungBaby • Comicraft

We had only 3 TV channels then.

Adamantium—Fang • Comicraft

Unlike today, when we have 150+.

Adamantium—Talon • Comicraft

150 CHANNELS? YEAH.

Alchemite—BoldItalic • Comicraft

AND NOTHING TO WATCH.

Alchemite—Italic • Comicraft

BUT I DIGRESS. AS I SAID,

Alchemite—Regular • Comicraft

WE READ COMICS A LOT.

AstroCityInt—BoldItalic • Comicraft

WE LEARNED LOTS OF STUFF

AstroCityInt—Italic • Comicraft

JUST BY READING COMICS.

AstroCityInt—Regular • Comicraft

LIKE: CRIME DOES NOT PAY

Bithead—Bark • Comicraft

AND GOOD GUYS WIN.

Bithead—Byte • Comicraft

THE COMICS TAUGHT US LOTS OF THINGS.

BrontoBurger—Medium • Comicraft

BrontoBurger—WellDone • Comicraft

SKINNY GUYS AT THE BEACH...

CarryOnScreaming • Comicraft

WHERE SOME BULLY KICKED SAND IN

Chills • Comicraft

THE SKINNY GUYS' FACE. RATS!

ClobberinTime—Crunchy • Comicraft

THE GIRLS LAUGHED; POOR GUY.

ClobberinTime—Smooth • Comicraft

He left humiliated. But...

Comicrazy—BoldItalic • Comicraft

the skinny guy saw an ad

Comicrazy—Italic • Comicraft

in the back of a comic book,

Comicrazy—Roman • Comicraft

FOR CHARLES ATLAS. BODYBUILDER!

Destroyer—Open • Comicraft

THE GUY ANSWERED THE AD, AND

Destroyer—Outline • Comicraft

BEFORE LONG, HE WAS STRONG!!

Destroyer—Solid • Comicraft

He went back to the beach, and this time,

DivineRight—Regular • Comicraft

HE KICKED BUTT! BIG TIME. YEAH!

DoubleBack—Future • Comicraft

EVEN THE ADS TAUGHT US.

I WAS NEVER A SKINNY KID,

BUT I NEVER KICKED SAND AT A

SKINNY GUY. I KNEW BETTER.

I HAD READ THE ADS. THEY'D GET ME BACK.

I WASN'T ABOUT TO HAVE THEM GET STRONG, AND FIND ME.

COMICS BROUGHT OUT SOME REAL FEARS.

LIKE THE SCARY COMICS. THEY WORKED.

I'D READ THEM AT BEDTIME.

And then, I'd hide under the bed covers.

I finally found the solution to this problem.

The fears never went away. No, not at all.

I just stopped reading that stuff.

C

C Superman was a big favorite of mine.

Hooky—Solid • Comicraft

I almost named my 2nd child "Clarke".

IncyWincySpider • Comicraft

EXCEPT SHE WAS A GIRL.

JimLee—BoldItalic • Comicraft

CLARK KENT—REPORTER.

JimLee—Italic • Comicraft

I WANTED TO BE A WRITER, TOO.

JimLee—Regular • Comicraft

I WANTED X-RAY VISION!!!

JoeMad—BoldItalic • Comicraft

DON'T EVEN ASK ME WHY.

JoeMad—Italic • Comicraft

BECAUSE I WON'T TELL YOU.

JoeMad—Regular • Comicraft

I REALLY LIKED SUPERMAN.

KissAndTellInt—BoldItalic • Comicraft

ONCE AN ALLERGIST ASKED

KissAndTellInt—Italic • Comicraft

"YOU HAVE ANY ALLERGIES?"

KissAndTellInt—Regular • Comicraft

"JUST KRYPTONITE," I SAID, SERIOUSLY.

Manganese—Open • Comicraft

HE DIDN'T HAVE ANY MEDICINE FOR THAT ONE.

Manganese—Outline • Comicraft

GUYS IN MY NEIGHBORHOOD LOVED COMICS.

Manganese—Solid • Comicraft

EVERY SO OFTEN, WE'D TRADE COMIC BOOKS.

Meltdown • Comicraft

ONE GUY WOULD PULL A WAGON FULL.

MonsterMash • Comicraft

HE'D GO TO HIS FRIENDS' HOUSES AND TRADE.

PhasesOnStunInt • Comicraft

I always liked Archie. And Jughead.

PulpFiction • Comicraft

AND VERONICA. WOW!

Resistancels—Futile • Comicraft

VERONICA. SHE WAS HOT!

Resistancels—Useless • Comicraft

MY HEART THROBBED!

RunningWithScissors • Comicraft

But she was a cartoon!

SchoolsOut—Open • Comicraft

Even so, Veronica was IT!

SchoolsOut—Solid • Comicraft

SHE WENT TO RIVERDALE HIGH.

Sez—Who • Comicraft

JUGHEAD WAS A REALLY FUNNY GUY.

Sez—You • Comicraft

And Archie's Rival—Reggie, the rich kid.

Spills • Comicraft

C

Comic Books Were a Major Medium.

We Didn't Have CNN.

Or Cable TV at All...

So Kids Spent a Lot of

Time Reading Comic Books. All Very Much "G" Rated.

Not to Mention the Comics

that appeared in all the daily newspapers.

There Were Lots of Stories

to be found in the "funny papers" every day.

There was a coach named Gil Thorpe, a nice guy.

And Little Abner Yokum!

Li'l Abner Was a Huge Hit.

And Daisy Mae Was "R" Rated.

I mean, her outfits showed a lot of flesh.

YuletideLog • Comicraft

Even for a comic strip. Oh, Daisy Mae!!

Zoinks • Comicraft

LITTLE ABNER WAS A HUGE SUCCESS.

Buffalo Joe—BoldOblique • TypeArt

THE STRIP BECAME PART OF OUR POP CULTURE.

Dead Zone—Bold • TypeArt

"SADIE HAWKINS DAY" WAS A DOGPATCH THING.

Dead Zone—Medium • TypeArt

OK. DOGPATCH WAS THEIR HOME. IN THE HILLS.

Dead Zone—Regular • TypeArt

WE AREN'T TALKING HOLLYWOOD HILLS.

Horror Show—Regular • TypeArt

Sadie Hawkins Day was where

Scratchpad—Italic • TypeArt

women could pursue men,

Scratchpad—Regular • TypeArt

CATCH THEIR MAN, AND THEN MARRY HIM...

Sideshow—Oblique • TypeArt

IN HIGH SCHOOLS ALL OVER THE

Sunday Best—Oblique • TypeArt

USA, "SADIE HAWKINS DAY"

Sunday Best—Regular • TypeArt

MEANT GIRLS COULD ASK GUYS.

Sunday Best—Shadows • TypeArt

C

WHAT A CONCEPT. GIRLS COULD

ASK OUT THE GUYS. (1950S)

TODAY THINGS HAVE CHANGED.

I don't think they have "Sadie

Hawkins" dances anymore. Today,

a girl can ask a guy to go out. I think

that's a very good change. Instead

of "Sadie Hawkins Day", now we

could have "Steven Hawkin Day"

and girls could ask out nerds.

Not that being a nerd isn't OK.

Being a nerd is definitely OK;

ask Bill Gates, Member FDIC.

If I had Bill Gates money:

I would do a lot of stuff.

Some very good things, and a

few really selfish, fun things.

I WOULD GIVE A LOT OF MONEY TO

FUND SCHOLARSHIPS AT UNIVERSITIES.

AND THEN, THERE'S "WORLD PEACE."

I WOULD GIVE MONEY TO EVERY

MISS AMERICA CONTESTANT WHO

WOULD AVOID SAYING,

"I WANT WORLD PEACE."

Is there anyone who doesn't want world peace?

OK. I forgot about those people who throw bombs.

C ANYWAY, IF I HAD GATES' MONEY

Bertram • ITC/Fontek (Creative Alliance)

I WOULD DO SOME GOOD THINGS

Boink • ITC/Fontek (Creative Alliance)

and then I would just buy stuff.

Britches—Script • Fonthaus (Creative Alliance)

Selfish Stuff, just for ME.

Comic Strip Classic Italic • G. Mariscalchi (C.A.)

I would buy 365 pair of sox.

Comic Strip Classic Regular • G. Mariscalchi (C.A.)

EACH YEAR, I'D BUY 365 PAIR OF SOX.

Comic Strip Regular • G. Mariscalchi (C.A.)

THERE'S NOTHING LIKE THE FEEL

Comic Strip Italic • G. Mariscalchi (C. Alliance)

of new sox on your feet.

Comic Strip Poster • G. Mariscalchi (C. Alliance)

And I'd have a lot of really neat ties.

Comix • Richard Yeend (Creative Alliance)

EXCEPT, I DON'T WEAR TIES,

Davison Zip Bold • Photolettering (C. Alliance)

but ties are so darned neat.

Dynamo • Creative Alliance

There are lots of great tie designs.

Fancy Extended • Fonthaus (Creative Alliance)

Too bad they're all upside down.

Fancy Extended Outline • Fonthaus (C. Alliance)

To me, they're upside down.

Fumo Dropshadow • Mecanorma (C. Alliance)

What else would I want to buy?

Graphite—Black • David Siegel (C. Alliance)

Every style of Gucci loafer available.

Graphite—BlackCondensed • David Siegel (C.A.)

And, lots of blue jeans.

Graphite—BlackExtended • David Siegel (C.A.)

Yeah, I'd wear Gucci loafers with blue jeans! I would.

Graphite—BlackNarrow • David Siegel (C.A.)

Every day is "Casual Day".

Graphite—BlackWide • David Siegel (C.A.)

I'd buy a new Wilson A2000 glove,

Graphite—Bold • David Siegel (C. Alliance)

even though I'm too old to play baseball anymore.

Graphite—BoldCondensed • David Siegel (C.A.)

The smell of a new ball glove...

Graphite—BoldExtended • David Siegel (C.A.)

the smell of a new ball glove is like flowers in spring.

Graphite—BoldNarrow • David Siegel (C.A.)

Ask any guy who played.

Graphite—BoldWide • David Siegel (C. Alliance)

Ask any guy who ever played the game.

Graphite—Demi • David Siegel (C. Alliance)

The smell of a new glove, and a new baseball...

Graphite—DemiCondensed • David Siegel (C.A.)

C

C Baseball was THE game.
Graphite—DemiExtended • David Siegel (C.A.)

When I was growing up, baseball was THE game.
Graphite—DemiNarrow • David Siegel (C.A.)

We played all day, 'til dark.
Graphite—DemiWide • David Siegel (C.A.)

Some days, we would bat 30 times.
Graphite—Light • David Siegel (C. Alliance)

Today, kids don't know that joy. Too much stuff to do.
Graphite—LightCondensed • David Siegel (C.A.)

Now, it's "batting practice," five cuts
Graphite—LightExtended • David Siegel (C.A.)

and then lay down a bunt. FIVE cuts! That's no way to learn.
Graphite—LightNarrow • David Siegel (C.A.)

When I was growing up,
Graphite—LightWide • David Siegel (C.A.)

we all wanted to play in the majors.
Graphite—Regular • David Siegel (C. Alliance)

None of us ever made it, though. Not one.
Graphite—RegularCondensed • David Siegel (C.A.)

Young dreams die hard.
Graphite—RegularExtended • David Siegel (C.A.)

I remember the day my "big league" dream died.
Graphite—RegularNarrow • David Siegel (C.A.)

A new kid moved to town.
Graphite—RegularWide • David Siegel (C.A.)

He came over one day, "Wanna play catch?"

GraphiteBlackCondOblique • David Siegel (C.A.)

"Sure," I said. We went out.

GraphiteBlackExtendedOblique• D. Siegel (C.A.)

"Hit me some flies," he said to me.

GraphiteBlackOblique • David Siegel (C.A.)

So I picked up a bat and hit to him three times.

GraphiteBoldCondOblique • David Siegel (C.A.)

He caught each one.

GraphiteBoldExtended • David Siegel (C.A.)

Then he came in to hit to me.

GraphiteBoldOblique • David Siegel (C.A.)

I stood where he had been; he hit a ball to me.

GraphiteDemiCondOblique • David Siegel (C.A.)

It went 40 feet behind me.

GraphiteDemiExtendedOblique • D. Siegel (C.A.)

As I turned and looked, my heart (gulp)

GraphiteDemiOblique • David Siegel (C.A.)

as I turned and looked, my heart began to ache.

GraphiteLightCondOblique • David Siegel (C.A.)

This new kid was better than me

GraphiteLightExtendedOblique • D. Siegel (C.A.)

and he was a year younger then me.

GraphiteLightOblique • David Siegel (C.A.)

My Major League Dream died that day.

GraphiteRegCondOblique • David Siegel (C.A.)

C From that day on, baseball

GraphiteDemiExtendedOblique • D. Siegel (C.A.)

never meant quite as much to me.

GraphiteDemiOblique • David Siegel (C.A.)

So I began to make a new "career plan." Plan B.

GraphiteLightCondOblique • David Siegel (C.A.)

Plan B was to become a writer.

GraphiteLightExtendedOblique • D. Siegel (C.A.)

As it turned out, an advertising writer.

GraphiteLightOblique • David Siegel (C.A.)

That career worked out pretty well. Still is.

GraphiteRegCondOblique • David Siegel (C.A.)

If I had been a baseball player,

GraphiteRegExtendedOblique • D. Siegel (C.A.)

I would have been a "utility infielder",

GraphiteRegularOblique • David Siegel (C.A.)

NOT A STAR, CERTAINLY NOT A SUPERSTAR.

Laura • ITC/Fontek (Creative Alliance)

I WOULD HAVE BEEN A BETTER COACH THAN A BALL PLAYER.

Ragtime • ITC/Fontek (Creative Alliance)

BUT, THINGS WORKED OUT OK.

Squash MN • Mecanorma (Creative Alliance)

I STILL DREAM OF BASEBALL.

Squash MN Ot • Mecanorma (Creative Alliance)

IN MY DREAMS I'M UP THERE.

ActionPacked • Fonthead

I'M IN THE MAJOR LEAGUES.

BUT I'M NOT IN THE GAME YET.

I'M GOING TO PINCH HIT,

BUT I NEVER GET IN THE GAME.

AND IN THOSE DREAMS MY TEAM

IS ALWAYS THE CINCINNATI REDS

OR THE NEW YORK YANKEES.

C

And, I'd get some neat cars. Old cars.

Kobalt—Black • flashfonts

The cars of today are nice but,

Kobalt—Bold • flashfonts

THEY JUST DON'T HAVE THE STYLE....

Kobalt—Kartoon • flashfonts

THE STYLE OF THE 1950'S CARS.

Love—Open • flashfonts

I MEAN, LOOK AT THE '53 CHEVY,

Love—Solid • flashfonts

OR A 1956 CHEVY BEL AIR,

Love—Stoned • flashfonts

or, the ultimate, the '57 Chevy.

Magneto—Bold • flashfonts

Compare any 1957

Magneto—BoldExtended • flashfonts

with a 2001,

Magneto—SuperBoldExtended • flashfonts

and the old car wins.

NeonStream • flashfonts

I love to see old cars on the road; and in my driveway.

Ojaio—Light • flashfonts

So, if I had all the money of Bill Gates, after World Peace,

Ojaio—Regular • flashfonts

I WOULD BUY SOME VERY FUN 50'S CARS.

Peace—Open • flashfonts

FIRST CAR I WOULD BUYZ NO DOUBT.

Peace—Outline • flashfonts

R

IT WOULD BE A 1961 FORD FALCON.

Peace—Solid • flashfonts

The Ford Falcon Futura was my first.

Primitiv Black • flashfonts

First new car: a 1961 Falcon Futura.

ProgressivRegular • flashfonts

I was just 18, and

Raceway • flashfonts

I saw it there in the window, Love!

Rocket • flashfonts

I FELL IN LOVE WITH THE 1961 FALCON FUTURA.

RocketGothic • flashfonts

My heart skipped a beat.

Streamline—Light • flashfonts

The moment I saw Her,

Streamline—LightExtended • flashfonts

I KNEW I HAD TO HAVE HER BECAUSE SHE ALREADY HAD ME

Jackrabbit's Bar & Grill • Synfonts

I took her home with me.

Omaha • Synfonts

You never forget the first car.

Omaha—Thin • Synfonts

Payment $76.67

Trumen • Synfonts

I had her 4 yrs-

college years.

White exterior,

red interior,

bucket seats,

I can feel her now. I see her.

Ten years ago, I began to have

dreams about her.

I KNEW WHY.

I WANTED

MY CAR BACK

Someday The Car Will Return

and I will have my best car again

Did you ever see a Rolls Royce Silver Cloud? With huge front fenders?

THAT IS THE ULTIMATE OLD CAR

EXCEPT FOR THE 1961 FALCON.

THE ROLLS IS A CLASSIC.

IMAGINE HAVING AN OLD ROLLS.

and driving it through McDonald's at lunch, and ordering a burger.

Then, when you get served, ask "Could I have some grey poupon?"

That would be a lot of fun. Especially if the car has right-hand drive.

Why do the English drive on the right of the car, and we on the left?

I don't know the answer to that one. Someday, I will look up the answer.

Where will I look up that information? Why, on the internet, of course.

The internet has just about everything you could possibly want to know

except, much of the stuff on the internet just isn't true. Or even real.

There's a lot of satire on the internet. Many people don't know...

many people can't tell satire from actual, real stuff.

A friend sent me a very concerned e-mail about "Satanistic Harry Potter" and kids.

Seems like this article said that Harry Potter was replacing Jesus in kids' hearts.

The article painted a pretty vivid picture of Potter's influence, and had a quote from a 10-year old girl.

The girl was quoted as saying, "After reading Harry Potter, I just don't have any interest in church now."

Yes, my friend was most concerned about the state of things in Harry Potter's world.

Only one problem. He failed to check the source of the article. Yes, check the SOURCE!

What was the source? A satirical web site—www.onion.com. Check it out. It's extremely funny.

And nothing in it is real. Not even close to real.

Like before the 2000 election, there was one item:

It had a photo of Bill Clinton wearing a neat uniform...

much like Col. Khadaffi wears...

The article's headline was

"Clinton suspends elections

Declares himself President...

CLINTON 'PRESIDENT FOR LIFE' "

That's what the article said. Nice idea.

Yes, onion.com is a funny web site.

CHECK IT OUT SOME TIME. FUNNY.

Just don't send copies to friends

about the "worrisome" events.

ANOTHER GREAT WEB SITE THAT IS COOL...

IT HAS A GREAT UNIQUE CONCERN.

Check out www.darwinawards.com.

DARWIN AWARDS PAYS TRIBUTE, SORTA, TO THOSE

WHO DIED IN SOME STUPID WAY...AND THE

DARWIN AWARD IS A SPOOF, BASED ON

THE FACT THAT BY DYING STUPIDLY, EARLY ON,

THESE POOR FOLKS HAVE DEPRIVED FUTURE

GENERATIONS OF THEIR SHALLOW GENE POOL.

Seems kind of gruesome, at first, anyway,

but check out darwinawards.com and see

just how stupid some people can be.

Of course, it's the final act of stupidity for them.

One guy decided to sleep in a dumpster. They found him

at the city dump. In about 100 pieces. Dumb.

One "winner" was juggling a hand grenade. A live one.

Except when it exploded, he was the dead one.

Another Darwin "winner" had a big bar tab--180 bucks.

Instead of paying, he had one last drink, then left

THE BAR AND JUMPED IN A RIVER, HOPING TO SWIM AWAY

and died not paying the bar bill.

He was a better drinker than

he was a swimmer. Too bad.

His "last drink" WAS his last.

At least he saved 180 bucks.

There was a guy who tried to

SIPHON GAS FROM A GAS TANK.

HE COULDN'T DO IT.

THE GAS WASN'T COMING UP.

HE WAS BAFFLED. SO...

...he needed to see

R EXACTLY WHAT THE

PROBLEM WAS. HE

decided that he needed more light to see,

so this bright fellow lit a match to see better.

Ka-BOOM. Another one bites the dust.

Back last winter, two toll collectors had

a big snowball fight. With snowballs.

One of the guys reached out and scooped some snow off a truck—a MOVING truck.

Not a very smart idea. He got his hand caught in the truck, and was dragged to his death.

ANOTHER GUY, IN GHANA 23-YEARS

old, bought a solution to

protect himself from unfriendly tribesmen.

He and 15 of his friends bought a magic potion.

THE POTION WAS SUPPOSED TO HELP.

THE SOLUTION WAS TO BE USED TO MAKE

THEM BULLETPROOF.

YES, THAT'S WHAT I SAID,

"MAKE THEM BULLETPROOF."

HE USED THE POTION.

HE RUBBED IT ON HIS BODY FOR TWO WEEKS. TWO LONG WEEKS.

NOW, IT WAS TIME to test the potion.

So, he volunteered to stand before his friends

AND TEST THIS SOLUTION. READY. AIM. FIRE.

IT DIDN'T WORK. (SURPRISE.)

The guy who sold the stuff was

BEATEN BY THE GUY'S FRIENDS...

Premier Shaded • ITC/Fontek (C. Alliance)

BUT, UNFORTUNATELY, THE FELLOW WHO WAS NOT

Queensbury • Fonthaus (Creative Alliance)

BULLETPROOF WILL BE DEAD FOR A LONG TIME.

QueensburyRules • Fonthaus (Creative Alliance)

A HOSPITAL PATIENT WAS IN AN OXYGEN TENT.

Rennie Mackintosh Bold • ITC/Fontek (C. A.)

HE WAS TOLD NOT TO SMOKE. HE DIDN'T LISTEN.

Rennie Mackintosh Light • ITC/Fontek (C. A.)

WHEN HE LIT UP THE FIRE STARTED

Rennie Mackintosh Ornaments • ITC/Fontek (C.A.)

BUT he was ashamed to get help.

Retail Script • ITC/Fontek (Creative Alliance)

HELP CAME—TOO LATE.

Roquette • ITC/Fontek (Creative Alliance)

HE WAS BURNT TO A CRISP .

Sinaloa • ITC (Creative Alliance)

actually, He was Toast. Ha!

Sitcom • Fonthaus (Creative Alliance)

AND HE SMOKED ONE LAST TIME.

SitcomExpert • Fonthaus (Creative Alliance)

yes, THE Darwin awards are fun.

SitcomOutline • Fonthaus (Creative Alliance)

In a very, very perverse way....

SitcomOutlineExpert • Fonthaus (C. Alliance)

Whatever happened to the "Most Likely to Succeed" Awards?

USED TO BE, IN HIGH SCHOOLS

every year, someone won the

Most Likely to Succeed award,

and then everyone waited...

THEY WAITED FOR 20 YEARS OR SO,

to see if the person "Most Likely to Succeed"

actually did succeed. Or whether he wound up driving a taxi in some faraway city.

Some years ago, a Former Governor

became a Taxi Driver in Chicago,

of all places. True Story. Really.

I KID YOU NOT. OK

The guy didn't do too well After Politics. But It could have been worse.

It Could Have Been a LOT Worse..."How?" you ask me. Well, I'll tell you.

Agfa Waddy 27 • Hideaki Wada (C. Alliance)

Some years later, Another Governor,

Agfa Waddy 124 • Hideaki Wada (C. Alliance)

from the Very Same State where the Chicago Taxi Driver

Agfa Waddy 125 • Hideaki Wada (C. Alliance)

HAD SERVED, FOUND

Agfa Waddy 211 • Hideaki Wada (C. Alliance)

HIMSELF LIVING IN GOVERNMENT HOUSING ONCE AGAIN. ONLY THIS TIME,

Agfa Waddy 213 • Hideaki Wada (C. Alliance)

he wasn't in the Governor's Mansion. He was In Federal Prison.

Agfa Waddy 28 • Hideaki Wada (C. Alliance)

True Story. Again. (What Else?)

Agfa Waddy 83 • Hideaki Wada (C. Alliance)

Would I lie to you? Not in a book like this. "No Way," he said.

Agfa Waddy 97 • Hideaki Wada (C. Alliance)

The Second Governor (the one who went to prison)

Whiskey • ITC/Fontek (Creative Alliance)

actually escaped prison earlier.

Xylo • ITC/Fontek (Creative Alliance)

There was a Bribery Scandal,

Zaragoza • ITC/Fontek (Creative Alliance)

and the governor was implicated for

Zeppelin • (Creative Alliance)

taking an "Illegal Payoff", you know, a Bribe.

Ziggy • ITC/Fontek (Creative Alliance)

THEY ACTUALLY FOUND THE $.

YES, THE AUTHORITIES FOUND THE MONEY IN HIS DESK. (BANKS WERE TOO RISKY, I GUESS.)

SO WHEN THEY FOUND THE BRIBE MONEY IN HIS DESK, THEY

ARRESTED THE GUV ALONG WITH THE GUY WHO MADE THE BRIBE, &

FOR WHATEVER REASON, THE GUY WHO BRIBED THE GOVERNOR,

The Briber, went on trial first.

And, a jury of his peers said "Guilty."

And the Poor Fellow admitted his guilt and went off to jail.

NOW IT WAS TIME TO TRY THE GUV.

SO WHAT HAPPENED?

Well, the Briber was already in jail,

convicted of Making the Bribe That the Guv Took.

BUT WHAT HAPPENED? WELL...

After a short deliberation, the jury said,

"NOT GUILTY" AND THE GOOD GOVERNOR WALKED.

BUT THE BAD MAN STAYED IN JAIL EVEN

THOUGH THE 2ND TIRAL BASICALLY SAID

THE BRIBE NEVER HAPPENED.

Penmanship ain't what it used to be.

Perceval—Bold • 2Rebels

Neither is the use of good grammar.

Perceval—BoldItalic • 2Rebels

C

Learning to write cursive in 2nd grade.

Perceval—Italic • 2Rebels

And in the third grade, as well.

Perceval—Regular • 2Rebels

AND IN FOURTH GRADE. AND 5TH.

Mission • Aerotype

ALL THAT PRACTICE WRITING

Pitchfork • Aerotype

and you know what? I still print, not write.

Cezanne Regular • P22

When did I give up on cursive? Maybe it was in my freshman year.

DaVinci Forward • P22

I discovered I couldn't read my writing.

DaVinci Backwards • P22

So the easy solution was to stop writing and start printing.

Hopper Edward • P22

Just like when I was in first grade, basic printed letters.

Hopper Josephine • P22

It was so much easier to read my class notes printed.

Michelangelo Regular • P22

When I wrote, I couldn't read it later.

Monet Impressionist • P22

Of course, I had to learn things the hard way. Drat!

i was taking this class in American History 101

C

and for the first few weeks, I wrote the notes.

I should have printed them, but no,

I was still concerned with "penmanship" like in 3rd grade.

Except my penmanship wasn't easy to read.

Especially when I wrote fast, as in taking notes.

Anyway, I wrote cursive back then, but I shouldn't have.

I should have printed, just the way I do today. Every day.

Today, I can READ my printing.

I even have a couple of different styles.

My use of cursive was my downfall in History 101.

I took great notes in History. Wrote almost every word I heard.

So when I began to study my Notes for a test,

Sanvito Light • Adobe (Creative Alliance)

I found that Benjamun Qfanklin was important,

Sanvito Roman • Adobe (Creative Alliance)

C

not to mention JuanQuince A

Nadianne Bold • Agfa (Creative Alliance)

And Retsy Poss, the Flag Lady,

Nadianne Book • Agfa (Creative Alliance)

and Gorj Vashyngten, first Resident.

Nadianne Condensed Bold • Agfa (C. Alliance)

The list went on and on. It was a long night

Nadianne Condensed Book • Agfa (C. Alliance)

as I studied history like no one else had.

Nadianne Condensed Medium • Agfa (C. A.)

So when the test came, I wrote.

Nadianne Medium • Agfa (Creative Alliance)

I wrote down just what I had studied.

Isabella • Agfa (Creative Alliance)

I wrote about the Revolution in 1176.

Amigo • Arthur Baker (Creative Alliance)

And I wrote about the "purfuit of Hapineff". Imagine that.

Marigold • Arthur Baker (Creative Alliance)

I should known about "pursuit of happiness".

Oxford • Arthur Baker (Creative Alliance)

But, no. I had studied a bit too hard. Word for word.

Pelican • Arthur Baker (Creative Alliance)

Gorj Vashyngten crossed the Peiaware River.

Visigoth • Arthur Baker (Creative Alliance)

Thomas Lesserson was the father of Reomcracy.

Calligraphica • Arthur Baker (Creative Alliance)

Needless to say, the professor wasn't impressed.

Calligraphica Italic • Arthur Baker (C. Alliance)

When the tests came back, I had high expectations.

ColdMountain • Arthur Baker (C. Alliance)

Unfortunately, my grade didn't match my expectations.

ColdMountain—Italic • Arthur Baker (C. A.)

Prof. Dirck Parkin spoke to me.

HiroshigeSansBlack • Arthur Baker (C. Alliance)

With a big red letter on my paper.

HiroshigeSansBlack Italic • Arthur Baker (C. A.)

His note was printed, not written.

HiroshigeSansBold • Arthur Baker (C. Alliance)

So I took his hint and printed notes.

HiroshigeSansBold Italic • Arthur Baker (C. A.)

From that day forward, I printed stuff.

HiroshigeSansBook • Arthur Baker (C. Alliance)

Even now, I print instead writing cursive.

HiroshigeSansBook Italic • Arthur Baker (C. A.)

I do write my name, but like a doctor.

HiroshigeSansMedium • Arthur Baker (C. A.)

That means it's impossible to read it.

HiroshigeSansMedium Italic • Arthur Baker (C.A.)

C

Don't Get me wrong; I love fine calligraphy. ABQabcdefghijkl is so pretty.

Mercator • Arthur Baker (Creative Alliance)

A DEFGKLM NPQRST VWY Bek, MstVxyz

MercatorSwash • Arthur Baker (C. Alliance)

Kinda neat! Rather elegant & classy, ain't it?

Basilica • Creative Alliance

Where's the good grammar? Ask me later.

Floridian Script • Creative Alliance

That is a Whole Different Issue for me. Grammar.

Quill • Creative Alliance

But for now, let's talk cursive.

LucidaCalligraphy • Bigelow & Holmes (C. A.)

And printing. As in handwriting.

LucidaCasual • Bigelow & Holmes (C. Alliance)

Yes, Calligraphy can be pretty.

LucidaCasual—italic • Bigelow & Holmes (C. A.)

And it can send very nice subtle messages.

Belltrap • Bo Berndal (Creative Alliance)

It reeks of elegance and class. And more.

Boscribe • Bo Berndal (Creative Alliance)

e.g.:   The Queen of England invites you.

Vivaldi • Title Wave Studios

Imean if the Queen is going to invite

Gianpoggio Bold • Bo Berndal (Creative Alliance)

someone to tea, SHE won't print it. NO!

Gianpoggio BoldItalic • Bo Berndal (C. Alliance)

Heavens NO! The Queen uses calligraphy.

As any good Queen certainly should do.

Me? I'll just print stuff for now.

Anyway, I don't invite people to tea

and probably won't be doing so.

I INVITE PEOPLE TO BROWN BAG LUNCH

AS IN "HOW ABOUT A SUB?"

and of course, a Diet Pepsi.

You know, I should have sold ads

in this book: Product Endorsements.

DAVE LIKES DIET PEPSI

HEY, a lot of people will see this book.

I mean, movies have products.

Movies have products on screen.

The companies pay to have them there.

C

How about this book shipped by FedEx?

Or, "This book done on Apple Computers."

We are Macintosh People. Totally.

I see Macs all the time on TV & in movies.

I think Apple provides the computers for them

and those people don't even use them.

They're just props. Hey, we USE Macs.

You'd think that Apple would read this &

send me a NEW G4 Macintosh. Right?

I mean, everyone reading this uses computers.

So the Apple People should see the value of this

and send me a new Macintosh. Lotta RAM.

PhyllisInitials • Creative Alliance

C

Just in case Apple wants to do this,

Mecurius Black • Club Type (Creative Alliance)

send it to me personally. "To Dave."

Mecurius BlackItalic • Club Type (C. Alliance)

Otherwise, someone else will open the package

Mecurius Light • Club Type (Creative Alliance)

and she'll say "What a nice present just for ME!"

Mecurius LightItalic • Club Type (C. Alliance)

And next thing you know, I won't get it.

Mecurius Medium • Club Type (C. Alliance)

So, if you're at Apple Computer, when you

Mecurius MediumItalic • Club Type (C. Alliance)

send the G4 Computer, be sure to send it to DAVE.

BolideScript • Fonthaus (Creative Alliance)

Thanks in advance. Macs are Number One.

Clichee • Fonthaus (Creative Alliance)

And if anyone from Pepsi has the same

Clichee—Bold • Fonthaus (Creative Alliance)

idea, you can send a couple dozen cases a month

Clichee—Bold Oblique • Fonthaus (C. Alliance)

to the office, and we'll happily consume them.

Clichee—Oblique • Fonthaus (Creative Alliance)

Who Knows? We might put the can in a photo...

Contrivance • Fonthaus (Creative Alliance)

I just had this idea...a very, very good idea. Listen.

Let's say that Pepsi sends a lot of stuff

all because we mention Diet Pepsi in this really good book.

Hey, it's called Product Placement. Right?

So if it's good for Pepsi to send us products cause we

really, really like them and use them, and because we

mention Pepsi in this great book,

THEN HOW ABOUT OTHERS?

If it's good for Pepsi, why not

OTHER products for us, Too?

Do you know how much I LOVE a BMW?

I mean, the 750i is just a GREAT car!!

Not To Mention the Z3. (Send 2, OK?)

C

And, did I ever tell you just how great RR is?

Oxalis Light • Franck Jalleau (Creative Alliance)

We're talking Rolls-Royce here. The ONE.

Oxalis Regular • Franck Jalleau (C. Alliance)

C

YOU KNOW, THE QUEEN RIDES IN A ROLLS.

Virgile • Franck Jalleau (Creative Alliance)

IF I HAD A ROLLS, I'D INVITE HER TO TEA.

Virgile Bold • Franck Jalleau (Creative Alliance)

I would send my driver for her.

Maiandra Black Italic • Galápagos (C. Alliance)

Imagine, my driver & the Queen...

Maiandra Black • Galápagos (Creative Alliance)

The only driver I own is a Callaway

Maiandra Demi Bold Italic • Galápagos (C. A.)

and I can't even drive it straight.

Maiandra Demi Bold • Galápagos (C. Alliance)

If I had a Rolls, I wouldn't even care.

Maiandra • Galápagos (Creative Alliance)

I mean hitting a ball straight is nice,

Maiandra Italic • Galápagos (Creative Alliance)

but it doesn't compare with a Rolls-Royce.

Longhand • Garrett Boge/Letterperfect (C. A.)

So, if you're from Rolls-Royce, please, sir,

Longhand Bold • G. Boge/Letterperfect (C. A.)

please send me a Rolls-Royce for free.

Evita Regular • Gerard Mariscalchi (C. Alliance)

Send me a Rolls-Royce, and I will

BriemScript—Black • Gunnlauger Se Briem (C.A.)

have a photo made: the car & me.

BriemScript—Bold • Gunnlauger Se Briem (C.A.)

C

It will appear on the dust cover of

BriemScript—Light • Gunnlauger Se Briem (C.A.)

every book that I ever do from now on.

BriemScript—Med. • Gunnlauger Se Briem (C.A.)

Really. And, I will send that same

BriemScript—Reg. • Gunnlauger Se Briem (C.A.)

photo to all the people I went

BriemScript—UltraBd. • Gunnlauger Se Briem (C.A.)

to High School with…especially to those

Inkspot • Howard Cuttle (Creative Alliance)

I didn't like (who didn't like me).

InkspotBold • Howard Cuttle (Creative Alliance)

I'll also send the photo to a couple of girls,

InkspotLight • Howard Cuttle (C. Alliance)

girlfriends from college, who dumped me.

Crusader—Regular • Ian Patterson (C. Alliance)

And I'd send one to my high school math teacher.

Humana Script Bold • ITC (Creative Alliance)

the one who told me I wasn't "college material". HA!

Humana Script Light • ITC (Creative Alliance)

O.K. Rolls Royce, you just got a full page and more

Humana Script Medium • ITC (Creative Alliance)

in this really great Font Book. Imagine

the value of this "unsolicited" mention.

C

I'll be looking for the Rolls delivery truck soon.

I'm not picky. Any color will be OK by me.

Hey, anyone from Mercedes-Benz out there?

Imagine having me drive a Mercedes convertible

all over town—YOUR nice car. Yeah!

THINK "PRODUCT PLACEMENT—DAVE"

and people would say "Beautiful car." I would

tell them just how great your 560SL convertible really is. Don't forget

the pictures...lots of photos...

send me a roadster, and the photo will be on

the dust jacket of every book I do from now on.

Every book I ever do, from now on until I'm…

Bible Script • ITC/Fontek (Creative Alliance)

Mercedes and Dave—what a photograph!

Blackadder • ITC/Fontek (Creative Alliance)

I have another great idea—what a photo this would be.

Blaze • ITC/Fontek (Creative Alliance)

Get a Rolls, and the Mercedes, and ME.

BradleyHand • ITC/Fontek (Creative Alliance)

Consider that. Rolls and Mercedes,

BradleyHand Bold • ITC/Fontek (C. Alliance)

the two classiest cars I can think of.

BradleyHand Italic • ITC/Fontek (C. Alliance)

Hey—let's toss in a Jaguar. O.K.?

Braganza • ITC/Fontek (Creative Alliance)

Anyone out there from Jaguar? Listen…

Braganza Light • ITC/Fontek (Creative Alliance)

SEND ME A NEW JAGUAR, SOON.

Braganza SC • ITC/Fontek (Creative Alliance)

PICTURE THIS: A PHOTO OF ME AND

Braganza Light SC • ITC/Fontek (C. Alliance)

THE JAGUAR, THE ROLLS, & THE MERCEDES CONVERTIBLE.

Cancione • ITC/Fontek (Creative Alliance)

And THAT photo will be on EVERY dust jacket

Challenge Bold • ITC/Fontek (Creative Alliance)

of EVERY book that I ever do. From now on.

Challenge Extra Bold • ITC/Fontek (C. Alliance)

C

And, I'll also send that photo to those

Champers • ITC/Fontek (Creative Alliance)

college girlfriends who dumped me. Yeah!

Choc • ITC/Fontek (Creative Alliance)

That will be fun. I think. Hey, wait, I just realized

Choc Light • ITC/Fontek (Creative Alliance)

there might be a downside to all this.

Coconino • ITC/Fontek (Creative Alliance)

What if they get this nice photo of me and the Rolls

Cult • ITC/Fontek (Creative Alliance)

and the Jaguar and the Mercedes Roadster

Cyberkugel • ITC/Fontek (Creative Alliance)

and they look at the photo and say, "Who is that?"

Deelirious • ITC/Fontek (Creative Alliance)

Who's the gray-haired guy with all the nice cars? Who is he?

Demian • ITC/Fontek (Creative Alliance)

Worse yet, they don't even remember me. Not at all.

Demian Bold • ITC/Fontek (Creative Alliance)

What if they didn't even remember my name?

Ellipse • ITC/Fontek (Creative Alliance)

Imagine, I go to all the trouble of getting 3 cars—

Ellipse Bold • ITC/Fontek (Creative Alliance)

the best three cars in the world, by the way—

Ellipse Bold Italic • ITC/Fontek (C. Alliance)

I get those three cars, and have a fine photographer

Ellipse Italic • ITC/Fontek (Creative Alliance)

C

create a Very Nice Photograph of ME and the three wonderful cars.

And they don't remember me.

What if I turn out to be merely a "footnote" to them?

A footnote in their life story.

Something like "guy from History Class".

HISTORY CLASS! FLASHBACKS.

What if they remember me only as the

nameless guy from History Class who didn't do too well.

THE GUY WHO COULDN'T EVEN WRITE.

THE GUY SO SLOW THAT HE PRINTED.

Maybe I won't send them the photo after all.

But, hey, people from Rolls, Jaguar,

and Mercedes Benz, don't let

C

tHis one, LittLe GLitcH stop you.

Send your car along to me, and I'll have a

C

photo of me and the Car on each book—

a Mercedes right on the dust jacket. Yes, I promise.

Only one problem with the photo: There will be no "driving" shot with the wind in my hair.

I'm afraid of having a "gray" sky, which would blend with my hair;

it would look like my hair was eaten by the sky.

LET'S NOT CALL ATTENTION TO MY GRAY HAIR.

The college girls wouldn't know me.

They would say, "He had a flat top,"

and it sure wasn't gray. Not back in college, for sure.

Somebody once said to me, "When did your hair turn gray?"

I said, "When I stopped using Grecian Formula."

By the way, THAT was NOT a product placement.

I'm not endorsing Grecian Formula. Sorry guys.

C

I decided to let it gray, just to see it.

Then one of my kids said I looked "very distinguished".

So, I settled for a "distinguished" look.

BETTER THAT THAN BAD COLOR.

I know a guy with green hair. Or orange hair.

Look, Ma, right ahead. Green hair!

But he didn't use Grecian Formula. Nope.

Maybe he used food coloring. Seems like it was.

So, every time I see my gray hair in the mirror, I think about

how much better it looks than orange. Or green. Or purple.

OF COURSE, IF I WERE YOUNGER, BLUE

or maybe orange, or even green might look good.

Skylark • ITC/Fontek (Creative Alliance)

But I'm a little **too** "mature" for green hair.

Smudger • ITC/Fontek (Creative Alliance)

C

CAN YOU SEE A 50-SOMETHING GUY—

Spirit • ITC/Fontek (Creative Alliance)

green hair, spiked, in a board meeting?

Squire • ITC/Fontek (Creative Alliance)

And all the guys in pin-striped suits

Squire Extra Bold • ITC/Fontek (C. Alliance)

looking at this old guy with green hair, saying, "Hello, Gentlemen.

Stranger • ITC/Fontek (Creative Alliance)

I am your Board Chairman, Mr. Green."

Styleboy • ITC/Fontek (Creative Alliance)

Nah. Not in the world where I live.

Stylus Bold • ITC/Fontek (Creative Alliance)

Even orange hair wouldn't fly there.

Stylus Regular • ITC/Fontek (Creative Alliance)

Nor blue, or purple, or green or yellow, or whatever color. Nope.

Tiger Rag • ITC/Fontek (Creative Alliance)

Many years ago, Roxanne, the barber,

Tiranti Solid • ITC/Fontek (Creative Alliance)

wanted to color my hair "blond".

Trackpad • ITC/Fontek (Creative Alliance)

"Blond," she said. "Like a surfer guy." "Go for it," I told her.

Ulysses • ITC/Fontek (Creative Alliance)

THE ENTIRE TIME THAT I

was in her chair, waiting for the color to

C

happen, I thought about the Beach Boys'

song, "Surfer Girl". "Little Surfer,

LITTLE GIRL, MAKES

my heart..." was in my mind; couldn't get it out.

I pictured myself driving a Mercedes convertible

at the Beach. Yeah. Me—Surfer Blond.

My hair blowing in the wind; salty air.

i LET MY MIND GO THERE: DAVE, SURFER GUY.

And then, finally, when my hair was dry, she got the mirror.

When I looked at myself, I was totally speechless.

I DIDN'T LOOK LIKE A SURFER GUY.

NOT AT ALL! I cried, "Help Me."

GreeneGreene • Judith Sutcliffe (C. Alliance)

"I look like BIG BIRD," I said.

Kiilani • Judith Sutcliffe (Creative Alliance)

Flashback to Easter when I was a young kid,

KufiScript • Judith Sutcliffe (Creative Alliance)

YOU REMEMBER "EASTER CHICKS"?

Renasci • Lennart Hansson (Creative Alliance)

MY QUICK MIND SAID, "I LOOK LIKE

Ghiberti • Letterperfect (Creative Alliance)

little baby chickens." And I did. I did look like a baby chicken,

Göteborg • Letterperfect (Creative Alliance)

THE KIND THEY DYED YELLOW.

Manito • Letterperfect (Creative Alliance)

Those poor chicks, dyed yellow by

OldClaude • Letterperfect (Creative Alliance)

PEOPLE WHO SURELY HAD TO KNOW

OldClaudeSC • Letterperfect (Creative Alliance)

that those poor baby chicks would soon die

Spumoni • Letterperfect (Creative Alliance)

at the hands of little kids who got them,

Stockholm • Letterperfect (Creative Alliance)

Did those chicks have a happy Easter?

TomboyBold • Letterperfect (Creative Alliance)

At least they didn't wind up as Sunday dinner.

TomboyLight • Letterperfect (Creative Alliance)

C

Anyway, once I had my hair colored yellow

TomboyMedium • Letterperfect (C. Alliance)

QUITE A BIT LIKE A BABY CHICKEN, I

Uppsala • Letterperfect (Creative Alliance)

C

decided that was the last unnatural color job.

Ashtray—Empty • Lunchbox (Creative Alliance)

Right then I said, "Better gray and

Ashtray—Full • Lunchbox (Creative Alliance)

distinguished, than yellow and like Big Bird."

Cirrus • M. Mastandrea/T-26 (Creative Alliance)

Hey, you know, a Silver Gray Mercedes would match my hair.

Civilite Normal • Majus Corporation (C. A.)

wht hggkkRe εɔεŋQEthcteʃgh k ɣɔtɓwpzʃŋt

Civilite Alternates • Majus Corporation (C. A.)

Isn't the previous font line very nice? Great look.

TwoVooDoo • Mark Harris (Creative Alliance)

After ALL, this is ʌ font book. Right?

Planet Sans Bold • Mat Planet (Creative Alliance)

fjttwRfffɓeeɔɔtⲧⲚ⫲wfffɓffiThLʌwɓ

Planet Sans AltBold • Mat Planet (C. Alliance)

And the sʌme for the Line ʌbove. Extrʌs

Planet Sans Book • Mat Planet (C. Alliance)

fffɓffiThⳒⲉttRfffɓeeɔɔtⲧⲚLʌyttw

Planet Sans Alt Book • Mat Planet (C. Alliance)

Wow. Same for The Line above. Good

Rondo • Mecanorma (Creative Alliance)

Those "ligatures" and special letters

make a nice addition to those fonts.

C

After all, this IS a font book. Don't forget.

Even though, there is a lot of stuff to read here.

Like the fact that a Silver Gray Mercedes

matches my hair (natural color) perfectly.

Hey, Mercedes Guy, think about that.

Not only will I be driving your car,

I will be endorsing your car

all the time, I'm driving it.

And even when I'm NOT driving it,

I will be promoting your car COLOR.

Like, people would see me at the mall, and say

They would say "Hey, that distinguished guy

has hair the exact color of a Mercedes."

And then they would all want to buy a car

the same color as my car—my Mercedes.

I mean, this is really starting to make sense:

Mercedes gives me a car, and sales

go up, up, up all because I show the

Mercedes in the photos on

every book jacket I do. Forever.

I mean, you guys at Mercedes

will need another factory just

to meet the demand for cars.

All because you sent me a Roadster.

C

This is a very sound marketing strategy.

Anybody at Mercedes reading this?

Hey, Mr. Rolls-Royce? Do you see the possibilities?

If it works for Mercedes, it can

certainly work for you as well. Dave = Rolls.

You know, Rolls-Royce could bring

back the Silver Cloud model. Just like my hair.

This is REALLY a good idea, Mr. Rolls-Royce.

I mean, you guys make several thousand Rolls every year, right?

So who is going to miss just one of them? Send it to me: Dave.

SEND ME A ROLLS-ROYCE, PLEASE, MR. ROLLS. THE SILVER CLOUD SEEMS JUST RIGHT.

AND just watch the image (and sales) go up.

People will say, "Dave has a silver Rolls."

Yep. They see me in a silver Rolls

Stellar Zeta • Panache Typography (C. Alliance)

and they will immediately want one as well,

Postcard • Perry Whittle (Creative Alliance)

C

not to mention the fact that the photo

Postcard Alternate • Perry Whittle (C. Alliance)

in the book will also include the Rolls.

Postcard—Bold • Perry Whittle (C. Alliance)

Think of all the dust jackets with the Rolls on it.

Postcard—Italic • Perry Whittle (C. Alliance)

Why every font user in the world will want one.

Dorothea • Philip Bouwsma (Creative Alliance)

Yes. All designers will prefer the finest car, like the Queen & her mother have. Nothing finer than a good Rolls.

Ludovico Smooth • Philip Bouwsma (C. Alliance)

All designers love the Rolls like the Queen owns. And they want one the same color as my hair. Got that, Mr. Rolls?

Ludovico Woodcut • Philip Bouwsma (C. A.)

And just Look at this font: Rolls-Royce SuzySpade

Ludovico Woodcut—Flourishes • P. Bouwsma (C.A.)

Think how this would affect all the designers

Mantegna—Italic • Philip Bouwsma (C. Alliance)

who use this book. They would

Neuhengen • Philip Bouwsma (Creative Alliance)

immediately (and naturally) think, "You drive a Rolls-Royce" and your image is

Ophelia Italic • Philip Bouwsma (C. Alliance)

greatly enhanced. Oh, yes, it would be.

Percival • Philip Bouwsma (Creative Alliance)

PEOPLE SEE YOU DRIVING A ROLLS, AND YOU

Pompeii Capitals • Philip Bouwsma (C. Alliance)

then become a better designer—at least in their minds.

Sallando Italic • Philip Bouwsma (C. Alliance)

I mean, you drive a Rolls, so you

Thalia Italic • Philip Bouwsma (C. Alliance)

must be an excellent designer,

Trieste • Philip Bouwsma (Creative Alliance)

A WONDERFUL DESIGNER, BECAUSE

Wolfdance • Philip Bouwsma (Creative Alliance)

if you weren't a world-class designer,

Benguiat Frisky Bold • Photolettering (C. A.)

you would NOT be driving

Benguiat Frisky • Photolettering (C. Alliance)

a Rolls-Royce, now would you? I mean,

Trophy Oblique • Photolettering (C. Alliance)

the Queen could have any car.

Gararond Bold • Pierre Di Sciullo (C. Alliance)

But the Queen chooses a Rolls-Royce.

Gararond Bold Italic • Pierre Di Sciullo (C. A.)

What does that say about the Queen & Rolls?

Gararond Light • Pierre Di Sciullo (C. Alliance)

The Queen knows good cars, I would say,

Gararond Light Italic • Pierre Di Sciullo (C. A.)

and if the Queen has a Rolls...

Gararond Medium • Pierre Di Sciullo (C. A.)

C

If it's good enough for the Queen,

Gararond Medium Italic • Pierre Di Sciullo (C.A.)

it's good enough for anyone—even world-class designers

SkippySharp • S. McFadden/Chank Diesel (C.A.)

like the ones who are using this book. Yes.

Andy—Bold • Steve Matteson (Creative Alliance)

Once again, this makes marketing sense.

Andy—BoldItalic • Steve Matteson (C. Alliance)

So, you people in Marketing at Rolls-Royce,

Andy—Italic • Steve Matteson (C. Alliance)

send me a Rolls-Royce. Even if you don't have

Andy—Regular • Steve Matteson (C. Alliance)

a Silver Cloud color to match my hair.

Fineprint • Steve Matteson (Creative Alliance)

GL   fb c ff ggfhffifjfk   fttvw

Fineprint Alt • Steve Matteson (C. Alliance)

ffggfhfjfk   fttvww   fflfjfhcfkffl   ft

Fineprint Alt Light • Steve Matteson (C. Alliance)

More nice extra font characters above.

Fineprint Light • Steve Matteson (C Alliance)

All you people in Marketing at Rolls...

Fineprint Swash One • Steve Matteson (C. A.)

remember to send me the car.

Fineprint Swash One Light • S. Matteson (C. A.)

After all, it's a good marketing strategy.

Fineprint Swash Two • Steve Matteson (C. A.)

C

And to the people at Jaguar, don't forget me.

Fineprint Swash Two Light • S. Matteson (C. A.)

If you want to be pictured on a dust jacket

Amanda • Tom Rickner (Creative Alliance)

C

with a Rolls-Royce, Mercedes,

Amanda—Bold • Tom Rickner (C. Alliance)

and me, the silver-haired, distinguished-looking guy,

Boomerang • Type Revivals (Creative Alliance)

get with it and send me a Jaguar. Soon.

Saltino • Type Revivals (Creative Alliance)

BECAUSE DESIGNERS BUY CARS.

Wildstyle • Vincent Connare (Creative Alliance)

King-Like Deft Artists Need Really Quick Waffles Yes. Rghjkrstvwyz!

Americratika • Fonthead

What was that sentence about? Do you know?

AppleSeed • Fonthead

Was that supposed to make any sense at all?

BadDog • Fonthead

No. It wasn't supposed to Make Any Sense. None.

BlackBeard • Fonthead

It was simply a sentence that displayed All the Neat Letters.

Carnation • Fonthead

ANYWAY, THE PURPOSE OF THIS BOOK IS TO SHOW FONTS—

DanceParty • Fonthead

All 5,000 Fonts that appear in this book.

DraftHand • Fonthead

All 5,000 of them. Do you think people will count them?

WILL ANYONE KNOW IF THERE ARE FEWER FONTS?

C

Someone will write me a letter about it for sure.

A picky quiet person will tell me if there are just 4,987 fonts.

"Dear Mr. Carter," the letter will start. "I bought your book because

I TRULY BELIEVED THAT IT CONTAINED

5,000 fonts, but when I counted them, I found that it doesn't. You are 13 short."

And the letter will go on to berate me, to demean my math skills, and tell me how bad I am.

AND THE LETTER WILL GO ON FOR 8, MAYBE

even 9, pages to read on and on...

The Writer will conclude in his letter

that he never would have

BOUGHT THE BOOK IF HE

had only known that it had fewer than

5,000 fonts—NEVER, EVER have

C

purchased it if he had known The Truth;

the book had fewer than 5,000 Fonts so

HE WOULD NEVER HAVE BOUGHT SAID BOOK.

AND HE WILL DO SOME CALCULATION

concluding that the "missing" 13 fonts

represent a specific, small percent of

The Sale Price of Reader's Book, and I basically cheated

AND DIDN'T GIVE THE BUYER HIS

Money's Worth. The letter will rant on about

the conspiracy that the global cartel

of math teachers do not teach kids to even be able to

count the number of fonts here. Finally

Fette Fraktur • Title Wave Studios

the accusation will fly, "Can't you even

Fette Gotisch • Title Wave Studios

count? Your math skill is lacking. Did you

Linden • Title Wave Studios

not study? Apparently not very hard."

Lydian • Title Wave Studios

Then I will answer, "You may be right."

Lydian Bold • Title Wave Studios

C

Did you ever want to write a "Top 10" list?

Hector—Bold • 2Rebels

Why should David Letterman have a

Hector—BoldComposite • 2Rebels

monopoly on doing a TOP 10 LIST?

Hector—BoldExtended • 2Rebels

Why should he? WHY? Well, he shouldn't.

Hector—Carre • 2Rebels

I mean, other people have ideas, too.

Hector—Composite • 2Rebels

Like, I have my own Top 10 List.

Hector—Extended • 2Rebels

My Top 10 Reasons why dogs are better than cats—

Hector—Photocopy • 2Rebels

Reason Number 10: Litter Boxes (Need I say more?)

Hector—Regular • 2Rebels

No. 9: Try calling a cat. See what happens. Nothing.

Hector—Rounded • 2Rebels

NO. 8:   CATS SPRAY

Tsjecho • 2Rebels

NO. 7: CATS WON'T EAT TABLE SCRAPS.

VintageGothic–Black Face • 2Rebels

NO. 6: THAT SILLY "PURRING". YUCK!

VintageGothic–Italique • 2Rebels

NO. 5: TONGUES LIKE SANDPAPER!!!

VintageGothic–Lefty • 2Rebels

NO. 4: WHINEY LITTLE CAT VOICES.

VintageGothic–Regular • 2Rebels

NO. 3: CATS HAVE FISH BREATH.

VintageGothic–Shadow • 2Rebels

NO 2: CATS ALWAYS LICK THEMSELVES.

VintageGothic–WhiteFace • 2Rebels

AND THE NUMBER ONE TOP

VintageGothic–WhiteFaceItalique • 2Rebels

REASON WHY DOGS ARE

Constructivist Block • P22

MUCH BETTER THAN CATS

Constructivist Line • P22

IS THE MOST BASIC AND

Constructivist Regular • P22

OBVIOUS REASON. NO. 1: CATS

Constructivist Square • P22

don't know WHERE to lick.

Johnston Underground • P22

IF YOU ARE OFFENDED BY THIS,

Johnston Underground Bold • P22

IF YOU ARE A TRUE CAT LOVER,

Koch Neuland • P22

don't write me; don't e-mail me. OK?

Adepta—Extrabold • Treacyfaces

Because I have 3 cats. THREE. (There!)

Alambic—Bold • Treacyfaces

B

Actually, no one "owns" cats.

Cats simply live with people

who are the care givers

because cats are independent.

Very independent.

Like I said earlier, try to call a cat.

Watch what happens. Nothing.

Actually, cats own people, I think.

Morning time comes, and

cats wake up people. Meow.

The whiney voice must be heard

YOU CANNOT JUST LIE IN BED WHEN

the CAT WANTS TO EAT.

When the cat wants to eat, he does.

Niteweit—BoldItalic • TypeArt

And, if the cat wants to go outside

Niteweit—Italic • TypeArt

and it happens to be midnight…

Niteweit—Regular • TypeArt

B

IF THE CAT WANTS OUT, HE GETS OUT. WHO CAN SLEEP WITH

Spaced Out—Regular • TypeArt

a cat whining in your ear? I can't do it.

Xheighter Condensed—Bold • TypeArt

You think I never had a cat? This cat's name

Xheighter Condensed—BoldItalic • TypeArt

was DARYL, and whatever he wanted, he got. Even if it was 3:00 a.m.

Xheighter Condensed—Italic • TypeArt

Actually, DARYL was one of three sons born to a Siamese cat mother "Thai".

Xheighter Condensed—Regular• TypeArt

And a scoundrel father. He was a yellow tabby.

Xheighter—Black • TypeArt

I don't think he and Thai ever even met. That is

Xheighter—BlackOblique • TypeArt

I don't think they were formally introduced.

Xheighter—BlackOriginal • TypeArt

As a cat owner, I am a little offended by that.

Xheighter—Light • TypeArt

But as a male, I am a little envious of Scoundrel.

Xheighter—LightOblique • TypeArt

Anyway, Thai was outside on the deck one day

Xheighter—LightOriginal • TypeArt

AND THAI WAS "IN SEASON."

Black Boton Bold • Albert Boton (C. Alliance)

Male Kitty, the Scoundrel, visited, quickly,

Aura • Creative Alliance

AND GAVE MY KIDS A SEX ED LESSON—FAST.

Logoform Bold • Bo Berndal (Creative Alliance)

"WHY IS THAT CAT BITING THAI?" LAUREN ASKED.

Logoform Regular • Bo Berndal (C. Alliance)

Well, there is no simple answer to that question.

Cosmic • Chank Diesel (Creative Alliance)

I mean, I'm not quite sure that cats have foreplay.

Black Tulip • ITC/Fontek (Creative Alliance)

Although I am pretty sure I wasn't going to explain that to a kid of 9.

Compacta • ITC/Fontek (Creative Alliance)

I'm not sure I want to explain that to anyone, any age.

Compacta Bold • ITC/Fontek (Creative Alliance)

So, about 8 weeks later, Thai had three kittens. All sons.

Compacta Italic • ITC/Fontek (Creative Alliance)

AND ALL OF THEM WERE BLACK. SOLID BLACK. EXCEPT TWO,

Machine • ITC/Fontek (Creative Alliance)

WHO HAD A FEW WHITE HAIRS UNDER THEIR NECK.

Machine Bold • ITC/Fontek (Creative Alliance)

SO WHAT DID WE NAME THE CATS?

Princetown • ITC/Fontek (Creative Alliance)

THE NAMES SEEMED PRETTY OBVIOUS.

Superstar • ITC/Fontek (Creative Alliance)

Remember THE NEWHART SHOW?

Fette Mittelschrift • Title Wave Studios

Where he was Dick Loudon, and had the bed and breakfast?

HadrianBold • Letterperfect (Creative Alliance)

B

That was a popular TV show when the

Headline Bd • Monotype (Creative Alliance)

3 kittens were born. So, the kittens'

Impact • Monotype (Creative Alliance)

names just had to be:

Placard Cn • Monotype (Creative Alliance)

Larry, Daryl, & Daryl. We kept Daryl. He lived

Placard Cn Bd • Monotype (Creative Alliance)

FOR 16 YEARS AND WHEN HE

Diesel • Fonthead

died, we were sad. He was a special cat.

Block • Title Wave Studios

Daryl was a lot like a dog.

Block Bold • Title Wave Studios

How? You could call Daryl and he would come.

Block Condensed • Title Wave Studios

And he would follow us on walks. Really.

Fette Engschrift • Title Wave Studios

Back to "Top Ten" lists:

ONCE YOU START WRITING THESE, YOU CAN'T QUIT.

Here is another Top Ten List,

My Top Ten Reasons why

MOZART IS NOW AND WILL

ALWAYS BE BETTER THAN DEION SANDERS.

NO. 10: MOZART NEVER, EVER,

questioned the decision of an umpire.

No. 9: Mozart never held out for more money.

No. 8: Mozart never declared himself a "free agent".

No. 7: Mozart never refused to talk to a reporter.

No. 6: Mozart never was a "hot dog".

(There isn't enough sauce in America for Deion.)

No. 5: Everything Mozart did was great.

NO 4: MOZART COULD PLAY MANY

MANY, MANY INSTRUMENTS.

DEION COULD PLAY ONLY 2 PRO SPORTS.

NO. 3: MOZART HAD A BETTER HAIRDO.

No. 2: Mozart's career lasted a lifetime.

No. 1: Mozart's life is a movie,

an Academy Award winning movie.

Final Bonus: You can buy Mozart CDs.

Don't get the idea that I hate baseball—

NOT TRUE. BASEBALL HAS BEEN VERY GOOD.

Baseball just isn't what it once was.

Any kid who grew up in the 1950s,

ANY kid of the fifties,

will certainly tell you

about baseball then

and now. No comparison.

PROOF: A)WILLIAMS, B)MUSIAL

NEED MORE EXAMPLES?

O.K. Let's go back to Ted Williams...

I mean the guy lost over five years to two different wars,

and he still hit 521 home runs, with a lifetime .344 average.

Not to mention the fact that he is the last man to hit .400.

Not impressed by that figure? Do you know that he hit .406?

He hit .406 back in 1941. That was over 60 years ago.

How many batters have come and gone in 60 years?

Maybe thousands. How many have hit .400?

Not one. Zero. Nobody. Hasn't happened in 60 years.

OK, so someone is going to bring up Mark McGwire.

And his 70 home runs in one season. And I'll say "So what?"

So McGwire hit 70 in one year? And how many did Sosa hit?

And in the same year? Wait a minute—TWO guys

break the Record that stood over 35 years?

Has anybody out there ever had a class in Statistics? Is this an Outlier?

When you have a statistic like THAT, look for an aberration.

There is some reason WHY

two hitters break the record

and do it in the SAME YEAR. Look for some reason.

Like, were the baseballs Juiced that year? Or,

maybe it was due to pitching.

How many "bad" pitchers

were in the majors that year?

Look at some numbers.

In 1961, when Maris hit 61 home runs,

there were 16 teams. Total.

Sixteen. Now, there are 30 teams. Aha....

What does that mean? It means that

if you assume each team has ten pitchers,

then back in 1961, there were 160

Major League Pitchers. And now, with 30 teams,

THERE ARE 300 MAJOR LEAGUE PITCHERS.

That's nearly twice as many.

TODAY, THERE ARE 140 PITCHERS IN THE MAJORS

Twist Four • Christian Schwartz (C. Alliance)

who would be in Triple-A, or worse,

CutamondBasic • Fonthaus (Creative Alliance)

if there were 16 teams instead of 30.

CutamondOldStyle • Fonthaus (C. Alliance)

Look at the number—140 pitchers in the majors,

LettresEclatees • Fonthaus (Creative Alliance)

guys who would be in the minors

Droplet • H. Nguyen/T-26 (Creative Alliance)

if this were 1961. Figure it out.

DropletExtra • H. Nguyen/T-26 (C. Alliance)

Pitching is a tad weaker now

DropletLite • H. Nguyen/T-26 (Creative Alliance)

than it was back then. Just look.

Aftershock • ITC/Fontek (Creative Alliance)

How many "major league pitchers" of today would be

Carumba • ITC/Fontek (Creative Alliance)

PITCHING BATTING PRACTICE

Carumba Hot Caps • ITC/Fontek (C. Alliance)

if they were playing back in 1961.

Chiller • ITC/Fontek (Creative Alliance)

And a lot of these guys have $5 million contracts,

Chipper • ITC/Fontek (Creative Alliance)

only because they are left handers,

Coventry—Heavy • ITC/Fontek (C. Alliance)

They have a lifetime winning record.

Coventry—Medium • ITC/Fontek (C. Alliance)

That's something like 78-83. Geeeeez!

Coventry—Thin • ITC/Fontek (C. Alliance)

OK. I THINK BASEBALL

DigitalWoodcutsBlack • ITC/Fontek (C. A.)

IN THE 1950S WAS BETTER.

DigitalWoodcutsOpen • ITC/Fontek (C. A.)

Basically, how many pitchers

Eastwood • ITC/Fontek (Creative Alliance)

of today could even walk in the

Farmhaus Normal • ITC/Fontek (C. Alliance)

shadow of Warren Spahn? Spahn?

Farmhaus Not So Normal • ITC/Fontek (C. A.)

Best left-handed pitcher. EVER.

Gramophone • ITC/Fontek (Creative Alliance)

The numbers back it up—363 wins, lifetime.

Hollyweird • ITC/Fontek (Creative Alliance)

No left-handed pitcher ever won more.

Jaft • ITC/Fontek (Creative Alliance)

And, remember that Spahn was over 26.

Jiggery Pokery • ITC/Fontek (Creative Alliance)

TALKING BASEBALL

Kendo Initials • ITC/Fontek (Creative Alliance)

Warren Spahn didn't get his first win

Kendo • ITC/Fontek (Creative Alliance)

until he was 26-years old—OLD.

Not because he was in the minors. No.

Seems like there was a war going on. Spahn didn't get

a Draft Deferment. Like most of the players, he wound up in uniform.

BUT ONCE HE WAS BACK, HE WON

and he won a lot. He pitched until he was 42.

How many of today's pitchers are

in a class with Warren Spahn?

MAYBE ONE. ROGER CLEMENS.

And how many players HAVE the class of Spahn?

Probably none. Warren Spahn ☆ Class.

Don't agree with my view of Baseball Today?

Don't write to me. Please. Don't e-mail.

When I was in college, I worked for a prof.

who was a Major Authority.

In fact, this book is dedicated to him.

Tom Turnbull was a top educator in

the field of Graphics and Typography.

TOM, ALONG WITH RUSSELL BAIRD,

wrote the DEFINITIVE text...I mean to say

Turnbull & Baird wrote THE book on

Graphics of Communication.

THE BOOK WAS USED IN NEARLY EVERY

college class in raptics.

It's still a major text, now in its 7th or 8th edition.

I mean, the book was TOPS.

Every so often, someone would write to Tom

Roughedge • R. Howell/T-26 (Creative Alliance)

WITH A CRITIQUE OF THE BOOK.

Commonworld • S. Farrell/T-26 (C. Alliance)

TOM WOULD READ EACH LETTER.

Entropy • S. Farrell/T-26 (Creative Alliance)

And he would answer each one. He would write a note

Freakshow—RealScary • T. Brei/T-26 (C. A.)

at the bottom of the letter: "You may be right," he would say.

FreakshowScary • T. Brei/T-26 (Creative Alliance)

That is my standard response, as well.

Handwrite–Inkblot • T. Brei/T-26 (C. Alliance)

Things I have learned as

Toxica • Title WaveStudios

I have written this book include: I love the letter S like f.

LucifersPension—Gothic • Vintage Type Library

I also learned that I have a short attention span.

LucifersPension—Roman • Vintage Type Library

YES. I ADMIT IT. I HAVE A SHORT ATTENTION SPAN.

Typewriter—Telegram • Vintage Type Library

I CAN GO FROM TOPIC TO TOPIC

Bessie • Fonthead

about as fast as a NASCAR Driver in a pileup.

Blearex • Fonthead

SPEAKING OF NASCAR, I HAVE TO ADMIT I DON'T GET IT.

Brolga • Fonthead

The noise is way too much and I don't understand

the Go in a circle-Go in a circle-Go in a circle

for a couple of hundred times and so on...

The Races ALWAYS attract hundreds of

thousands of people...all the time, hundreds

of thousands of people, but not me.

I'D RATHER ENDURE PHYSICAL PAIN THAN GO.

I'd rather have a sigmoidoscopy

Than Go to A Nascar Race. Really I would.

WHICH ReMINDS Me, MY MOTHER TOLD Me NEVER GO

OUT WITH DIRTY UNDERWEAR

BECAUSE YOU MIGHT BE IN AN ACCIDENT & END UP IN THE E.R.

Some jobs are taken just for fun

Billes • 2Rebels

Such as the Casting Director for movies.

Caaarc • 2Rebels

Casting Directors are really important,

Craaac • 2Rebels

but no one thinks about what they do.

Gagarin—Gregor • 2Rebels

JUST TO SEE HOW IMPORTANT THEY ARE,

Gagarin—Hektor • 2Rebels

consider some movies, and

Gagarin—Igor • 2Rebels

change the cast, just slightly;

LaPlaya • 2Rebels

Look What Happens...Oh!

LaserBeam—Medium • 2Rebels

Imagine Woody Allen in Psycho,

Manomessa • 2Rebels

right? In the Tony Perkins role.

Manomessa—Bucata • 2Rebels

See what I mean. Casting is crucial.

Nameless—Bold • 2Rebels

And picture Pee Wee Herman in ANY

Nameless—Regular • 2Rebels

role that Jack Nicholson had. Ha.

Napoleon—roman • 2Rebels

CAN YOU SEE PEE WEE HERMAN
ThinMan—Drunk • 2Rebels

in the five Easy Pieces restaurant?
Vague—Normal • 2Rebels

Imagine Pee Wee telling a waitress,
Vague—Outline • 2Rebels

"Hold that between your knees,"
AngleBold • flashfonts

and you see just what I mean.
AngleIn • flashfonts

Yes. Casting is very important.
AngleUltra • flashfonts

IMAGINE KERMIT THE FROG
BadTyp • flashfonts

taking the place of...let's say, oh,
HaarlemBlack • flashfonts

Cary Grant. Yes, Kermit can be suave.
HaarlemWhite• flashfonts

What a concept. Kermit the Frog,
Albers—One • P22

the green frog, instead of Mel Gibson—
AlbersTwo • P22

Kermit the Frog in The Patriot.
Albers Three • P22

(And Miss Piggy, not Julia Roberts.)
Bagaglio 3D • P22

84

Or how about Kermit, not Jackie Chan?

Bagaglio Flat • P22

CAN YOU SEE KERMIT IN AN ACTION FILM?

Il Futurismo Velocita • P22

HIS MAIN DEFENSE WOULD BE TO:

Il FuturismoRegular • P22

GO LIMP. AS LIMP AS A DISH RAG. GET IT? KERMIT

Parrish Hand • P22

the Frog IS a dish rag. A green one.

Ticonderoga • Title Wave Studios

But, it would be nice to have his fame.

Dada • P22

EVEN IF HE IS ONLY A DISH RAG,

FFLW Exhibition Light • P22

HE IS A VERY WEALTHY DISH RAG.

FFLW Exhibition Bold • P22

WONDER WHO HAS MORE MONEY,

FFLW Exhibition Regular • P22

JACKIE CHAN OR KERMIT THE FROG? INTERESTING.

FFLW Terracotta Regular • P22

ONE THING IS SURE. JACKIE BRUISES EASIER.

FFLW Terracotta Alternates • P22

KERMIT NEVER BRUISES. LUCKY.

GD&T Frames • P22

HE HAS A STUNT DISH RAG.

GD&T No Frames • P22

Once you buy into Kermit as real, you

start thinking of him as a real, live person...

then you wonder a lot of stuff.

Does he get tired of wearing green?

I mean, as much as you like one suit

AFTER AWHILE

YOU WOULD GET

tired of green.

Does Kermit have

a tailor? What

other color

would Kermit want to be, and,

if he changed the color, maybe

he would get daring, and

get a new style that's just right for him.

(I mean, Kermit's pants are really tight.)

Wonder if he has the same tailor

as Pee Wee Herman? Just maybe...

In fact, it is possible that

Kermit the Frog and Pee Wee Herman

are the SAME person. Think about it.

Have you ever seen Kermit

and Pee Wee together? No!

When you think about their voices,

they sound a little bit alike. Sorta.

Just imagine Pee Wee singing

"It isn't easy being green." It could be true.

Could you picture Kermit as the

star of Pee Wee's Big Adventure?

Well, yes. I can see Kermit starring in that movie, can't you?

And, I think that Pee Wee and Kermit would have the same defense.

If either were to be attacked, they would simply GO LIMP. Right.

Somehow, I can see Miss Piggy falling big time for Pee Wee.

And once I think about it, I can see Pee Wee falling for Miss Piggy.

Actually, stranger things have happened. In Hollywood, especially.

Want an example? Well, let's take Tom Arnold...see what I mean?

I mean, who do you think made better life choices, Tom or Pee Wee?

And let's not even get into Julia Roberts &

Lyle Lovett. Is he the poster child for ugly?

Can you see John Wayne & Kermit

in a movie, Wayne as the bad guy,

Kermit as sheriff? I always

thought John Wayne was playing

"John Wayne" in every movie;

he just happened to change hats and shirts.

S O M Y T H E O R Y I S

T H E R E A R E A C T O R S

and there are "personalties."

"Personalities" always play themselves,

but only because they are NOT actors.

Actors, on the other hand, are truly gifted.

They act. Let's take a couple of extreme examples.

DUSTIN HOFFMAN IS AN ACTOR CAPITAL A

Freakshow—Oblique • TypeArt

BILL MURRAY IS A PERSONALITY. CAPITAL P.

Frontline—Regular • TypeArt

THAT'S NOT TO IMPLY THAT MURRAY ISN'T

Hammerhead—Regular • TypeArt

TALENTED. HE IS QUITE ENTERTAINING,

Junglemania—Oblique • TypeArt

BUT IN EVERY MURRAY MOVIE, HE PLAYS

Junglemania—Regular • TypeArt

THE SAME GUY. HE JUST HAS DIFFERENT

Junglemania—Staggered • TypeArt

NAMES. GROUNDHOG DAY WAS HIS BIOGRAPHY.

Junglemania—StaggeredOblique • TypeArt

EVERY DAY, SAME STORY.

Puzzler—Bold • TypeArt

DON'T GET ME WRONG.

Puzzler—BoldOblique • TypeArt

I LIKE BILL MURRAY. I DO.

Puzzler—Oblique • TypeArt

IN GHOSTBUSTERS, HE

Puzzler—Regular • TypeArt

was very entertaining, very funny.

Strangelove—Bold • TypeArt

But he was playing Bill Murray. Himself.

Strangelove—BoldItalic • TypeArt

90

A Good Case Could Be Made That

Strangelove—Italic • TypeArt

Kermit The Frog Isn't Truly

Strangelove—Regular • TypeArt

an Actor, but a Personality.

Sundance—Bold • TypeArt

Can You Imagine Kermit

Sundance—BoldItalic • TypeArt

being Cast as The Lone

Sundance—Italic • TypeArt

Ranger? And Kermit certainly

Sundance—Regular • TypeArt

Can't Play Tonto Either. He Might Be

Tolstoy—Oblique • TypeArt

Able To Play The Great Horse, Though.

Tolstoy—Regular • TypeArt

Kermit Could Play the part of Silver, the great horse.

What The Hell—Oblique • TypeArt

Of Course, he would have to change colors. No green

What The Hell—Regular • TypeArt

It Doesn't Make Sense to have a Green Colored Horse Named Silver. Not at All.

DeccoModernNormal • A. Hullinger/T-26 (C. A.)

Or, Could You Imagine The Lone Ranger Getting on Kermit the Horse, and as he prepares to go into the west, says, "Hi-Yo, Green"?

Technique • A. Roe/T-26 (Creative Alliance)

No, Kermit the Frog would have to have a Costume Change in Order to Play the Part of the Great Horse, Silver, in the Lone Ranger.

TechniqueLight • A. Roe/T-26 (Creative Alliance)

91

IMAGINE AN ACTORS' STRIKE, AND

PalazzoCaps • ABCDesign (Creative Alliance)

all the Animal Actors Decide to Not Cross the Picket Line. And then

Birch • Adobe (Creative Alliance)

Lassie will

Blackoak • Adobe (Creative Alliance)

NOT WORK. SHE'S ON STRIKE.

CiceroCaps • Adobe (Creative Alliance)

But a few animal actors WILL work. A Cat

Gothic 13 • Adobe (Creative Alliance)

Named Daryl says "I will work. Hire me as Lassie."

Poplar • Adobe (Creative Alliance)

And the Producer hires him.

Serpentine Bold • Adobe (Creative Alliance)

All goes Well until Lassie,

Serpentine BoldOblique • Adobe (C. Alliance)

THE CAT, IS SUPPOSED TO GO

Serpentine Bold—small caps • Adobe (C.A.)

FOR HELP. THE ACTING CAREER

Serpentine BoldOblique—sm cap • Adobe (C.A.)

of Daryl as a Dog is over. Because no matter how he tries, Daryl is NOT an actor at all.

Willow • Adobe (Creative Alliance)

Daryl is no actor; He's a Personality. See?

AdvertisersGothicLight • Creative Alliance

So, Let's Get Back to Bill Murray. OK?

TriumIn • Agfa (Creative Alliance)

I think it would be fun to lunch with him.

It's kinda like I already think I know him.

HE'S HIM. I THINK PLAYING

golf with him would be fun, but

he still isn't an ACTOR.

Dustin Hoffman is an actor.

Take Rain Man, for example. He acts.

He creates a character you believe.

In Tootsie, same thing. He acts.

You even buy into the whole premise.

Same as in Wag the Dog. Great.

Remember "The Graduate"?

Young Dustin Hoffman. Just a kid. Still classy.

That movie had one of the most famous movie scenes ever,

THE ONE WITH ANNE BANCROFT,

LOVELY ANNE BANCROFT

who happens to be Mel Brooks' wife.

Anyway, the famous scene is also

the poster for the movie—Anne Bancroft taking off a stocking, Dustin looking on

and his character saying, "Are you trying to seduce me, Mrs. Robinson?"

I bet every college boy who ever saw that movie lusted for Anne Bancroft.

I know that I did. And I know that my friends did, too—a LOT, for a LONG time.

THAT WAS BEFORE OLDER WOMEN ACTUALLY SEDUCED YOUNGER MEN. (DARN IT.)

I saw Anne Bancroft recently on the Tony Awards.

She is over 70 now and lookin' good.

She was there with Mel Brooks, genius.

Mel Brooks is also her husband, as I said.

Mel Brooks is one of

the most creative people of our generation.

HE WAS A YOUNG WRITER FOR "YOUR SHOW OF SHOWS" IN THE 1950S, THE SID CAESAR SHOW.

HE STARTED DOING MOVIES

a little later, writing AND producing back in the 1960s.

His first was "The Producers".

This was one of the best comedies ever,

but *it* didn't impress the critics.

What did/do they know? Nonetheless, a small group of people

REALIZED HOW GOOD THIS MOVIE WAS, AND ITS POPULARITY GREW—

VERY SLOWLY. BUT IT WAS AVAILABLE ON TAPE, AND BY THE TIME THAT THE AFI,

which is the American Film Institute, named the 100 Best Comedies of all time, it was near the top.

IN 2001, MORE THAN 30 YEARS AFTER THE MOVIE CAME OUT, IT WAS A BROADWAY SHOW. NO, THAT'S AN UNDERSTATEMENT. IT BECAME THE

most honored Broadway show of all

time, winning 12 Tony awards,

What an ironic situation.

The movie, "The Producers", was about two

producers who created a Broadway show.

The show HAD to be a flop, because they

had swindled all the investors.

They sold something like 2500% of the show

to little old ladies who invested because the older producer "boinked" them. So, if

THE SHOW FLOPPED, THEY DIDN'T

have to pay back the investors, and they had MANY more investors than were needed.

Mel Brooks created this.

Mel Brooks created the show in which The Producers simply HAD to create a major FLOP.

What was the name

of the show they did? "Springtime for Hitler". Yes,

the movie had a Broadway show inside the movie.

Great concept. The killer scene features the song "Springtime for Hitler and Germany".

(EXTRA CHARACTERS FOR THE ABOVE FONT: AGJKMNRSUWY akrswy)

JUST IMAGINE GOOSE-STEPPING DANCERS IN A BUSBY BERKELEY STYLE. SUCH IMAGINATION.

(EXTRA CHARACTERS FOR THE ABOVE FONT: AGJKMNRSUWY AGJKRSUWY)

But in the end, the two producers get caught, and wind up going to prison.

and while in prison, they do the same thing, creating a musical

and taking in far too many investors. Great movie. Great musical.

That was just Mel Brooks' first movie. Many think that his best one was "Blazing Saddles".

The "noisy beans" scene around the campfire was an all–time classic. A breakthrough, really.

Others think that "Young Frankenstein" was his all-time best movie. Remember that one?

SpireExtraLight • Fonthaus (Creative Alliance)

Gene Wilder was the great-grandson of the original Doctor Frankenstein,

SpireExtraLightExpert • Fonthaus (C. Alliance)

and he eventually followed in the Footsteps of the original Doctor Frankenstein,

SpireMonoline • Fonthaus (Creative Alliance)

By the way, Gene Wilder also starred in "The Producers". Gene Wilder is an actor, not a personality,

SpireMonolineExpert • Fonthaus (C. Alliance)

Tom Hanks is an Actor. No. Tom Hanks is an ACTOR.

Stadion • Fonthaus (Creative Alliance)

I MEAN, HE DOESN'T PLAY HIMSELF.

Trio—Bold • Fonthaus (Creative Alliance)

JUST THINK OF TOM HANKS IN "BIG." GREAT.

Trio—Light • Fonthaus (Creative Alliance)

NOW, WITH THAT START, REMEMBER HIM

Trio—Medium • Fonthaus (Creative Alliance)

in "Forrest Gump". Now THAT was acting. He BECAME Forrest Gump.

Trois Regular • Fonthaus (Creative Alliance)

And think of the movie "Philadelphia".

Link Bold • Gerard Mariscalchi (C. Alliance)

and "Saving Private Ryan". Great performances.

Link Bold Italic • Gerard Mariscalchi (C. A.)

Every time Tom Hanks acts, he CREATES a character.

Link Italic • Gerard Mariscalchi (C. Alliance)

That's the difference between actors and personalities.

Link Regular • Gerard Mariscalchi (C. Alliance)

"Saturday Night Live" has produced

Briem Akademi Bold • G. Se Briem (C. Alliance)

many personalities and a few actors.

Briem Akademi Bold Bsl • G. Se Briem (C. A.)

Looking for an actor? Dan Ackroyd.

Briem Akademi Bold Oblique • G. S. Briem (C.A.)

Yes, Dan Ackroyd is quite an actor.

Briem Akademi Comp Bold • G. Se Briem (C. A.)

Remember him in "Dragnet"? He simply became Joe Friday. Jack Webb would be very proud.

Briem Akademi Comp Bold Bsl • G. S. Briem (C.A.)

And when he was in "Driving Miss Daisy", he created a totally new character, a man of the south.

Briem Akademi Comp Bold Oblique • G. S. Briem (C.A.)

He had to CREATE that character, because it wasn't his "personality" that we saw.

Briem Akademi Comp Light • G. Se Briem (C. A.)

And as I mentioned before, Bill Murray is always Bill Murray. That doesn't make him a bad person though.

Briem Akademi Comp Light Bsl • G. S. Briem (C.A.)

It's just that there is a big difference between actors and personalities.

Briem Akademi Comp Light Oblique • G. S. Briem (C.A.)

One of my favorite "stars" of all time is a personality, not an actor.

Briem Akademi Comp Medium • G. S. Briem (C.A.)

That doesn't mean that I have any less respect for Mary Tyler Moore.

Briem Akademi Comp Medium Bsl • G. S. Briem (C.A.)

But whenever you see MTM, you see her personality. She just doesn't create new characters.

Briem Akademi Comp Medium Oblique • G. S. Briem (C.A.)

Want to know a good actor? Surprise!

Briem Akademi Cond Bold • G. Se Briem (C. A.)

Robin Williams is an excellent actor

Briem Akademi Cond Bold Bsl • G. S. Briem (C.A.)

even though his "foundation" is his personality.

Briem Akademi Cond Bold Oblique • G. S. Briem (C.A.)

Somehow, he transcends that and is

Briem Akademi Cond Light • G. Se Briem (C.A.)

able to create believable characters.

Briem Akademi Cond Light Bsl • G. S. Briem (C.A.)

And as much as I like Candace Bergen,

Briem Akademi Cond Light Oblique • G. S. Briem (C.A.)

I don't think of her as an actor. She's always Candace.

Briem Akademi Cond Medium • G. S. Briem (C.A.)

Same with Jane Curtin, one of the "Saturday Night Live".

Briem Akademi Cond Medium Bsl • G. S. Briem (C.A.)

As good an entertainer as Jane Curtin is,

Briem Akademi Cond Medium Oblique • G. S. Briem (C.A.)

she is not really an actress.

Briem Akademi Light • G. Se Briem (C.A.)

Want a good contrast to Jane?

Briem Akademi Light Bsl • G. Se Briem (C.A.)

John Lithgow. He is an ACTOR.

Briem Akademi Light Oblique • G. Se Briem (C.A.)

Just compare his character in

Briem Akademi Medium • G. Se Briem (C.A.)

the great movie "Princess Caraboo".

Briem Akademi Medium Bsl • G. Se Briem (C.A.)

Compare his character in

Briem Akademi Medium Oblique • G. S. Briem (C.A.)

"Princess Caraboo" with his role

Havergal Book • Holly Goldsmith (C. Alliance)

in "Third Rock From the Sun"

Havergal Heavy • Holly Goldsmith (C. Alliance)

and you will see just how much

Havergal Light • Holly Goldsmith (C. Alliance)

of an ACTOR John Lithgow is.

Havergal SemiBold • Holly Goldsmith (C. A.)

And how about Steve Martin?

Binary Bold • ITC (Creative Alliance)

I'm not sure about Steve Martin.

Binary Light • ITC (Creative Alliance)

I think he may be an actor, and

Mona Lisa Solid • ITC (Creative Alliance)

I base that on his role in "Father of the Bride". But when you

Roswell Two • ITC (Creative Alliance)

LOOK AT MOST OF HIS MOVIES, HE SEEMS TO PLAY STEVE MARTIN, I THINK. JON LOVITZ?

Roswell SC Two • ITC (Creative Alliance)

He started out as a personality. Yeah, that's the ticket. Then you

Roswell Three • ITC (Creative Alliance)

SEE HIM IN "A LEAGUE OF THEIR OWN" AND YOU SEE HE CAN ACT. YEAH, I'M AN ACTOR,

Roswell SC Three • ITC (Creative Alliance)

not just a personality. Yeah, that's the ticket, Jack.

Plakette DemiBold • Title Wave Studios

DID YOU KNOW THAT JULIA ROBERTS GETS $20 MILLION PER MOVIE?

And Jim Carrey gets about the same?

Is Jim Carrey a personality, or an actor?

I think he used to be a personality.

Then, he turned into an actor.

ONCE HE DID "THE TRUMAN SHOW", HE GOT TO ACT.

And when he played Andy Kaufmann,

as Kaufmann, he really ACTED.

I think that all personalities

WOULD LIKE TO BE ACTORS,

IF THEY COULD. BUT IT AIN'T EASY.

When you look at some of the old "B" movies,

you can see just how tough it is to be an actor.

So Julia Roberts gets $20 million per?

Forkbeard • ITC/Fontek (Creative Alliance)

She can't even hit a curve ball. Or dunk.

Gill Display Compressed • ITC/Fontek (C. A.)

I wonder who makes more money?

Gill Kayo Condensed • ITC/Fontek (C. Alliance)

Julia Roberts, or, say, the guy

Green • ITC/Fontek (Creative Alliance)

WHO INVENTED THE SLINKY? I WONDER.

Harvey • ITC/Fontek (Creative Alliance)

Does a movie star make more than,

Klepto • ITC/Fontek (Creative Alliance)

say, a pretty productive baseball star? Who's worth it?

Latino Elongated • ITC/Fontek (C. Alliance)

That would be an interesting study. One thing to remember, as this study is done...

Mekanik • ITC/Fontek (Creative Alliance)

baseball players don't get a "percent of the gross" the way movie stars do.

Mekanik Italic • ITC/Fontek (Creative Alliance)

And remember, movie stars

MotterCor • ITC/Fontek (Creative Alliance)

get income from overseas.

MotterCor Con • ITC (Creative Alliance)

Of course, if their movie flops, the "gross" is just that.

Orbon Black • ITC/Fontek (Creative Alliance)

Baseball players seem to have these long-term contracts

Orbon Bold • ITC/Fontek (Creative Alliance)

that pay off no matter what. Sign an 8-year contract

Orbon Light • ITC/Fontek (Creative Alliance)

while you're a top pitcher, a 20-game winner, and

Orbon Regular • ITC/Fontek (Creative Alliance)

then WHAM!

Ozwald • ITC/Fontek (Creative Alliance)

The rotator cuff blows. You're toast.

Pump • ITC/Fontek (Creative Alliance)

As a pitcher, it's over for you, basically,

Pump Demi Bold • ITC/Fontek (C. Alliance)

unless Dr. Frank Jobe performs miracle surgery on you.

Regatta Condensed • ITC/Fontek (C. Alliance)

But even if you never pitch again, you just might

Rundfunk • ITC/Fontek (Creative Alliance)

WIND UP GETTING MILLIONS OF DOLLARS WHILE YOU'RE HOME.

Serengetti • ITC/Fontek (Creative Alliance)

I mean, just how much is A-Rod worth, anyway?

Stoclet Bold • ITC/Fontek (Creative Alliance)

Doesn't anybody understand the

Paddington Bold • Title Wave Studios

word "overpaid"? You want to know what really hacks me off? I'll

Verkehr • ITC/Fontek (Creative Alliance)

tell you anyway. What really bothers me is

Waterloo Bold • ITC/Fontek (Creative Alliance)

when teams pay marginal players MILLIONS, and pay stars

Integral • Jim Marcus (Creative Alliance)

OUTLANDISH MEGA-BUCKS. AND THEN...

then they think they deserve

a new Stadium—for free.

THEY WANT THE LOCAL

TAXPAYERS TO BUILD A NEW

stadium for them—FOR FREE. They say,

"We can't afford to do it ourselves, and if you want us to

pay for it ourselves, we'll just have to move

TO ~~SOME OTHER CITY~~ WHERE THEY LOVE US."

THAT'S JUST WHAT THEY TELL THE LOCAL PEOPLE. "BUILD IT FOR US, OR WE LEAVE."

THEY SAY, "WE CAN'T AFFORD TO BUILD IT ON OUR OWN."

But they can sign an outfielder who hit .262

AND GIVE HIM A HUGE CONTRACT.

I MEAN, THEY PAY MILLIONS...

Neuland Inline • Keystrokes (Creative Alliance)

let's take the A-Rod contract. It's

Informal Black • Keystrokes (Creative Alliance)

something like $272 million,

Isabell Bold • Title Wave Studios

over years. What if they paid him "ONLY"

Aleksei—Disturbed • L. Tsalis/T-26 (C. Alliance)

$200 million? That was more than anyone else

Aleksei—Inline • L. Tsalis/T-26 (C. Alliance)

offered him. So, they pay him "just" $200 million,

Aleksei—Solid • L. Tsalis/T-26 (Creative Alliance)

and then they use the other $72 million

Crane Light • Lennart Hansson (C. Alliance)

to help pay for the new stadium.

Crane Light Italic • Lennart Hansson (C. A.)

They can afford to build the stadium

Crane Medium • Lennart Hansson (C. Alliance)

themselves by paying the players just a few million less.

KochOriginal • Letterperfect (Creative Alliance)

I MEAN, HOW CAN THEY SAY, "WE'RE POOR,"

Kolo Narrow • Letterperfect (Creative Alliance)

& THEN GIVE THESE HUGE CONTRACTS?

Kolo Regular • Letterperfect (Creative Alliance)

BUD SELIG: HOW ABOUT

Kolo Wide • Letterperfect (Creative Alliance)

Do you really think that Derek Jeter will

refuse to play for a measly $10 million

A YEAR, INSTEAD OF $16 MILLION?

WILL HE BE POLITE? "NO, THANKS,

GEORGE. I'M GOING TO WORK AT UPS"?

NO. THESE SALARIES ARE SO UNREAL.

What do the owners have in mind?

Does anyone realize that during the

entire decade of the 1990s, only five

teams made money?

OUT OF 30 TEAMS, ONLY FIVE MADE A PROFIT

FOR THE ENTIRE DECADE. 25 OF THEM LOST MONEY.

Is this any way to run a business?

IT'S A RIDICULOUS WAY

TO RUN A BUSINESS, BUT

as long as there are "greater fools"

with deep pockets out there—people to buy the team—this madness

will continue. Madness! I am

MAD, MAD AS HELL, AND

I am not going to take it any more. I will NOT go to a ball game again.

I TOOK THE PLEDGE IN

1994 after the stupid strike

THAT CANCELLED THE WORLD SERIES. I TOOK A

baseball vow "never again".

In the summer of 1995,

My resolve was tested greatly. I was in Boston.

I was in Boston, and, yes,

Fenway Park was beckoning me.

I had never been to Fenway.

I had never seen the Green Monster.

I was given a free ticket.

A FREE ticket to a Red Sox game at Fenway. What a temptation.

WHAT TO DO, WHAT TO DO?

GREEN MONSTER. TEDDY BALLG

TED WILLIAMS. LEFT FIELD.

TEMPTATION WAS HUGE. TED .406

Finally, I reached a "compromise".

I went to the ball park. Smelled the popcorn.

Watched batting practice. Heard the crowd.

D

Saw the Green Monster, in person. Got a little misty.

TED WILLIAMS IN MY MIND. BUT WHAT ABOUT MY PLEDGE? YOU ASK.

I HAD to see the wall. **315 feet.**

HAD to go there. HAD to pay tribute to Ted Williams. HAD to.

And I did. I knelt before the altar of Theodore S. Williams

with all the reverence of a priest at mass.

I HAD BEEN WHERE TED PLAYED. I WAS THERE.

I KNEW I WOULD SOMEDAY TELL

FUTURE GENERATIONS OF MY TRIP.

They would hear me describe Fenway.

I will also tell them about the day I met Ted.

THEY WILL HEAR ABOUT HOW I SPENT AN AFTERNOON WITH HIM, DOWN IN ISLAMORADO, IN 1985.

AND THEY WILL HEAR THE LEGEND OF

THE GREAT TED WILLIAMS.

THEY WILL HEAR OF MY VISIT WITH HIM IN FLORIDA.

They will hear about Ted's Dalmatian, Slugger.

They will hear how I got my own dog,

a dalmatian named Buster, because of that trip.

They will hear about how I watched

Ted and Slugger, and saw

this magical bond between Man and Dog, Ted & Slugger.

And I wanted a dog like Slugger.

So I got Buster, who became my best friend (and only son),

soon after that. They will hear how Buster

lived with us for almost 11 years,

and when he died, it was like losing my best friend.

BECAUSE HE WAS MY BEST.

BUSTER WAS MY BEST FRIEND.

WHEN I TELL THE STORY

OF TED WILLIAMS, I WILL

D always talk about Buster, and how he was

the result of my visit with Ted Williams that day in '85.

When I talk about the day, I will say that 10 years

later I visited

Fenway Park_

And I kept my

"no more baseball games" pledge that day, even though I went to Fenway. Yes,

I saw the Green Monster, thought about Ted (and Buster), got misty.

And before the game started, I hailed a taxi.

When I was in Junior High School, Gum Chewing in class

Allise • Fonthead

was somewhere between being a Capital Crime and a Mortal Sin. Every teacher was on

BattleStation • Fonthead

THE LOOKOUT FOR A GUM SUSPECT. IF

Engravers Litho Cond Bold • Title Wave Studios

THEY HAD HAD POLICE IN THE HALLS,

Engravers Roman • Title Wave Studios

LIKE TODAY, THEY WOULD BE THE

Goliath • Fonthead

Gum Police. Some of the more daring students

Navel • Fonthead

smuggled gum into class.

ReadOut • Fonthead

We would try to chew

ReadOut Super • Fonthead

CHEWING GUM WITHOUT

RedFive • Fonthead

BEING SEEN. IT WAS TOUGH BUT

Binner • Title Wave Studios

we all tried to do it. And we always got caught.

Caslon Antique • Title Wave Studios

WE WERE ALWAYS CAUGHT CHEWING GUM.

Engravers Litho Cond • Title Wave Studios

The Punishment was very severe.

Cipollini Bold • Title Wave Studios

THE SENTENCE FOR GUM CHEWING

Copperplate Gothic • Title Wave Studios

WOULD BE TO GET "PADDLED".

Copperplate Gothic Bold • Title Wave Studios

TODAY, THEY WOULD CALL IT "CHILD ABUSE".

Copperplate Gothic Cond • Title Wave Studios

BACK THEN, IT SEEMED PROPER.

Copperplate Gothic Cond Bold • Title Wave Studios

I didn't understand why a teacher

Coronado • Title Wave Studios

should spank a student for chewing

Dynamo • Title Wave Studios

GUM IN CLASS, BUT IT HAPPENED ALL THE TIME.

Eldamar • Title Wave Studios

YES, IT EVEN HAPPENED TO ME.

Elefont • Title Wave Studios

Where do babies come from?

Greco-In • 2 Rebels

PINK IS FOR GIRLS()

Minimex • 2 Rebels

Blue, of course, is for little baby boys.

Mediterano • Aerotype

So, where do babies come from?

Saber • flahfonts

I THINK EVERY PARENT DREADS

Acropolis • P22

the day that the kids ask the

Kells Round • P22

QUESTION, "WHERE DO BABIES COME FROM?"

Kells Square • P22

"MEMPHIS" IS WHERE.

Victorian Gothic • P22

That's what one of my children said. "Babies come from Memphis."

Victorian Swash • P22

"HOW DO YOU KNOW THAT?" I ASKED.

Brahn Mufun • Synfonts

"BECAUSE MY FRIEND TOLD ME THAT.

Brahn Mufun—Bold • Synfonts

She and her sister were both born in Memphis."

Grayletter—TenWeight • Treacyfaces

Babies come from Memphis too.

Foreign Language–Oblique • TypeArt

⌐⌐⊦ ⊃⌐⊃ ⊐⌐⌐⌐⌐⊦ ⌐⌐⌐⌐ ⊦⌐⌐⌐⌐.

Foreign Language—Regular •TypeArt

You weren't born in Memphis, I told her.

"Oh," she said, then sat silently for awhile.

"So where DO babies come from?"

"Oh." I said, while I thought about it awhile.

Then I had the answer. "St. Louis," I said.

That was not the answer she wanted.

I was suddenly into an area where I

was not especially familiar. Ugh!

So, I did what any good father would do,

"Go ask Your Mother," I said. "She knows."

So we began Sex Education 101, like that.

Next thing you know, we were in a book.

WE WERE IN A BOOK STORE, BUYING A BOOK

Eccentric • Agfa (Creative Alliance)

that A Friend had recommended to Us.

Raphael • Agfa (Creative Alliance)

The friend had three daughters, and said it was a Very Good Book.

Basque • Creative Alliance

So we bought that book, then and there.

OldEnglish • Creative Alliance

The title of the book was this:

Uncial • Creative Alliance

"Where Did I Come From?"

Wedding Text • Creative Alliance

So, we took the new book home.

LucidaBlackletter • Bigelow & Holmes (C.A.)

THE NEW BOOK WAS FOR

Benedikt Bold • Bo Berndal (Creative Alliance)

OUR TWO LOVELY & INQUISITIVE

Benedikt Light • Bo Berndal (Creative Alliance)

daughters who had asked Questions: "Where

Johabu • Bo Berndal (Creative Alliance)

do babies come from?" They had

Unotype • Bo Berndal (Creative Alliance)

the question, and now they had

Unotype Bold • Bo Berndal (Creative Alliance)

this great book to give them the answer.

Vadstenakursive • Bo Berndal (Creative Alliance)

The book would answer their

NeoBold • C. Segurat/T-26 (Creative Alliance)

questions about babies and stuff like that.

Skjald • Creative Alliance

the book was really well done. it was very complete;

Revolution • D.Carter/T-26 (Creative Alliance)

it covered the Subject in very small steps. Just right for kids.

BrunnhildeOne • Fonthaus (Creative Alliance)

With each step, the book gave information just a little more complex.

BrunnhildeTwo • Fonthaus (Creative Alliance)

P

We showed the book to our daughter.

Iona Regular • Gerard Mariscalchi (C. Alliance)

We showed her the book, and then put it

Agincourt • ITC/Fontek (Creative Alliance)

among the other books on her shelf

Blackmoor • ITC/Fontek (Creative Alliance)

such as Dr. seuss books—cats & hats—

Frances Uncial • ITC/Fontek (Creative Alliance)

SO THAT WHEN SHE WAS LOOKING

Kanban • ITC/Fontek (Creative Alliance)

at books, THIS book would be

Korigan Bold • ITC/Fontek (Creative Alliance)

there, and she could move along at

Korigan Light • ITC/Fontek (Creative Alliance)

her own pace, in her own time.

Minska Bold • ITC/Fontek (Creative Alliance)

she could move at her own pace.

Minska Light • ITC/Fontek (Creative Alliance)

SO, AS WEEKS PASSED, WE NOTICED

Minska Medium• ITC/Fontek (Creative Alliance)

she would read this book

Simran • ITC/Fontek (Creative Alliance)

very often. Sometimes she would

AlbanyTelegram • J. Marcus/T-26 (C. Alliance)

READ DR. SEUSS, AND THEN

SkreechCaps • J. Marcus/T-26 (Creative Alliance)

she would read "Where Did I Come From?"

ArabiaFelix • Judith Sutcliffe (Creative Alliance)

What an Interesting Combination

Mesopotamia • Judith Sutcliffe (C. Alliance)

of Books-cats in hats, along with

Hindendburg • Keystrokes (Creative Alliance)

green eggs and ham, green eggs

Percolator Regular • Lunchbox (C. Alliance)

and where babies come from.

Percolator Bold • Lunchbox (Creative Alliance)

SOMEWHERE ABOUT MID-BOOK, THE DETAILS

Percolator—Small Caps • Lunchbox (C. Alliance)

got a little more detailed: Sex Ed 102,

Percolator—Text • Lunchbox (Creative Alliance)

or maybe even Sex Education 201.

Replicant • Lunchbox (Creative Alliance)

P

For example, the "parts" are named

(Mctckcvckychef Ligatures for above)

and the parts are described.

(Thfjlafbchttoofftvryft Ligatures for above)

So our daughter was reading, aloud,

words such as: "It's called a Vagina."

AND THERE WAS EVEN ANOTHER SENTENCE THAT TOLD

JUST HOW TO PRONOUNCE THE WORD "VAGINA",

which a lot of people call "Virginia".

The book made it very simple though.

"Vagina rhymes with North Carolina."

Thanks to this book, Sex Education

was made a little less stressful for me

P

except for the evening when we had company.

Goudy Text • Monotype (Creative Alliance)

We invited some friends over for dinner that night

Goudy Text Lombardic Caps • Monotype (C. A.)

and somewhere between the main course

Wittenberger Fraktur • Monotype (C. Alliance)

and dessert, our daughter felt the

Wittenberger Fraktur Bd • Monotype (C. A.)

NEED TO TALK, AND SHE DID.

Ginko • Paul Pegoraro (Creative Alliance)

"I have a new book," she said.

AureusUncial • Philip Bouwsma (C. Alliance)

Nobody Said Anything to That.

Clemente Rotunda • Philip Bouwsma (C. A.)

She continued talking. "And you

Connach • Philip Bouwsma (Creative Alliance)

know what I learned today?"

Connach—Historical • Philip Bouwsma (C. A.)

Nobody knew what she had learned,

CresciRotunda • Philip Bouwsma (C. Alliance)

so she told us what she had learned.

Francesca • Philip Bouwsma (Creative Alliance)

"Vagina rhymes with North Carolina," she said.

Francesca Gothic • Philip Bouwsma (C. Alliance)

And all conversation Came to a Halt.

Hrabanus • Philip Bouwsma (Creative Alliance)

P

121

THE ROOM WAS REALLY

Lombardic Capitals • Philip Bouwsma (C. A.)

Silent. Nobody Said A Word. It was

Monmouth • Philip Bouwsma (Creative Alliance)

Quiet Like We've Never Heard Before.

Poggia Bookhand • Philip Bouwsma (C. Alliance)

Our Daughter Used This as an Opening,

Polenta Black Italic • Philip Bouwsma (C. A.

Good Kid That She Was, to Tell All of Us,

Polenta Italic • Philip Bouwsma (C. Alliance)

"You Know I Really Liked That Book.

Ramsey • Philip Bouwsma (Creative Alliance)

I LEARNED SOME NEW WORDS AND

Abbot Uncial • Richard Yeend (Creative Alliance)

some other new things in that book."

Simplex • Type Revivals (Creative Alliance)

We all Anticipated Just Exactly

Odilia • Zezschwitz (Creative Alliance)

what she would tell us next. Quickly,

Peignot • Title Wave Studios

SHE SAID, "BOYS HAVE PEANUTS."

Pericles • Title Wave Studios

Do you ever look at a book,

and then do you ever wonder where

the writer was when he wrote that?

Sometimes, the introduction in the book will tell the answer.

The answer. I Remember Reading Books

WHERE THE AUTHOR SAID, "I

G

AM WRITING THIS WHILE

overlooking the Atlantic Ocean

in Ibiza. Or, I am writing this from

my Penthouse in the luxurious Hotel...

or, as I sit here, Mt. Everest in the distance"

from a castle in Belgium, or France.

Or from the 2nd home in Aspen.

Or on the Queen Elizabeth II, 3 days

out of London, on the water on

the way to New York.

maybe the writer is on the Delta Queen on the Ohio.

Or perhaps on the Orient Express (a mystery, of...)

You get the idea. Writers

are supposed to write their

words from exotic places, places like

Katmandu or the Embassy

in Rome. The image that I had

was that people who wrote books were

supposed to write from romantic, faraway places.

Wonder why I have that thought in mind

ScratchNsniff—Regular • 2 Rebels

at this Particular Moment? Well,

Scritto Politto Freako • 2 Rebels

here is why: I am writing these words now

SemiSans • 2 Rebels

Let me tell you, it's Not the Cayman Islands. No.

Toxin—Spotless • 2 Rebels

WHERE AM I? IN BOSTON. (I KNOW IT

Bellamie—Oblique •TypeArt

SEEMS LIKE A GOOD START, NOT BAD.)

Bellamie—Regular •TypeArt

But I'm not writing this

Bighead—Bold •TypeArt

from the Back Back here,

Bighead—BoldOblique •TypeArt

nor from my suite at

Bighead—Oblique •TypeArt

The Four Seasons Hotel.

Bighead—Regular •TypeArt

No. I'm writing this from

Braindead—Bold •TypeArt

Gate 84 at Logan Airport

Braindead—BoldOblique •TypeArt

in Boston, Massachusetts.

Braindead—Oblique •TypeArt

Not exactly what I had

in mind, not my choice,

for a place to write

these words that you are

reading right now. I could

think of a lot more glamorous places to write this book.

For example, I'm close to Martha's Vineyard right now.

I'm also close to Edgartown, which is a very famous place.

And I'm not that far away from Nantucket. No, not far at all.

THAT would be a nice place to write this book.

Just imagine looking out to the Atlantic Ocean as I

write this book, sipping a nice Merlot and writing

an occasional word — between sips on Nantucket.

Sitting there **on** Nantucket Island,

sea breeze in my face, at my laptop

computer, which, by the way, is an Apple.

Apple Computer. Macintosh. G4. Titanium.

ANYONE THERE FROM APPLE?

REMEMBER "PRODUCT PLACEMENT"?

THINK OF THE VALUE TO MACINTOSH WHEN

PEOPLE WHO BUY THIS BOOK SEE **THAT**

IT WAS **PRODUCED** ON A **MAC,** ON YOUR

VERY BEST LAPTOP COMPUTER. MAYBE

YOU WILL WANT TO SEND ME A GIFT...ANYWAY,

I digress. I was Talking About Being on Nantucket. Every time

I think of that lovely place, I smile, and think back...

Somehow, I always think back to Junior High School.

Even though that was a long time ago, I think back to those days

whenever I hear Nantucket. Yes I do.

It wasn't because of geography, either.

Gee, Junior High School was so long ago.

But some things you remember like they happened yesterday.

One of my strongest memories of Junior high School was

every October, we watched the World Series.

Yes, we watched the World Series

on TV in CLASS. Kids today would say "at

NIGHT?" because they don't remember

ANY WORLD SERIES PLAYED IN THE DAY.

THEY DON'T REALIZE THAT ONCE UPON A TIME,

way back then, World Series games

Variator Three • J. Marcus/T.26 (C. Alliance)

were all played in the daytime and

Bludgeon • Jon H. Clinch (Creative Alliance)

somehow, the schools thought

Adolescence • Lunchbox (Creative Alliance)

that the World Series was important

Outahere—Bold • Lunchbox (Creative Alliance)

enough to bring in TV sets and have

Outahere—Light • Lunchbox (Creative Alliance)

them in "study hall" so kids

Outahere—Regular • Lunchbox (C. Alliance)

with a late afternoon study hall could watch the game.

Sabotage • Lunchbox (Creative Alliance)

We got to watch the games on TV

Helix • M. Renberg/T-26 (Creative Alliance)

unless we happened to have class.

Fur—ExtraRounded • P. Sahre/T-26 (C. Alliance)

If we had class then, we could not watch.

Fur—ExtraRounded—Light • P. Sahre/T-26 (C.A.)

I remember being in Science

FacsimiledBold • Plazm (Creative Alliance)

When Don Larsen pitched his

FacsimiledLight • Plazm (Creative Alliance)

perfect game. Not on TV, though.

Rufnu • Plazm (Creative Alliance)

A friend had a transistor radio

Residoo • Roger Luteyn (Creative Alliance)

AND WOODY TOLD ME

Osprey • S. Farrell/T-26 (Creative Alliance)

ABOUT IT. YES, WOODY MOORE

DoomsDay • Fonthead

told me about Don Larsen's

Gritzpop • Fonthead

PerfeCt Game. The neWW s

GritzpopGrunge • Fonthead

came in the Middle of Science class one

Ladybug • Fonthead

October afternoon at advance School.

Mondo—Loose • Fonthead

THAT'S WHEN. NOW, EVERY TIME

WashMe • Fonthead

I hear Don Larsen's Perfect

Ebola—Kikwit • Vintage Type Library

game Mentioned, I always

Ebola—MarburgBlackVomit • V. Type Library

think about that Science Class

Ebola—Reston • Vintage Type Library

in OctOber 1956 whEn

Ebola—SudanCrashing • Vintage Type Library

Woodie Moore Told me.

Ebola—Zaire • Vintage Type Library

Did you ever see a sign that made you look twice?

Prints Charming—Oblique • TypeArt

I mean, some signs defy logic; the words say one thing

Prints Charming—Regular • TypeArt

but your mind goes somewhere else with it.

Prints Charming—Version • TypeArt

Like the sign that said "Satellite Parking".

Prints Charming—VersionOblique • TypeArt

Satellite Parking? A Real Satellite?

Overfield—BoldScript • Treacyfaces

Is there really a PARKING PLACE for SATELLITES?

Saginaw—Bold • Treacyfaces

WHO IN THE WORLD (or galaxy) IS GOING TO

Saginaw—Light • Treacyfaces

CIRCLE EARTH IN A SATELLITE, LOOKING

Saginaw—Medium • Treacyfaces

for a place to park it?

2 RebelsUn • 2 Rebels

And if you did, exactly how much would

LeScript—Big • 2 Rebels

Satellite Parking cost? I have thought about

LeScript—Bold • 2 Rebels

that for a while, and I wonder who

LeScript—Regular • 2 Rebels

decided to call that place "Satellite Parking".

LeScript—Thin • 2 Rebels

131

"Satellite Parking" needs a

Quattr'occhi • 2 Rebels

better name, a new label, a change in identity,

Brophy Script • Creative Alliance

Like maybe "Parking Lot B". Or whatever.

Citadel Script • Creative Alliance

Yesterday, I saw another sign.

Commercial Script • Creative Alliance

It was also a little off the wall in its true meaning.

Flemish Script II • Creative Alliance

The sign said "Watch Battery Replacement Here".

Florentine Script II • Creative Alliance

Why in the world would anyone want to watch a battery

French Script • Creative Alliance

being replaced? I mean, it's not exactly high level entertainment, is it?

Helinda Rook • Creative Alliance

There are certainly many things to do that are

Jasper • Creative Alliance

more fun than watching a battery being replaced. If this

Liberty • Creative Alliance

were such Major Entertainment, there would be an

Mahogany Script • Creative Alliance

annual awards show for all those who are involved in the

Original Script • Creative Alliance

replacement of batteries, wouldn't there?

Riviera Script • Creative Alliance

An awards program for those who Replace Batteries

CaflischScript Bold • Adobe (Creative Alliance)

as in: Best Supporting Role in Battery Replacement.

CaflischScript Regular • Adobe (C. Alliance)

And categories such as Truck Batteries, and

Mistral • Adobe (Creative Alliance)

Car Batteries, not to mention other categories such

Carl Beck • Bo Berndal (Creative Alliance)

as AA Batteries, and smaller roles,

Maricava • Bo Berndal (Creative Alliance)

AAA Batteries. When I see signs with a word with a double meaning

HighScript 20 • Bruno Trico (Creative Alliance)

why do I always find the OTHER meaning in signs and things?

HighScript 20 Italic • Bruno Trico (C. Alliance)

Today I saw a sign that didn't have a double meaning, but it

HighScript 40 • Bruno Trico (Creative Alliance)

was still a very amusing sign. "This Door Must Always be Closed".

HighScript 40 Italic • Bruno Trico (C. Alliance)

That's exactly what the sign said. I read it over again to be sure.

HighScript 80 • Bruno Trico (Creative Alliance)

What does that mean, anyway? The door must never be opened?

HighScript 80 Italic • Bruno Trico (C. Alliance)

My first thought was "Why is the door there, then?

Epaulet • C. Macgregor/T-26 (Creative Alliance)

Wouldn't it have just been better off as a wall?"

CarmineTango • Creative Alliance

Then I noticed that the door was not locked or anything.

Chaplin • Creative Alliance

"Golly," I thought. "What if I opened the door?"

Charme • Creative Alliance

I looked around, expecting to see the Door Police.

Coronet • Creative Alliance

If the Door Police were there, I didn't see them.

Coronet Bold • Creative Alliance

I couldn't help myself.

Salut • Creative Alliance

After looking all around for ""the authorities", I went over to the door and opened it.

Amethyste • Fonthaus (Creative Alliance)

"Perhaps there was a Silent Alarm," I thought.

BernhardBrushscript • Fonthaus (C. Alliance)

No. It didn't happen. Nobody came after me.

Carpenter • Fonthaus (Creative Alliance)

And I left the door open. I expected the Sky to Fall, or

CopperplateScript • Fonthaus (Creative Alliance)

something else bad to happen. But, no. Life went

FrenchLetters—Plain • Fonthaus (C. Alliance)

on just like it did before I opened the door.

FrenchLetters—Raised • Fonthaus (C. Alliance)

Then, I noticed Something Very Curious.

Jawbox • G. Hustwit/Exploding Font Co. (C. A.)

With the door open, the sign was blocked.

Jawbox Chanky • G. Hustwit/Exploding Font Co. (C.A.)

5

No one could even see I had violated the rule.

Jawbreaker • G. Hustwit/Exploding Font Co. (C.A.)

No one knew that I was a Perpetrator, nearly a criminal.

Marnie Regular • Gerard Mariscalchi (C. A.)

Gosh, I had broken a Major Rule...Yet

Toots Extended • Gerard Mariscalchi (C.A.)

A Passerby Could Not Know. Would Not Know.

Toots Regular • Gerard Mariscalchi (C. Alliance)

(Did that line read like it was written by Dr. Seuss? I think so.)

Aristocrat • ITC/Fontek (Creative Alliance)

A Passerby, He Would Not Know. Could Not Know. Sam I am.

Balmoral • ITC/Fontek (Creative Alliance)

So there I was, picturing me, wearing a Dr. Seuss Hat

Bickley Script • ITC/Fontek (Creative Alliance)

Breaking The Rules of Society, and not only that, I'm Writing Like Seuss, Sam I am.

Bordeaux Script • ITC/Fontek (C. Alliance)

Did I open a Closed Door? Yes.

Bronx • ITC/Fontek (Creative Alliance)

I opened a Closed Door. Sam I Am. Help me.

Cancellaresca Script • ITC/Fontek (C. Alliance)

All of a sudden, I'm caught in a Seuss-like world

Clover • ITC/Fontek (Creative Alliance)

all because I opened a door, broke a rule.

Coptek • ITC/Fontek (Creative Alliance)

Broke a Rule, you Motley Fool. No one should ever break a rule.

Dartangnon • ITC/Fontek (Creative Alliance)

No one should ever break a rule, motley fool.

EdwardianScrBol • ITC/Fontek (C. Alliance)

Don't break a rule, you motley fool.

EdwardianScrBolAlt • ITC/Fontek (C. Alliance)

Especially in Dr. Seuss-Land. What will the kids say?

EdwardianScrReg • ITC/Fontek (C. Alliance)

So there I was, standing by the Open Door, on the floor.

EdwardianScrRegAlt • ITC/Fontek (C. Alliance)

In my mind, I was wearing the Long Tall Hat, like a cat

Flamme • ITC/Fontek (Creative Alliance)

My mind said, "Close the Door. Fast." I did.

Fling • ITC/Fontek (Creative Alliance)

And just like that, I escaped Seuss Land, and immediately felt better.

Freestyle Script • ITC/Fontek (Creative Alliance)

But, for the rest of the day, I had this cloud over my head.

Freestyle Script Bold • ITC/Fontek (C. Alliance)

All day I realized that I Broke a Rule.

Gigi • ITC/Fontek (Creative Alliance)

And we don't want to break any rules, now do we? Boy,

Glastonbury • ITC/Fontek (Creative Alliance)

was I ever glad the Door Police were not around.

Gravura • ITC/Fontek (Creative Alliance)

What If I had encountered the Door Police?

Greyton Script • ITC/Fontek (Creative Alliance)

Right away, I would have been "Branded for Life".

Inscription • ITC/Fontek (Creative Alliance)

Right. Branded. "He Opens Doors...

Isadora • ITC/Fontek (Creative Alliance)

the ones that say 'Keep Closed'."

Isadora—Bold • ITC/Fontek (Creative Alliance)

And, of course, that would wind up on my Record.

Johann Sparkling • ITC/Fontek (Creative Alliance)

On the dreaded "Permanent Record". Gads!

Katfish • ITC/Fontek (Creative Alliance)

The Permanent Record. Oh No!!

Kick • ITC/Fontek (Creative Alliance)

Is there anything worse? No.

Kulukundis • ITC/Fontek (Creative Alliance)

My word, right away I knew that there was

Lightnin • ITC/Fontek (Creative Alliance)

No Worse Fate than the Permanent Record.

Marguerita • ITC/Fontek (Creative Alliance)

Fears of youth: getting a misdeed on your record.

Mistral Light • ITC/Fontek (Creative Alliance)

FOREVER BRANDED. AS A DOOR OPENER. PERMANENT.

Mistral SC Light • ITC/Fontek (Creative Alliance)

There is a story about an old man who had been

Musica • ITC/Fontek (Creative Alliance)

very ill and now he was dying. He called his grandson to

Pablo • ITC/Fontek (Creative Alliance)

his deathbed. "I must tell you, before I die…"

Pendry Script • ITC/Fontek (Creative Alliance)

5

"Before I die, I must tell you...

Peters Miro • ITC/Fontek (Creative Alliance)

You must know, Grandson,

Peters Miro Too • ITC/Fontek (Creative Alliance)

before I... Really, there are few things more

Rage Italic • ITC/Fontek (Creative Alliance)

important than..." The grandson came closer

Rapier • ITC/Fontek (Creative Alliance)

to listen to his grandfather's Words of Wisdom.

Redonda Fancy • ITC/Fontek (Creative Alliance)

"Grandson," he said, "The most important thing I can

Redonda • ITC/Fontek (Creative Alliance)

tell you is this: There is No Permanent Record."

Riva • ITC/Fontek (Creative Alliance)

How many rogues wish they knew that long ago?

Santa Fe • ITC/Fontek (Creative Alliance)

No Permanent Record? How many lives would have been changed

Savoye • ITC/Fontek (Creative Alliance)

by the simple knowledge that "Second Chances" do exist.

Scriptease • ITC/Fontek (Creative Alliance)

Actually, some people do learn this while young.

Tropica Script • ITC/Fontek (Creative Alliance)

Might this have been learned by Bill Clinton?

Vivaldi • ITC/Fontek (Creative Alliance)

Perhaps Bill Clinton did learn this at a young age. Right?

Young Baroque • ITC/Fontek (Creative Alliance)

One Question: What about transcripts?

Florens • Letterperfect (Creative Alliance)

Are transcripts a Permanent Record?

Florens Flourished • Letterperfect (C. Alliance)

Surely, transcripts are a Permanent Record.

Spring • Letterperfect (Creative Alliance)

Has anyone discovered that I made a D in Geology?

Spring Light • Letterperfect (Creative Alliance)

Not to mention another D in Astronomy. Well, I did.

Wendy Bold • Letterperfect (Creative Alliance)

That was how I fulfilled the Physical Sciences requirement.

Wendy Light • Letterperfect (Creative Alliance)

Physical Sciences Requirement: six credits.

Wendy Medium • Letterperfect (Creative Alliance)

Why did I do so poorly in those?

Brio • Mecanorma (Creative Alliance)

A few good reasons: no math background and "The Semester of

Dorchester Script • Monotype (C. Alliance)

Pam, and Bonnie and Too Many

Forte • Monotype (Creative Alliance)

College Girls and Too Little Time."

Monoline Script • Monotype (Creative Alliance)

That same semester of Bonnie & Pam

New Berolina • Monotype (Creative Alliance)

was the semester of Astronomy & Geology.

Pepita • Monotype (Creative Alliance)

With only 24 hours in a day, something had to go. (It was studying.)

Palace Script • Monotype (Creative Alliance)

Yes, I was supposed to be learning about Geology and Astronomy, but

Palace Script SemiBold • Monotype (C. Alliance)

really, there was no time to study.

Script Bd • Monotype (Creative Alliance)

What was a guy to do? Bonnie, or Pam, or Books?

Old Fashion Script • Creative Alliance

Well, may I assure you, books lost. Badly.

Old Fashion Script Flourishes • Creative Alliance

Bonnie and Pam have surely forgotten me.

Greyhound Script • Panache Typography (C. A.)

I am but a small footnote in their lives. Very small indeed

Carmela • Philip Bouwsma (Creative Alliance)

like "Senior Guy, Forgot His Name".

Saxony Script • Richard Yeend (C. Alliance)

But those 2 grades: D in Geology & Astronomy

Sackers English Script • Creative Alliance

are on my college transcript, forever, etched in stone. Forever.

Sackers Italian Script • Creative Alliance

Did You Ever Wonder Whatever happened to

Flowerpot • Fonthead

old Girlfriends from College. Whatever

Bernhard Tango • Title Wave Studios

became of them? Do we wonder just where they

Brody • Title Wave Studios

are today, and well, would they

remember you? That's the

Scary Part. Imagine bumping into

Someone you hadn't Seen For Maybe

30 years. Thirty Years is a Long Time,

a very long time. Here's a Scenario: You spot

Her in the mall and you Just Have to go

over and say, "Hello, Do You Remember me?"

She looks at you, then ignores you, like you weren't

Even There—Blank Stare. So you tell her

Your Name, and Then she says,

"I Really Don't Remember Anyone by that name."

And You slowly Slink Away, Ego Wounded. Forever.

TECHNOLOGY IS A WONDERFUL THING.

COMPUTERS MAKE LIFE EASIER

AND WE ALL BENEFIT FROM THE COMPUTER REVOLUTION.

IN THE LAST 40 YEARS, AMAZING

Things Have Happened with Computers.

they have become much more

powerful, and certainly less costly.

Today, the typical car has

150 computers. Yes, the typical car has 150 computers

on board the auto. Computers

control much of a newer car()s

operations. New cars

are FULL OF COMPUTERS.

The Typical Car of 2001 has More

Computing Power than the U.S.

Department of Defense Had in 1960.

Imagine that: your new car has

more computing power while

computer costs have plummeted.

An IBM 650 Mainframe Computer cost $10.

Make that $10 Million, back in 1960.

The laptop computer that I'm using now

has many times more computing power than that.

Yes, my G4 Macintosh Laptop has more power

than the IBM 650 from forty years ago.

My trusty Mac G4 Titanium Laptop (5 pounds) has more power

Than the $10 million IBM Mainframe had 40 years ago. And the big 360...

Foxfire—BoldItalic • Treacyfaces

The 360 took up a Lot of Space: like there was a whole room just for it.

Foxfire—Light • Treacyfaces

And, there was a full-time "Customer Engineer" assigned to it.

Foxfire—Medium • Treacyfaces

I mean, those things would often need maintenance, RIGHT THEN.

Foxfire—MediumItalic • Treacyfaces

So the Customer Engineer was on hand

Honeyspot—Bold • Treacyfaces

and he would Fix it immediately,

Honeyspot—Light • Treacyfaces

RIGHT THEN. imagine how

Zacron—Black • Treacyfaces

technology has affected

Zacron—Light • Treacyfaces

products of the automobile industry.

Amnesia—Light • TypeArt

For example, open the hood of a 1960s car.

Amnesia—LightOblique • TypeArt

Look down. You can see the ground.

Amnesia—Medium • TypeArt

Look under the hood of an older car, and

Amnesia—MediumOblique • TypeArt

you see the engine, a few wires,

Citymap Rounded—Bold • TypeArt

With a carburetor on top,

you see part of the transmission,

a few cables, and not a lot more.

A good mechanic today

can fix an old Car with

a hair pin. Look under the hood

of a new car. What do you see?

Lots and lots of stuff—

stuff that is confusing.

And if you know where to look, there will be a lot of Little Computers.

THOSE LITTLE COMPUTERS CONTROL

LOTS OF FUNCTIONS FOR THE NEW CAR.

The things you never think about are controlled by...

computers! For example, computers control the

Aspersion—Bold • Synfonts

air bags. Think about it: Those Air Bags Don't Work Alone.

Aspersion—Light • Synfonts

THEY must be told to deploy.

LEaD Lights—bold • Synfonts

When does the air bag deploy?

LEaD Lights • Synfonts

When a computer tells it to.

LEaD Lights—Bold • Synfonts

And do you want to know when

LEaD Lights—BoldItalic • Synfonts

you have a tire with low

LEaD Lights—Italic • Synfonts

air pressure?

Liquid Sex • Synfonts

Your Computer will

Liquid Sex—Italic • Synfonts

tell you: get air.

Liquid Sex—Out • Synfonts

Get Some Air For

Liquid SexHard edged and Empty • Synfonts

Your Left Front Tire. It Has Low Air Pressure.

NudE • Synfonts

You need to go to a service station for air.

NudE—bold • Synfonts

Yes, computers help with cars a lot.

One Problem. What is a "Service" Station?

Gas stations don't know what "service" is.

You pull in, pump your own gas, clean

your own window,

test your lights

(head and tail).

NOBODY EVER SAYS ANY MORE, "MAY I

check your oil?" Actually

"service" is no longer

THERE. SERVICE STATIONS

DON'T EXIST MUCH. GAS STATIONS

DAM EIDH HIMH DAM.

"Check your oil, sir?" he asked.

When was the last time you

had someone offer to check

your oil? Of course, with a

COMPUTER RUNNING

YOUR CAR...IMAGINE A COMPUTER

ONBOARD YOUR CAR THAT IS

ADVANCED ENOUGH TO SAY TO YOU,

"CHECKYOUROIL."

OF COURSE, NOW YOU GET

AN ON-SCREEN DISPLAY

WINDOW THAT TELLS

you when you are low on oil.

You know your oil is low, because you read

Serene • Fonthaus (Creative Alliance)

IT ON A MESSAGE ON

VanDoesberg • Fonthaus (Creative Alliance)

THE CONTROL

Mata—Bold • G. Samata/T-26 (Creative Alliance)

PANELS. THE

Mata—Condensed • G. Samata/T-26 (C. Alliance)

MESSAGE SAYS

Mata—CondensedBold • G. Samata/T-26 (C. A.)

YOUR OIL IS

Mata—Regular • G. Samata/T-26 (C. Alliance)

low so you need to add some oil

Lineale Regular • Gerard Mariscalchi (C. A.)

SOON OR YOU WILL HAVE A PROBLEM

Bitmax • ITC/Fontek (Creative Alliance)

WITH LOW OIL PRESSURE.

BuzzerThree • ITC/Fontek (Creative Alliance)

The car's 150 computers are watching out

Data Seventy • ITC/Fontek (Creative Alliance)

for You——Big Brother in your car. Low oil? The computer will flash a message for you on the screen.

Digitek • ITC/Fontek (Creative Alliance)

WHAT A WONDERFUL SYSTEM, TELLING YOU

LCD • ITC/Fontek (Creative Alliance)

WHAT YOU NEED FOR YOUR CAR. NOW.

Synchro • ITC/Fontek (Creative Alliance)

Imagine The Next Generation of On-Board Computers for Automobiles.

Teknik • ITC/Fontek (Creative Alliance)

Just Think About the Possibilities for On-Board Computers.

Union—Round • ITC/Fontek (Creative Alliance)

Voice Systems for Cars Remove the Need to Read the Display Information.

Union—Round Tight • ITC/Fontek (C. Alliance)

For Example, You Could be Driving Down the Highway,

Union—Square • ITC/Fontek (Creative Alliance)

and you would Hear a Voice Say, "Your Oil is Low" Like having a Butler

Union—Square Tight • ITC/Fontek (C. Alliance)

in your car. Well, let's take

Prosper Black • Joe Nicholson (C. Alliance)

this one step Further.

Prosper Black Italic • Joe Nicholson (C. Alliance)

You could customize the voice.

Prosper Bold • Joe Nicholson (Creative Alliance)

If you must have a "voice"

Prosper Bold Italic • Joe Nicholson (C. Alliance)

telling you, you could pick

Prosper Book • Joe Nicholson (Creative Alliance)

the voice you want. How about

Prosper Book Italic • Joe Nicholson (C. Alliance)

a John Wayne voice? "Your

Prosper Condensed Black • Joe Nicholson (C. A.)

oil needs changing, pardner."

Prosper Condensed Black Italic • Joe Nicholson (C. A.)

Or Eva Gabor, saying softly, just to you,

Prosper Condensed Bold • Joe Nicholson (C. A.)

"You Need an Oil Change Now, Dahling."

Prosper Condensed Bold Italic • Joe Nicholson (C. A.)

Or a Pee-Wee Herman Voice, "Change your

Prosper Condensed Book • Joe Nicholson (C. A.)

oil. Ha-ha!" How about Jack Nickolson's

Prosper Condensed Book Italic • Joe Nicholson (C. A.)

voice saying to you, "Your oil is low."

Prosper Condensed Light • Joe Nicholson (C. A.)

The Rules Say Add Some Oil to Your car

Prosper Condensed Light Italic • Joe Nicholson (C. A.)

and you don't want to break any rules,

Prosper Condensed Medium • Joe Nicholson (C. A.)

do you? That leads to More Possibilities

Prosper Condensed Medium Italic • J. Nicholson (C. A.)

for having mass customizing of voices.

Prosper Light • Joe Nicholson (Creative Alliance)

Say your teenage kid is driving the car.

Prosper Light Italic • Joe Nicholson (C. Alliance)

The on-board computers senses

Prosper Medium • Joe Nicholson (C. Alliance)

the car is getting low on oil, and

Prosper Medium Italic • Joe Nicholson (C. A.)

the car "knows" who's driving.

Prosper Open Black • Joe Nicholson (C. Alliance)

So the car needs oil, and the

Kid is driving; the system's

computer voice says to him,

"Hey Dude, it's time to add some oil"

What an interesting possibility. Every

driver could choose the voice and

the message would be customized.

How about a voice like Lt. Columbo

with a message like "You need to

tie up a couple of loose ends. Change

your oil?" Why, 150 computers on a

car seems like a 1950s idea—like

a 1950 idea for a Science Fiction Movie.

They don't make movies like that anymore.

Prosper Open Cd Medium • Joe Nicholson (C. A.)

There's Just Something About the old

Prosper Open Cd Medium Italic • J. Nicholson (C. A.)

Sci-Fi Movie from the 1950s and 60s.

Prosper Open Light • Joe Nicholson (C. Alliance)

They were always in Black & White.

Prosper Open Light Italic • Joe Nicholson (C. A.)

They never won any Academy Awards,

Prosper Open Medium • Joe Nicholson (C. A.)

but they were very entertaining.

Prosper Open Medium Italic • J. Nicholson (C. A.)

VINCENT PRICE.

Monolith Bold • Jun Tomita (Creative Alliance)

REMEMbER HIM

Monolith Light • Jun Tomita (Creative Alliance)

IN "THE FLY"?

Monolith Outline • Jun Tomita (C. Alliance)

WHAT A GREAT

Monolith Regular • Jun Tomita (C. Alliance)

CONCEPT. MAN BECOMES A FLY. WITH THE MAN FACE. I CAN

ZiP • Lennart Hansson (Creative Alliance)

STILL SEE THE FLY IN THE SPIDER'S WEB.

Baluster • M. Burlile/T-26 (Creative Alliance)

The poor man-fly is saying, "Help me-e-e-e-."

Isonorm • Mecanorma (Creative Alliance)

All the great movies about UFOs &

Isonorm—bold • Mecanorma (Creative Alliance)

flying saucers that invaded earth. Wow.

Teckno—Bold • Mecanorma (Creative Alliance)

AND THERE WERE SO MANY MOVIES...

Watch Ot • Mecanorma (Creative Alliance)

movies like "The Incredible Shrinking Man".

Zeitgeist • Monotype (Creative Alliance)

It was great. In SHRINKING MAN,

Zeitgeist Alt • Monotype (Creative Alliance)

there was a guy on his boat, and the

Zeitgeist Bd • Monotype (Creative Alliance)

boat went though a Strange Kind of Fog.

Zeitgeist Ca • Monotype (Creative Alliance)

The "fog" left a metallic kind of stuff on his skin, but he

Zeitgeist Cn • Monotype (Creative Alliance)

wasn't scared by all that. He was OK, he said.

Zeitgeist Cr Pv • Monotype (Creative Alliance)

The Next Day, though, his clothes didn't fit too well.

Zeitgeist It • Monotype (Creative Alliance)

HE WAS GETTING SMALLER.

Eon Age • Paul Prue (Creative Alliance)

AND THE NEXT DAY, EVEN SMALLER.

Galaxy Run • Paul Prue (Creative Alliance)

Soon, he was living inside a doll house.

Logan • Paul Prue (Creative Alliance)

IN ONE GREAT SCENE, HIS

System X3 • Paul Prue (Creative Alliance)

own cat almost attacked

Square40 • Segura/Reinert/T-26 (C. Alliance)

and ate him. That part

Square40—Oblique • Segura/Reinert/T-26 (C. A.)

was scary. And he kept

Square40—Outline • Segura/Reinert/T-26 (C. A.)

getting smaller and smaller.

Square40—OutlineOblique • Segura/Reinert/T-26 (C. A.)

One Day he wound up in his basement.

Eumundi Book—bold • Type Associates (C.A.)

His Wife could not find him

Eumundi Book • Type Associates (C. Alliance)

because he was so small. So small, in fact,

Eumundi Book Italic • Type Associates (C. A.)

that a match was like a log to him—a big log.

Eumundi Sans • Type Associates (C. Alliance)

The Match was Bigger Than He was. In the

Eumundi Sans Bold • Type Associates (C. A.)

end, he Kind of Disappeared. Actually, he

Eumundi Sans BoldItalic • Type Associates (C. A.)

wound up going down the water drain. Sad, but

Eumundi Italic • Type Associates (C. Alliance)

it was really a Good, Scary Sci-Fi Movie from the 50s.

AsimovSans • Fonthead

T

ARE YOU SCARED OF SPIDERS? ONE OF THE BEST SCIENCE

Beckett • Fonthead

FICTION MOVIES I EVER SAW

CyberMonkey • Fonthead

was made in the 1950s. it was

Mekanek • Fonthead

titled "Tarantula", and as

Millennnia • Fonthead

YOU MIGHT IMAGINE, IT

Network • Fonthead

WAS ABOUT A BIG SPIDER. THE

Sputnik • Fonthead

tarantula was already big, but he got a

Teknobe • Fonthead

whole lot bigger—and bigger. Typical Plot From the 50s because it dealt with an atomic

TekStencil • Fonthead

accident and everyone was

ZipSonik • Fonthead

FIXATED ON ATOMIC POWER AND

ZipSonik—Italic • Fonthead

ITS DANGERS. IN THE MOVIE, AN

ZipSonik—Sketch • Fonthead

ATOMIC ACCIDENT CAUSED A

ZipSonik—SketchItalic • Fonthead

Spider to mutate through drastic growth.

Function Display • Title Wave Studios

THE SPIDER WAS ALREADY IN A

BAD MOOD AND BY THE TIME He

GOT LOOSE, HE WAS 100-FEET LONG.

A 100-FOOT LONG SPIDER IN A BAD MOOD—

THAT'S NOT SOMETHING YOU WANT TO MEET.

I ALWAYS LIKE TO SEE JUST

which actors were in those

movies. Tarantula's cast

had Leo G. Carroll. He

was also in Topper, a

humorous representation

of ghosts among the living.

AND HE PLAYED A SCIENTIST IN TARA

Leo G. Carroll played a Mad Scientist.

MicroSquare • Title Wave Studios

And as I have already pointed out,

MicroSquare Bold • Title Wave Studios

though the scientist may have been

MicroSquare BoldOblique • Title Wave Studios

mad, the Spider wasn't in the best of

MicroSquare Oblique • Title Wave Studios

MOODS HIMSELF. ANOTHER ACTOR IN

MicroSquare SC • Title Wave Studios

TARANTULA WAS THE GUY WHO PLAYED

MicroSquare SC Bold • Title Wave Studios

Mr. Ziffle in Green Acres.

OCR A • Title Wave Studios

He was in Tarantula, a

OCR B • Title Wave Studios

MOVIE ABOUT A HUGE SPIDER.

Orator • Title Wave Studios

WHAT IF ARNOLD THE PIG WAS HUGE?

Orator Oblique • Title Wave Studios

WHEN I GROW UP, I WANT TO BE A CARPENTER.

Frankenstein—Regular • TypeArt

OR MAYBE A POLITICIAN◊ WHAT

Handex • 2 Rebels

DO YOU WANT TO BE

Kidy—CapsBlack • 2 Rebels

WHEN YOU GROW UP? i

Kidy—CapsRegular • 2 Rebels

WANT TO BE A CARTOONIST

Lolo • 2 Rebels

I WANT TO DRAW COMIC BOOKS

Mariasfont—Bold • 2 Rebels

AND WRITE FUNNY STUFF AND LAUGH

Mariasfont—Medium • 2 Rebels

AND LAUGH A LOT AT MY FUNNY STUFF.

Cage Text • P22

ToyBox Blocks • P22

WANT TO BE A KID FO

ToyBox BlocksLine • P22

WANNA BE A KID FORE

ToyBox BlocksSolid • P22

WANT TO BE A KID FO

ToyBox BlocksSolidBold • P22

I Want To Be a Kid Forever. There.

ToyBox Regular • P22

I SAID IT, AND I'M GLAD

I DID. I WANT TO ALWAYS

be able to see the world

through the innocent eyes of a

child forever. Kids get up every

Morning, and can't wait for

each New Day to begin.

(NUDE DAY?!!! OH. NEW DAY.)

BECAUSE EVERYDAY IS A

NEW ADVENTURE

LIFE SHOULD

ALWAYS BE LIKE THAT

YOU SHOULD WAKE UP EACH

morning WITH A SENSE OF anticipation

ChauncyFatty • Chank Diesel (Creative Alliance)

of what that day may turn out to be.

ChauncyDeluxxe • Chank Diesel (C. Alliance)

Wake Up Each Day with Eagerness to

KidTYPE—Ruled • DS Design (Creative Alliance)

see just what good and

KidTYPECrayon • DS Design (Creative Alliance)

exciting things await you. Like...

KidTYPEMarker • DS Design (Creative Alliance)

having a 64 box of

KidTYPEPaint • DS Design (Creative Alliance)

CRAYOLA CRAYONS EVERYDAY,

Deco Initials • Fonthaus (Creative Alliance)

and you get to decide what

Gallo Serif • Fonthaus (Creative Alliance)

TO DO WITH THEM WHILE YOU ARE

Freeway • Ian Patterson (Creative Alliance)

HAVING YOUR BREAKFAST CEREAL

Hollywood • Ian Patterson (Creative Alliance)

OF COURSE. MAYBE QUAKER OATMEAL OR

Railway • Ian Patterson (Creative Alliance)

MAYBE CREAM OF WHEAT

ChauncyDeluxxe—bold italic • C. Diesel (C.A.)

OR MAYBE CHEERIOS

DinitialsNeg • ITC/Fontek (Creative Alliance)

IF YOU HAVE NOT EATEN ANY

Cheerios for awhile, then you

MUST HAVE A

BOWL OF CHEERIOS

FOR BREAKFAST

AND SEE JUST HOW IT FEELS

TO BE A KID AGAIN

THERE'S SOMETHING ABOUT

THEM THAT BRINGS BACK MEMORIES OF

WHEN YOU WERE A KID. CHEERIOS

were my favorite. I liked them best of all---

even though Wheaties was tempting.

BREAKFAST OF CHAMPIONS

was what the Wheaties box said. It was

Kidprint • Monotype (Creative Alliance)

pretty tempting to have Wheaties all

Kidprint Bold • Monotype (Creative Alliance)

the time, but I liked Cheerios

LangerBold • Paul Lang (Creative Alliance)

Better. And I still do. Oh...

LangerAltBold • Paul Lang (Creative Alliance)

I just had a Sudden Thought.

LangerBoldItalic • Paul Lang (Creative Alliance)

What If I Had Wheaties ALL

LangerAltBoldItalic • Paul Lang (C. Alliance)

the time, instead of Cheerios.

LangerItalic • Paul Lang (Creative Alliance)

Would I be a Champion Today?

LangerAltItalic • Paul Lang (Creative Alliance)

How I wonder. If only I had not

LangerRoman • Paul Lang (Creative Alliance)

ignored the Wheaties ads, would

LangerAltRoman • Paul Lang (Creative Alliance)

I BE ABLE TO PLAY GOLF BETTER?

Alligators • Philip Bouwsma (Creative Alliance)

Would I have been a PGA Champion?

ScottyNormal • S. Smith/T-26 (Creative Alliance)

WOULD I BE AS GOOD AS

Kiddo • Type Revivals (Creative Alliance)

Tiger Woods? Is it possible?! No Way.

SchoolOblique • Type Revivals (C. Alliance)

OK. So I'm glad I had Cheerios instead.

SchoolObliqueBold • Type Revivals (C. Alliance)

Seeing this font Just Gave Me a Flashback

SchoolObliqueDashed • Type Revivals (C. A.)

to First Grade, at Advance School. Yeah.

SchoolObliqueLined • Type Revivals (C. Alliance)

I Can Almost Smell the Chalk Dust and

SchoolObliqueLined—Bold • Type Revivals (C.A.)

I Can Certainly See the Blackboard.

SchoolScript • Type Revivals (Creative Alliance)

The Blackboards Were Still Black.

SchoolScriptBold • Type Revivals (C. Alliance)

By the time My Kids Were in School,

SchoolScriptDashed • Type Revivals (C. Alliance)

The Blackboards Had Become Green.

SchoolScriptLined • Type Revivals (C. Alliance)

But at Advance, they Were Black.

SchoolScriptLined—Bold • Type Revivals (C.A.)

I can still smell the scent of school chalk.

HippoCritic—Antics • Vintage Type Library

School Chalk Brings Back Memories of

HippoCritic—Flowerchild • Vintage Type Library

Miss Bessie Teaching Geography,

HippoCritic—Lollypops • Vintage Type Library

AND MISS THOMPSON'S PADDLE.

WroughtIron—Bombs • Vintage Type Library

I'M SURE SHE WAS A NICE LADY

WroughtIron—Cherries • Vintage Type Library

BUT SHE HAD THIS THING

WroughtIron—Maces • Vintage Type Library

about States and their Capitals. We had to learn all

Caterpillar • Fonthead

the states and their capitals. We had a big test about this,

Croissant • Fonthead

all 50 States and their 50 Capital Cities.

Dandelion • Fonthead

If you didn't get them ALL right, she would paddle you. I am serious about this.

Leaflet • Fonthead

If a teacher did that today, there would be court documents, and the

Leaflet Bold • Fonthead

whole Class Would be on Court TV. There would be indictments, witnesses, people

Leaflet Light • Fonthead

showing the Jury..."Will you

Pesto • Fonthead

Please Show the Jury Your Bruised Butt?" And I Would

SororityHack • Fonthead

have to show my bruise to a jury of Miss Thompson's peers, all

Submarine • Fonthead

BECAUSE I MISSED ONE.

Dresden • Title Wave Studios

And besides the smell of chalk,

Font Pirate • Synfonts

FROM ADVANCE GRADE SCHOOL ,

Milkshake • 2 Rebels

I can also smell The Lunch Room. Yumm.

StencilFull—Danse • 2 Rebels

There was a Very Nice Lady,

StencilFull—Negative • 2 Rebels

named Miss Silvey, who ran

StencilFull—NegativeDance • 2 Rebels

The Advance Lunchroom, and for the

StencilFull—Normal • 2 Rebels

Most Part, the food was Pretty Good. Except

StencilFull—Sans • 2 Rebels

ONCE A WEEK THEY HAD WEINERS AND

Wire—AndPlanks • 2 Rebels

Sauerkraut. And a pot

Obsolete • Aerotype

of Spinach. Yuck! The

Obsolete Bold • Aerotype

weiner was OK. I got

Obsolete Light • Aerotype

a slice of bread and it

Obsolete Outline • Aerotype

BECAME A HOT DOG.

Recycle Alternate • Aerotype

SO I ATE THAT FAST

Recycle Alternate Reverse • Aerotype

AND IT WAS GOOD. OK?

Recycle Outline • Aerotype

NEXT. I HAD DESSERT:

Recycle Reverse • Aerotype

A COOKIE, OR ICE CREAM

Recycle Standard • Aerotype

AND I WAS THROUGH WITH LUNCH—FAST.

Nyx • Adobe (Creative Alliance)

I never ever touched the

Courier • Adobe (Creative Alliance)

sauerkraut and I couldn't

Prestige Elite Bold • Adobe (Creative Alliance)

STAND the smell of the

Prestige Elite Bold Slanted • Adobe (C. Alliance)

DREADED SPINACH. GADS!

Stencil • Adobe (Creative Alliance)

I couldn't even stand

SchabloneLabel • Fonthaus (Creative Alliance)

the sight of it!!! Just

SchabloneLabelroughMask • Fonthaus (C.A.)

seeing spinach made me

SchabloneLabelroughNegative • Fonthaus (C.A.)

sick, woozy, nauseous.

SchabloneLabelrough Positive • Fonthaus (C.A.)

Seeing spinach made me sick then,

SchabloneRegular • Fonthaus (Creative Alliance)

and it still does today.

SchabloneRough • Fonthaus (Creative Alliance)

I could never stand that stuff. At all.

AmTypewriterCd—Bold • ITC (C. Alliance)

Anyway, there was this teacher who had

AmTypewriterCd—Light • ITC (C. Alliance)

Lunch Room Duty. All the time.

AmTypewriterCdMd • ITC (Creative Alliance)

And she was hung up on eating

AmTypewriter—Bold • ITC (Creative Alliance)

everything on your plate.

AmTypewriter—BoldItalic • ITC (C. Alliance)

She wanted you to Eat It ALL. OR,

AmTypewriter—Light • ITC (Creative Alliance)

you had to stay in the Lunch Room.

AmTypewriter—LightItalic • ITC (C. Alliance)

Everyday, she would announce,

AmTypewriterMd • ITC (Creative Alliance)

"Those who have eaten

AmTypewriterMd—Italic • ITC (C. Alliance)

EVERYTHING ON YOUR PLATE, MAY

Campaign • ITC/Fontek (Creative Alliance)

NOW LEAVE THE LUNCH ROOM AND GO PLAY."

Portago • ITC/Fontek (Creative Alliance)

WELL, YOU KNOW WHAT I HAD

Rubber Stamp • ITC/Fontek (Creative Alliance)

on my plate. I still had that

Bulletin Typewriter • Mecanorma (C. Alliance)

kraut and the smelly spinach.

Sayer—Interview • Mecanorma (C. Alliance)

So I wasn't allowed

Braggadocio • Monotype (Creative Alliance)

to go anywhere. I was

Courier LD Bold • Monotype (Creative Alliance)

stuck in the Lunch Room

Courier LD BoldItalic • Monotype (C. Alliance)

while all my friends were

Courier LD Italic • Monotype (Creative Alliance)

leaving to play outside.

Courier LD Regular • Monotype (C. Alliance)

Yes, the kids with clean

Courier PS • Monotype (Creative Alliance)

plates got to go outside

Courier PS Bd • Monotype (Creative Alliance)

and play now. But not me.

Courier PS Bd It • Monotype (Creative Alliance)

I sat there, kraut and

Courier PS It • Monotype (Creative Alliance)

smelly spinach on my plate.

Courier Twelve • Monotype (Creative Alliance)

And I got to watch while

Typewriter Elite • Monotype (Creative Alliance)

all My Friends were playing

Typewriter Gothic • Monotype (C. Alliance)

outside. At least, my friends

Typewriter • Monotype (Creative Alliance)

who ate all their food. My friends who

FuturaBlack • Neufville (Creative Alliance)

were less picky eaters, they got to

Breadline • Panache Typography (C. Alliance)

go out and play while I was

Chandler 42 Lite • Steve Mehallo (C. Alliance)

there frowning at kraut and

Chandler 42 LiteOblique • Steve Mehallo (C.A.)

spinach. Not fair. "This

Chandler 42 Medium • Steve Mehallo (C.A.)

isn't fair," I thought.

Chandler 42 MediumOblique • S. Mehallo (C.A.)

Then, finally, the Teacher

Chandler 42 Noir • Steve Mehallo (C. Alliance)

spoke again. Finally.

Chandler 42 NoirOblique • Steve Mehallo (C.A.)

"All those who have just

Chandler 42 Oblique • Steve Mehallo (C.A.)

one food item left..."

Chandler 42 Regular • Steve Mehallo (C.A.)

THOSE WITH ONE FOOD LEFT ON THEIR

plate could now go outside.

And play. In the meantime, we

Picky Eaters were being held

hostage inside. Held Hostage by

a teacher with a Strong Desire

to make us eat kraut and smelly

spinach. I think she was trying

to get us to eat food that was

GOOD FOR US, BUT SHE NEVER

SUCCEEDED. NO WAY! I STILL HAVE

NEVER EATEN KRAUT AND I STILL

HATE THE LOOKS OF SPINACH.

Dimeotype—Tape • TypeArt

hate spinach? I'm not

Firenza Text—Bold • TypeArt

sure what that teacher

Firenza Text—BoldItalic • TypeArt

accomplished with me.

Firenza Text—Italic • TypeArt

Nothing, I think. I still

Firenza Text—Regular • TypeArt

hate those two

Firenza —Bold • TypeArt

foods & I wonder

Firenza —BoldItalic • TypeArt

what the effect

Firenza —Italic • TypeArt

on me was for

Firenza —Regular • TypeArt

missing all that extra play time.

Keystoned—Bold • TypeArt

Did I become a sociopath?

Keystoned—BoldOblique • TypeArt

I don't know. If I were one, I'm

Keystoned—Oblique • TypeArt

not sure anyone would tell me.

Keystoned—Regular • TypeArt

DID ALL THAT MISSED PLAY TIME

HAVE A NEGATIVE EFFECT ON MY

ATHLETIC ABILITY? IF I HAD

EATEN ALL THAT FOOD, AND IF

I HAD BEEN ABLE TO PLAY A

LOT MORE OUTSIDE, WOULD MY

SKILL LEVEL IN SPORTS...WOULD I

have been more athletic? Would I

have become a baseball star? Maybe

I would've been a baseball star.

But as I think about it more, I don't

think so because I never ate

Wheaties, Breakfast of Champions.

When I got a little older, I

figured out what to do about

the Food Problem in the Lunch Room.

When I was a little older, I begged

my friends, and I discovered

brown bags and food from home.

I mean, I could actually take

my own lunch with Peanut

Butter and Jelly Sandwiches.

That was a good start. Then I

would toss in an apple or two.

(Yes, I gave one to the Teacher—

depending on who the teacher was.)

I always gave one to Miss Howes.

Writing Machine—BoldOblique • TypeArt

Known to all as "Miss Bessie".

Writing Machine—Light • TypeArt

But never to the "Spinach Lady".

Writing Machine—LightOblique • TypeArt

And I never gave one to

JohnDoe • Fonthead

MISS THOMPSON WHO PADDLED

GlaserStencil • Title Wave Studios

kids on a Whim (not to mention

Typewriter • Title Wave Studios

their rear ends). Why was she

Typewriter Bold • Title Wave Studios

like that? Who knows? There was

Typewriter BoldItalic • Title Wave Studios

one great teacher there; Coach Meredith

Typewriter Cond • Title Wave Studios

was a Role Model Before That Phrase Ever

Typewriter Cond Bold • Title Wave Studios

existed. Students looked up to him.

Typewriter Italic • Title Wave Studios

COACH MARVIN MEREDITH,

Carbon 14—Black Tape • Vintage Type Library

YOU WERE OK. THANKS.

Carbon 14—Neo • Vintage Type Library

WHERE I WENT TO GRADE

Carbon 14—Neo • Vintage Type Library

SCHOOL, THE BELL WAS

Carbon 14—Regular • Vintage Type Library

AN OLD STYLE BELL, JUST

Carbon 14—Stout • Vintage Type Library

like the Liberty Bell. And

Screenplay—OliverB • Vintage Type Library

it was in the Belfry,

Screenplay—RemingtonB • Vintage Type Library

Way up High. Every morning

Screenplay—SmithB • Vintage Type Library

Mr. Daniels rang the bell.

Screenplay—UnderwoodB • Vintage Type Library

And he rang the bell for Recess.

Typewriter—BlickCursive • Vintage Type Library

And to tell us Lunch was over.

Typewriter—BlickElectric • Vintage Type Library

Recess was a lot of fun.

Typewriter—Corona • Vintage Type Library

Red Rover was a big game

Typewriter—Olympia • Vintage Type Library

we played at recess.

Typewriter—Olympia—bold • V. Type Library

The Girls Would Jump Rope.

Typewriter—RemingtonPortable • V. Type Library

T

The guys would play ball.

Or They Would Run. Usually

they would run to where the

Girls Were Jumping Rope.

For a 6th Grade Kid, this was

the beginning of romance and love.

THE GUYS BEGAN TO NOTICE THE GIRLS, AT RECESS.

And though we didn't know it

This was puberty-at last!

What if Elvis were alive today?

Folk Art Block • P22

Of course, many think he is alive.

Folk Art Cross • P22

He Does Live in the Hearts & Minds

Folk Art Square • P22

Of Many People who love the

Folk Art—Stitch • P22

fifties, when Elvis was King. But

CyberZombie • Synfonts

what if elvis were still alive...he

Electric Weasel • Synfonts

would be 60+, but

Human Condition • Synfonts

He would still be Elvis.

löuD • Synfonts

If Elvis were alive, some

Nurse Ratchet • Synfonts

THINGS WOULD BE A LOT DIFFERENT.

Studded Leather Jackets • Synfonts

What things would change?

Graffiti • flashfonts

Well, there is at least one

Fiesta • Aerotype

industry that would not exist. No.

Indigo • Aerotype

Which industry would not exist, you ask me?

Looneywood Outline • Aerotype

Elvis impersonators, that's which industry.

Looneywood Regular • Aerotype

Sudden Thought: If Elvis Were Alive Today,

Looneywood Drop • Aerotype

Would He Have Gray Hair? Can You Picture Elvis With Silver Hair? Not me.

Saloon After • Aerotype

Perhaps Elvis would be appearing in Grecian Formula commercials—Jet Black.

Saloon Before • Aerotype

OR PERHAPS JUST FOR MEN HAIR COLORING. YES.

Double Vision—Oblique • TypeArt

FLYING ELVIS? THE MOVIE WOULD NEVER HAVE

Double Vision—Regular • TypeArt

BEEN MADE IF HE WERE ALIVE. WHAT WOULD

Eye Doctor—Oblique • TypeArt

ELVIS BE DOING TODAY IF HE WERE ALIVE?

Eye Doctor—Regular • TypeArt

Perhaps Infomercials. Imagine Elvis selling the merits of a bed.

Outlaw—Bold • TypeArt

THE ELVIS ADJUSTABLE BED WHAT A PRODUCT

Sidewalker—Regular • TypeArt

OR ELVIS & TEDDY BEARS

Wendy Woo—Oblique • TypeArt

GET YOUR LIMITED EDITION...

Wendy Woo—Regular • TypeArt

179

GET YOUR LIMITED EDITION

GENUINE ELVIS TEDDY BEAR.

WOULD ELVIS BE ON HSN?

ELVIS ON HOME SHOPPING+

OR HOW ABOUT ELVIS ON ABC-

HOW ABOUT ELVIS AS A GUY ON

MONDAY NIGHT FOOTBALL YEAH

IF DENNIS MILLER CAN DO IT

then why not Elvis? I Like it.

And since the topic is Elvis...

HE WAS NOT AN ACTOR

HE WAS A PERSONALITY

IN ALL HIS MOVIES

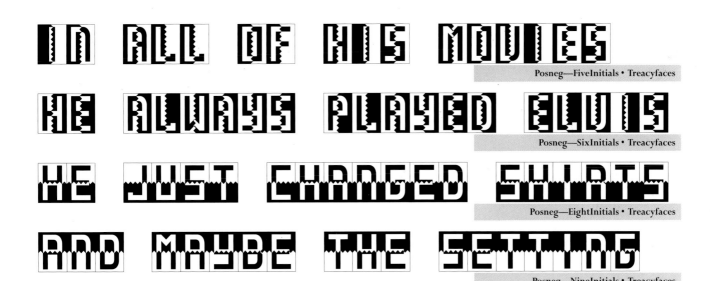

IN ALL OF HIS MOVIES

Posneg—FiveInitials • Treacyfaces

HE ALWAYS PLAYED ELVIS

Posneg—SixInitials • Treacyfaces

HE JUST CHANGED SHIRTS

Posneg—EightInitials • Treacyfaces

AND MAYBE THE SETTING

Posneg—NineInitials • Treacyfaces

his one really doesn't matter.

1BubbleBath—Light • 2 Rebels

whether he rode a horse or a Harley.

2BubbleBath—Regular • 2 Rebels

he was still Elvis. You know the deal.

3BubbleBath—Bold • 2 Rebels

It's just how things are, net: this looks like the way Hirschfeld signs his home.

Babbio—Alto • 2 Rebels

By the way, was there ever bad a better caricature artist than that Hirschfeld? I.D.

Babbio—Basso • 2 Rebels

The early Elvis Sun records are worth a lot of money.

Bereta • 2 Rebels

your ELViS 45rpm is hOSTage.

Blackmail—Regular • 2 Rebels

did elvis ever really wear blue suede shoes?

Design • 2 Rebels

actually, carl perkins did it first.

Graphic • 2 Rebels

HAVE YOU EVER BEEN TO GRACELAND?

IN MEMPHIS () TENNESSEE ()

American Shrine.

DOES ELVIS DESERVE SAINTHOOD

Saint Elvis? How does that

SOUND? SAINT ELVIS, KING OF ROCK AND ROLL.

Rock and Roll Too Bad

THAT AMERICANS DO NOT

Have Knighthood, as they do in Britain.

Wouldn't that be a hoot: Sir Elvis.

Wow! Imagine, the Queen Laying a Sword

ON HIS SHOULDER AND

182

saying, "In the name of the crown,

Chinchilla • Fonthead

I hereby dub thee, Sir Elvis." What a scene.

Chinchilla Black • Fonthead

Imagine Sir Elvis on TV, for Subway.

Chinchilla Dots • Fonthead

"Hello. I'm Sir Elvis," He would say, and then

CircusDog • Fonthead

HE WOULD SAY, "YOU KNOW,

DingleHopper • Fonthead

I LOST 240 POUNDS ON THE SUBWAY DIET.

Hopscotch • Fonthead

UH-HUH." AND ALL THOSE EXTRA

Hopscotch Plain • Fonthead

POUNDS HE PUT ON WOULD

HotCoffeeFont • Fonthead

BECOME A SOURCE OF INCOME

ShoeString • Fonthead

FOR SIR ELVIS, THE KING. I WONDER

ShoeString—Round • Fonthead

if Elvis ever met Kermit the Frog.

SpaceCowboy • Fonthead

Just picture Elvis and Kermit on tour together, singing together.

Stiltskin • Fonthead

They would sing "It's Not Easy Being Green".

Swizzle • Fonthead

I BET ELVIS NEVER WORE DIRTY

Blinddate • A. Roe/T-26 (Creative Alliance)

UNDERWEAR. JUST IMAGINE

BlinddateLight • A. Roe/T-26 (Creative Alliance)

WHAT WOULD HAVE HAPPENED IF ELVIS HAD BEEN WEARING

Epicure • A. Roe/T-26 (Creative Alliance)

DIRTY UNDERWEAR WHEN HE DIED. THE NATIONAL ENQUIRER

EpicureDecorative • A. Roe/T-26 (C. Alliance)

would have had a Field Day with that!

Giddyup • Adobe (Creative Alliance)

Just imagine the headlines:

Shuriken Boy • Adobe (Creative Alliance)

ELVIS RUSHED TO MEMPHIS

Kigali Block • Arthur Baker (Creative Alliance)

Emergency Room with Dirty Underwear,

Kigali Zigzag • Arthur Baker (Creative Alliance)

the headlines would shout. Shame! SHAME!

Sassafras • Arthur Baker (Creative Alliance)

And in that one moment, Elvis would serve future

Sassafras Italic • Arthur Baker (Creative Alliance)

generations of mothers because they would be able

Artisan Roman • Creative Alliance

to say, "Children, never, ever go out with

Artistik • Creative Alliance

Dirty Underwear. Remember what happened to Elvis."

Branding Iron • Creative Alliance

184

"REMEMBER WHEN ELVIS WORE

AshleyCrawford • Creative Alliance

DIRTY UNDERWEAR? NOT

AshleyInline • Creative Alliance

only did the Elvis Family have to

BetonExtraBold • Creative Alliance

ENDURE THE SHOCK OF HIS UNTIMELY

BeverlyHills • Creative Alliance

DEATH, but they also have to bear

Art Gallery • Bo Berndal (Creative Alliance)

forever the stigma of his being taken to an

Swingbill • Bo Berndal (Creative Alliance)

EMERGENCY ROOM WITH DIRTY UNDERWEAR. HORRORS! AND CHILDREN, LET THIS BE A LESSON TO YOU ALL. DO NOT SHARE YOUR

FlacoInline • C. Segura/T-26 (Creative Alliance)

RELATIVES. ALWAYS PUT ON CLEAN UNDERWEAR BEFORE YOU GO OUT. PUT ON CLEAN UNDERWEAR. DO YOU HEAR ME?"

FlacoSolid • C. Segura/T-26 (Creative Alliance)

Imagine, had Elvis died wearing

Time In Hell • C. Segura/T-26 (Creative Alliance)

dirty underwear. There would

Time In Hell—bold • C. Segura/T-26 (C. Alliance)

be nonprofit organizations

Time In Hell—italic • C. Segura/T-26 (C.A.)

USING HIS IMAGE AND ASKING

Eclipse • Creative Alliance

for $$$ for the undie-fortunate.

EgizianoBl • Creative Alliance

Imagine their commercials: Elvis song in background.

DEAD ELVIS PHOTO BEHIND

spokesperson. The Message:

Mothers do not EVER let your children go out

WEARING DIRTY UNDERWEAR.

Elvis took just one chance, and

LOOK WHAT HAPPENED TO HIM. HE DIED IN DISGRACE

because he failed to heed

HIS MOTHER'S WARNING ABOUT DIRTY UNDERWEAR.

SHAME! WHAT A SOCIAL STIGMA

ELVIS IS—NO MATTER HOW

NICE HIS HAIR LOOKED (AND HIS

HAIR DID LOOK NICE).

Sure, his hair looked good, but

Orbital • Chank Diesel (Creative Alliance)

the dirty underwear was

OrbusMultiserif • Chank Diesel (C. Alliance)

ALL THEY NOTICED IN THE

Zombie Different • Christian Schwartz (C.A.)

Emergency Room. No one said,

Zombie Regular • Christian Schwartz (C.A.)

"Nice hair." No. Everyone

AmplifierBold • F. Heine/T-26 (C. Alliance)

WHISPERED, "DIRTY UNDERWEAR."

AmplifierBoldSmallCaps • F. Heine/T-26 (C.A.)

And then they said, "Didn't

AmplifierLight • F. Heine/T-26 (C. Alliance)

HIS MOTHER EVER TELL HIM?"

AmplifierLightSmallCaps • F. Heine/T-26 (C.A.)

I KNOW MY MOTHER WOULD STILL BE VERY DISAPPOINTED IF I EVER

Agency—Open • Fonthaus (Creative Alliance)

HAD A WRECK IN DIRTY UNDERWEAR. THE

BrushSans—RimmedCond • Fonthaus (C.A.)

FAMILY WOULD DISOWN ME.

Cameo Outline • Fonthaus (Creative Alliance)

NEIGHBORS WOULD SHUN ME.

Cameo Outline Shaded • Fonthaus (C. Alliance)

IT'S JUST NOT WORTH THE RISK.

Cameo Solid • Fonthaus (Creative Alliance)

IF ELVIS WERE ALIVE TODAY,

Cleancut • Fonthaus (Creative Alliance)

WHAT KIND OF TU SHOWS

CrucibleLight • Fonthaus (Creative Alliance)

WOULD HE BE ON?

CrucibleMedium • Fonthaus (Creative Alliance)

HE MIGHT BE ON

CrucibleUltra • Fonthaus (Creative Alliance)

SUCH SHOWS AS Hollywood Squares.

DecoWave • Fonthaus (Creative Alliance)

"ELVIS TO BLOCK," someone would say.

Elroy • Fonthaus (Creative Alliance)

And on Very Special Days, Elvis would get to

EvaAntiqaHvyItSG • Fonthaus (C. Alliance)

be the Secret Square—quite an honor.

EvaAntiqaLtItSG • Fonthaus (Creative Alliance)

Imagine Elvis as the Secret Square.

EvaAntiqaLtItSGA • Fonthaus (Creative Alliance)

HEY, YOU KNOW WHAT ELSE?

Greco Adornado • Fonthaus (Creative Alliance)

HE MIGHT BE ON WHEEL.

Greco Solid • Fonthaus (Creative Alliance)

ELVIS ON Wheel of Fortune, Celebrity Week.

Heatwave • Fonthaus (Creative Alliance)

WHAT A TRINITY: ELVIS

Logotype • Fonthaus (Creative Alliance)

along with Pat Sajek and Vanna White. Hey I would watch that show.

Or, Elvis could be on Celebrity Jeopardy. He could be the only contestant ever who was both

a contestant AND the Answer to the Final Jeopardy question.

That would be an unusual event in Television History.

Alex Trebek would say, in his TV voice,

"The answer is: The King of Rock n Roll."

And Then They Would Play That Catchy Jeopardy Musical Theme.

You know the one. It gets in your head, and won't go away.

Drm De de de, Drm de de........ Drm de de de Drm de de de de.

AND AT THE END ALEX WOULD

ask each contestant for their answer. Elvis would be last, and only HE would have written the correct answer:

"Who is Elvis Presley?" Correct.

Elvis you are the winner...

AND ELVIS WOULD BE THE WINNER. AND HE WOULD COME BACK AGAIN TOMORROW.

Paleface—Black • Fonthaus (Creative Alliance)

ELVIS WOULD WIN A GAZILLION DOLLARS, BUT GIVE IT TO CHARITY.

Paleface—Lift • Fonthaus (Creative Alliance)

WONDER WHAT HIS FAVORITE CHARITY WOULD BE? GRACELAND? MAYBE.

Paleface—Open • Fonthaus (Creative Alliance)

OR PERHAPS THE ROCK AND ROLL HALL OF FAME, WHICH IS IN CLEVELAND. OH.

Paleface—Solid • Fonthaus (Creative Alliance)

If I mention the Rock and Roll Hall of Fame enough

RoslynGothic—Bold • Fonthaus (C. Alliance)

would they send me free tickets? Naw. Probably not.

RoslynGothic—Medium • Fonthaus (C. Alliance)

SO NEVER MIND ABOUT THAT ONE.

Round Sans Inline • Fonthaus (Creative Alliance)

ELVIS MIGHT GIVE HIS WINNINGS TO

Round Sans Outline • Fonthaus (C. Alliance)

THE NATIONAL HOT DOG MUSEUM

Round Sans Solid • Fonthaus (Creative Alliance)

WHO KNOWS?

Ramiz—Bold • G. Samata/T-26 (C. Alliance)

WHAT IF

Ramiz—BoldExt • G. Samata/T-26 (C. Alliance)

ELVIS HAD

Ramiz—Extended • G. Samata/T-26 (C. Alliance)

BEEN JAPANESE?

Ramiz—Regular • G. Samata/T-26 (C. Alliance)

Would he have still been Elvis? Probably not.

Baylac Regular • Gerard Mariscalchi (C.A.)

That's a little too deep for me to think

Goudy Handtooled • Creative Alliance

about. If Elvis were still alive,

BriemGauntletMedium • Gunnlauger Se Briem (C.A.)

would there be Elvis action figures, like GI Joe?

BriemGauntletNarrow • Gunnlauger Se Briem (C.A.)

Imagine an Elvis type doll.

BriemGauntletWide • Gunnlauger Se Briem (C.A.)

AND WHAT IF THE ELVIS ACTION FIGURE WERE CO-MARKETED

Anna • ITC (Creative Alliance)

WITH THE BARBIE DOLL? BARBIE MEETS ELVIS, HAWAIIAN STYLE?

AnnaSC • ITC (Creative Alliance)

WHAT A COMBINATION.

Beesknees • ITC (Creative Alliance)

Neat. Elvis and Barbie.

CenturyHan • ITC (Creative Alliance)

The set would come with a

CenturyHanIta • ITC (Creative Alliance)

big, long car, a Pink Cadillac.

CheltenhamHan • ITC (Creative Alliance)

Maybe the two of them could

CheltenhamHanIta • ITC (Creative Alliance)

have matching scarves—sold separately.

Mona Lisa Solid • ITC (Creative Alliance)

Who is the greatest TV detective?

And that includes the movies, too.

CHARLIE CHAN GETS MY VOTE.

THERE WERE A BUNCH OF GOOD CHAN MOVIES.

THEY STARTED IN THE 1930S

AND THERE WERE ACTUALLY

TWO different actors who played Chan.

Neither one of them was Chinese.

ONE WAS WARNER OLAND OF

SCANDINAVIAN DESCENT, NOT CHINESE.

The other was Sidney Toler, born in St. Louis, MO.

ANYWAY, BOTH WERE CHAN

TOLER & OLAND.

Remember the board game—Clue?

Bertie • ITC/Fontek (Creative Alliance)

YOU HAD TO GUESS WHO DID IT, WHERE, AND WITH WHAT.

Bluntz • ITC/Fontek (Creative Alliance)

JUST the mention of the name

Bodoni Brush • ITC/Fontek (Creative Alliance)

Colonel Mustard and I have flashbacks to my youth.

Bordeaux Display • ITC/Fontek (C. Alliance)

As in Col. Mustard did it

Buckeroo • ITC/Fontek (Creative Alliance)

in the Conservatory, with a Rope...no a Knife.

Burlington • ITC/Fontek (Creative Alliance)

There were some other "players" in the Clue Game,

Caribbean • ITC/Fontek (Creative Alliance)

LIKE MISS WHITE, AND PROFESSOR PLUM. GOOD NAMES FOR THEM;

Cherie • ITC/Fontek (Creative Alliance)

EACH PLAYING PIECE WAS A COLOR.

Chromium One • ITC/Fontek (Creative Alliance)

THE COLOR & NAME MATCHED.

Citation • ITC/Fontek (Creative Alliance)

THIS would be funny: Picture

Crillee Italic Inline Shad • ITC/Fontek (C.A.)

Columbo on TV, in his Raincoat, walking

Dancin • ITC/Fontek (Creative Alliance)

AROUND TYING UP LOOSE ENDS...

Emphasis • ITC/Fontek (Creative Alliance)

So Columbo finally says, "I have it."

Corinthian Bold • ITC/Fontek (C. Alliance)

The murderer is Colonel Mustard, and

Corinthian Bold Condensed • ITC/Fontek (C.A.)

Columbo would pause, smoke his cigar.

Corinthian Light • ITC/Fontek (C. Alliance)

Then he would say, "He did it in the hall."

Corinthian Medium • ITC/Fontek (C. Alliance)

COLUMBO WOULD SQUINT,

Epokha • ITC/Fontek (Creative Alliance)

AND SAY, "THE WEAPON WAS A PIPE."

Faithful Fly • ITC/Fontek (C. Alliance)

Do you know that Lt. Columbo never had a first name.

Fashion Engraved • ITC/Fontek (C. Alliance)

And as often as he mentioned his wife,

Flamenco Inline • ITC/Fontek (C. Alliance)

SAME FOR HER.

Flatiron • ITC/Fontek (Creative Alliance)

SHE DIDN'T HAVE A FIRST NAME, TOO.

Florinda • ITC/Fontek (Creative Alliance)

HAVE YOU FOUND ANY TYPOS YET?

Follies • ITC/Fontek (Creative Alliance)

A type book shouldn't have any.

Forest Shaded • ITC/Fontek (Creative Alliance)

Well, we tried our best,

Freddo • ITC/Fontek (Creative Alliance)

BUT THE TRUTH IS, WE HAVE A

Frankfurter • ITC/Fontek (Creative Alliance)

DYSLEXIC PROOFREADER. HONEST.

Frankfurter Highlight • ITC/Fontek (C. Alliance)

I MEAN, WHENEVER YOU SEE DOG,

Frankfurter Inline • ITC/Fontek (C. Alliance)

It's possible that GOD was intended.

Frankfurter Medium • ITC/Fontek (C. Alliance)

That's just the beginning…Possible

Frankfurter Medium—italic • ITC/Fontek (C.A.)

errors have many origins. First of all,

Harlow • ITC/Fontek (Creative Alliance)

(damn it Jim) I'm a writer, not a typist.

Harlow Solid • ITC/Fontek (Creative Alliance)

SO I JUST MIGHT HAVE WRITTEN

Hazel • ITC/Fontek (Creative Alliance)

some wrong word somewhere,

Highlight • ITC/Fontek (Creative Alliance)

and, miraculously, I may

Hornpype • ITC/Fontek (Creative Alliance)

have done it more than one time,

Ignatius • ITC/Fontek (Creative Alliance)

So, as you read this, please be gentle.

Impakt • ITC/Fontek (Creative Alliance)

AND IF YOU DO WRITE ME A NOTE, BE PREPARED FOR ME TO RESPOND WITH THE CLASSIC ANSWER: "YOU MAY BE RIGHT."

Iris • ITC/Fontek (Creative Alliance)

If you were to be Shipwrecked on

Ironwork • ITC/Fontek (Creative Alliance)

A DESERTED ISLAND, WHAT ONE

Isis • ITC/Fontek (Creative Alliance)

Book would you want to have with you? This

Jambalaya • ITC/Fontek (Creative Alliance)

one is worth thinking about, even though

Jambalaya Too • ITC/Fontek (Creative Alliance)

you may never be on an island alone.

Jellybaby • ITC/Fontek (Creative Alliance)

But Tom Hanks never thought he would

Jokerman • ITC/Fontek (Creative Alliance)

AND LOOK WHAT HAPPENED TO HIM & WILSON.

Juanita Condensed • ITC/Fontek (C. Alliance)

SO, WHAT BOOK WOULD IT BE?

Juanita Deco • ITC/Fontek (Creative Alliance)

I THINK I WOULD TAKE THE

Juanita • ITC/Fontek (Creative Alliance)

ENCYCLOPEDIA OF BASEBALL.

Juanita Lino • ITC/Fontek (Creative Alliance)

YES. THE ENCYCLOPEDIA OF BASEBALL. ONE BOOK.

Juanita Xilo Condensed • ITC/Fontek (C.A.)

MY SECOND CHOICE? EASY ONE.

Juanita Xilo • ITC/Fontek (Creative Alliance)

My second choice would be "The Lucifer Principle."

Juice • ITC/Fontek (Creative Alliance)

"The Lucifer Principle" is perhaps the best book

Klee • ITC/Fontek (Creative Alliance)

I EVER READ. NOTHING ELSE IS EVEN CLOSE.

Kokoa • ITC/Fontek (Creative Alliance)

Other choices: "Shoeless Joe" which was made into the movie "Field of Dreams".

Malstock • ITC/Fontek (Creative Alliance)

FIELD OF DREAMS IS MY FAVORITE MOVIE OF ALL TIME!

Mastercard • ITC/Fontek (Creative Alliance)

THERE ARE SEVERAL SCENES IN THE MOVIE

Mo Funky Fresh • ITC/Fontek (C. Alliance)

GUARANTEED TO MAKE YOU...

Montage • ITC/Fontek (Creative Alliance)

THOSE scenes will make you misty.

Motter Sparta • ITC/Fontek (Creative Alliance)

First One: "Daddy, there's a man on your lawn."

Oberon • ITC/Fontek (Creative Alliance)

The best one: When Archie Graham

Odessa • ITC/Fontek (Creative Alliance)

Crosses the foul line to save the

One Stroke Script Shaded • ITC/Fontek (C.A.)

Little Girl's Life, but is turned back into Doc.

Party • ITC/Fontek (Creative Alliance)

He turns back into Dr. Graham, and can't go...

Pink • ITC/Fontek (Creative Alliance)

ONCE HE CROSSES THE LINE, HE CAN'T GO BACK!!

Quadrus • ITC/Fontek (Creative Alliance)

Can you believe what Tiger Woods

has been able to accomplish?

Some say he is the Best Golfer Ever.

How many other sports have had a star

who was SO much better than all the rest?

In hockey, "The Great One" was super.

Number 99 was so much better

THAN EVERYONE ELSE. HE WAS LIKE A MAN PLAYING AMONG BOYS. NO ONE HAD NUMBERS LIKE HE DID.

OF COURSE, BABE RUTH WAS HEAD AND SHOULDERS

ABOVE EVERYONE ELSE—METAPHORICALLY & PHYSICALLY.

EVERYONE KNOWS HE HIT 60

HOME RUNS IN 1927. THAT WAS A RECORD.

DO YOU KNOW WHOSE RECORD HE BROKE?

ACTUALLY, Babe Ruth broke his own record. He had hit 59 homers in an earlier year.

Robotik • ITC/Fontek (Creative Alliance)

And whose record did he break before that? Not many people know that one.

Robotik Italic • ITC/Fontek (Creative Alliance)

Again, Ruth's 59 homers broke his own record.

Scriptek • ITC/Fontek (Creative Alliance)

The record before he hit 59? Do you know that one?

Scriptek Italic • ITC/Fontek (Creative Alliance)

The record before Ruth hit 59—was 29.

Scruff • ITC/Fontek (Creative Alliance)

THAT'S RIGHT. ONLY 29

Shaman • ITC/Fontek (Creative Alliance)

HOME RUNS WAS THE RECORD.

Shatter • ITC/Fontek (Creative Alliance)

Then Ruth hit 59 Homers to break that Record.

Silvermoon Bold • ITC/Fontek (C. Alliance)

That may have been the all-time greatest performance

Silvermoon Regular • ITC/Fontek (C. Alliance)

IN ALL OF SPORT HISTORY. JUST LOOK

Stenberg Inline • ITC/Fontek (Creative Alliance)

AT THE NUMBERS: HE ACTUALLY DOUBLED

Stenberg • ITC/Fontek (Creative Alliance)

THE PREVIOUS RECORD. HAS THERE

Strobos • ITC/Fontek (Creative Alliance)

EVER BEEN A GREATER FEAT?

Surfboard • ITC/Fontek (Creative Alliance)

CAN YOU THINK OF A MORE

Tag • ITC/Fontek (Creative Alliance)

impressive sports performance?

Typados • ITC/Fontek (Creative Alliance)

Ever wonder why William Henry Harrison

Vermont • ITC/Fontek (Creative Alliance)

IS NEVER FOUND ON ANY OF THE

Vintage • ITC/Fontek (Creative Alliance)

lists of Greatest US Presidents?

Vinyl • ITC/Fontek (Creative Alliance)

President Harrison had the misfortune

VinylOutline • ITC/Fontek (Creative Alliance)

of dying after only 30 days in office.

VinylSawthOut • ITC/Fontek (Creative Alliance)

President-Elect Harrison insisted on walking

VinylSawtooth • ITC/Fontek (Creative Alliance)

in the Inaugural Parade; the weather got to him.

Wanted • ITC/Fontek (Creative Alliance)

He got sick, and then he died. Dead.

Werkstatt Engraved • ITC/Fontek (C. Alliance)

After only 30 days as President.

Werkstatt • ITC/Fontek (Creative Alliance)

That may be one reason why

Zaragoza • ITC/Fontek (Creative Alliance)

THERE ARE NO STATUES OF HIM.

Zinjaro • ITC/Fontek (Creative Alliance)

NO HARRISON MONUMENT,

Slide • J. Marcus/T-26 (Creative Alliance)

EITHER, BUT HIS GRANDSON, BENJAMIN

Thornface—ExtraSharp • Jan Erasmus (C.A.)

HARRISON BECAME PRESIDENT LATER.

Thornface—SemiSharp • Jan Erasmus (C.A.)

BY THE WAY, A LOT OF THIS STUFF THAT I'M

Thornface—Sharp • Jan Erasmus (C. Alliance)

writing is from memory—a bad

AikikoPlain • Jasper Manchip (Creative Alliance)

memory perhaps. Not to mention

AikikoSans • Jasper Manchip (Creative Alliance)

THAT A LOT OF STUFF THAT I REMEMBER FROM

Commerce Gothic • Jim Parkinson (C. Alliance)

American History Class is...I seem to remember stuff

BlackRocks • Judith Sutcliffe (Creative Alliance)

from US History that is, well, not always exactly true.

BlackTents • Judith Sutcliffe (Creative Alliance)

For years, I believed Alexander Hamilton

Adastra • Keystrokes (Creative Alliance)

HAD BEEN ONE OF OUR PRESIDENTS. HIS NAME

Arwen • Keystrokes (Creative Alliance)

sounds like it. President Hamilton—it sounds good.

Elegant Inline • Keystrokes (Creative Alliance)

Then one day, not so long ago, I was talking about

Elegant Open Face • Keystrokes (C. Alliance)

the major accomplishments during

HIS SECOND TERM,

WHICH WAS WHEN HE SIGNED THE

EMANCIPATION PROCLAMATION.

AND PRESIDENT EISENHOWER WENT TO KOREA

WHERE THE HAPSBURG AGREEMENT ENDING

WORLD WAR II WAS

SIGNED—AT SEOUL KOREA,

I THINK—AND I KNOW—

some of the things I

remember are not

exactly correct, but they SEEM

pretty much true, especially at the time.

IT ISN'T OF HUGE IMPORTANCE TO ME RIGHT NOW. BUT, LET ME SAY

Devit • L. Tsalis/T-26 (Creative Alliance)

I NEED TO WARN YOU NOT

Bermuda Dots • Letterperfect (Creative Alliance)

TO USE ANYTHING IN

Bermuda Open • Letterperfect (C. Alliance)

THIS BOOK. NOTHING

Bermuda Solid • Letterperfect (C. Alliance)

YOU READ HERE SHOULD

Bermuda Squiggle • Letterperfect (C. Alliance)

BE USED AS A FOOTNOTE. TO DO SO IS TO RISK YOUR

Destijl • Letterperfect (Creative Alliance)

ACADEMIC FUTURE. THIS BOOK AND ITS CONTENTS WERE

Destijl Alternates • Letterperfect (C. Alliance)

CREATED · TO · SHOW

KrypticPlain • Letterperfect (Creative Alliance)

off type. This book is for typographic use and for fun only. Don't assume that

Silhouette • Letterperfect (Creative Alliance)

what you read here is for class. Nothing

Le Chat Noir • Luiz Da Lomba (Creative Alliance)

YOU READ HERE IS GUARANTEED ACCURATE EXCEPT

Moulin Rouge Outline • Luiz Da Lomba (C.A.)

FOR THE GREAT FONTS AND WHERE TO GET THEM.

Moulin Rouge Solide • Luiz Da Lomba (C.A.)

No animals were harmed during the work on the book.

Theatre Antoine • Luiz Da Lomba (C. Alliance)

How come Ben Franklin was never

Category—Fat • Lunchbox (Creative Alliance)

Elected President of the United States?

Category—Tall • Lunchbox (Creative Alliance)

Sometimes I think that there was a "deal" struck back in the Revolution.

Malaise—Tall • Lunchbox (Creative Alliance)

I think That Ben Franklin was maybe

Malaise—Text • Lunchbox (Creative Alliance)

Our Most highly-qualified

Promdate—Regular • Lunchbox (C. Alliance)

person to become president. Look at his resume and see what I mean.

Promdate—Tall • Lunchbox (Creative Alliance)

sure, washington was a war

Malaise—Text—bold • Lunchbox (C. Alliance)

HERO. AND THOMAS JEFFERSON

Artworld • Mecanorma (Creative Alliance)

was certainly a good guy, and even

Circus • Mecanorma (Creative Alliance)

John Adams has his supporters,

Estro • Mecanorma (Creative Alliance)

BUT SHOULDN'T BEN FRANKLIN HAVE BEEN

Category—Tall—italic • Lunchbox (C. Alliance)

President Ben Franklin? Why not?

Glowworm • Mecanorma (Creative Alliance)

He was one of the Geniuses of his time.

Glowworm Cp • Mecanorma (Creative Alliance)

HE INVENTED BIFOCALS.

AND THE FRANKLIN

STOVE (APPROPRIATELY NAMED).

NOT TO MENTION THE

BEN FRANKLIN STORES. YES,

Ben Franklin Invented the stores that bear his name. True.

HE FOUNDED A VERY FAMOUS

magazine, The Saturday Evening Post,

Benjamin Franklin did. So why was

BEN NOT ELECTED PRESIDENT

HE SHOULD HAVE BEEN

VOTE 4 PRESIDENT FRANKLIN

I THINK THERE WAS A CONSPIRACY—A DEAL.

HERE IS MY THEORY.

Falstaff Festival • Monotype (Creative Alliance)

TIRED OF CONSPIRACY

Falstaff • Monotype (Creative Alliance)

Theories? Well, hear me out. Here is my theory

Figaro • Monotype (Creative Alliance)

about why Ben Franklin was not elected President.

Gill Sans Ex Cn Bd • Monotype (C. Alliance)

LET US ASSUME THAT BEN

Gill Sans Sd • Monotype (Creative Alliance)

FRANKLIN and Jefferson were

Gill Sans Shadowed Lt • Monotype (C. Alliance)

BOTH Running For President, and

Imprint Sd • Monotype (Creative Alliance)

neither Franklin nor Jefferson

Imprint Sd It • Monotype (Creative Alliance)

Could Get the Majority Needed to win.

Kino • Monotype (Creative Alliance)

So, Franklin and Jefferson

Monotype Broadway • Monotype (C. Alliance)

MADE A DEAL—SURE.

Monotype Broadway Engraved • Monotype (C.A.)

The Deal Was well Planned, and until Now, it has Never Been Revealed.

Obsessed • Nazaroff/ChankDiesel (C. Alliance)

Franklin was the first to propose a solution.

Classic • Panache Typography (Creative Alliance)

FRANKLIN HAD AN IDEA.

TOM, YOU BE PRESIDENT.

THAT IS EXACTLY WHAT FRANKLIN SAID TO

JEFFERSON & THEN HE SAID, "I WILL

GET TO BE ON THE $100 BILL."

If you don't believe this conspiracy theory,

just check the next $100 bill you see.

And who is on it? Franklin. See? Conspiracy.

WHAT MORE PROOF DO YOU NEED?

(LACtAEACtGA LIGATURES FOR ABOVE)

THIS is the kind of stuff that

should be reported on

the front page of The National Enquirer.

But you have to find it in a Font Book.

Peregrine—Bold • Pysops (Creative Alliance)

Wouldn't it be interesting to see

Peregrine—Demi • Pysops (Creative Alliance)

this Story Broken on CNN, and

Peregrine—Regular • Pysops (Creative Alliance)

LARRY KING TALKING ABOUT

Peregrine—TitlingBlack • Pysops (C. Alliance)

this long secret Conspiracy, of just how Franklin

BandoleraA • Ray Cruz (Creative Alliance)

managed to get on the $100 Bill, and how the

BandoleroO • Ray Cruz (Creative Alliance)

Story First Appeared in a Font Book?

Cruz Swinger • Ray Cruz (Creative Alliance)

Who Knows, Maybe Other Well-

Acorn • Richard Yeend (Creative Alliance)

Hidden Facts will be brought to light

Bangor • Richard Yeend (Creative Alliance)

out of the depths of This book.

Broad Street • Richard Yeend (Creative Alliance)

Do You Think that A lot of other Stuff

Broad Street Text • Richard Yeend (C. Alliance)

YOU READ HERE IS ACTUALLY TRUE? IT'S POSSIBLE. HEY, THIS JUST MIGHT

Ringworld • Creative Alliance

be the next Dead Sea Scrolls.

Flexure • S. Farrell / T-26 (Creative Alliance)

The Dead Sea Scrolls, first translated

here. Just don't expect that

I'm going to become a Prophet.

(Gotta admit, I have more interest in Profit.)

That's the Result of My Going to Business School

"PROFIT," HE SAID.

NOT PROPHET.

M.B.A. TALK. YES

DEAD SEA

TRANSLATION 4U

DON'T KNOW MUCH

ABOUT HISTORY

ABOUT BIOLOGY

OTHER HISTORIC

MartiniAtJoesCameoOblique • S. Mehallo (C.A.)

LITTLE KNOWN

MartiniAtJoesCameoRetro • S. Mehallo (C.A.)

FACTS FROM OUR

MartiniAtJoesDimOutline • Steve Mehallo (C.A.)

NATION'S EARLY

MartiniAtJoesDimOutlineOblique • S. Mehallo (C.A.)

HISTORIC STUFF

MartiniAtJoesDimOutlineRetro • S. Mehallo (C.A.)

G. WASHINGTON

MartiniAtJoesOblique • Steve Mehallo (C.A.)

NEVER LIVED IN

MartiniAtJoesRetro • Steve Mehallo (C. Alliance)

WASHINGTON DC   TRUE

Tatoo • T. Klassen / T-26 (Creative Alliance)

Just don't footnote that. And

Werkman—Regurge • T. Tsalis / T-26 (C. Alliance)

as often as you see pictures

Werkman—Round • T. Tsalis / T-26 (C. Alliance)

of George Washington and

Werkman—Square • T. Tsalis / T-26 (C. Alliance)

Abe Lincoln together, it is

Quantum • Trevor Scobie (Creative Alliance)

Strange; they never met

Theory • Trevor Scobie (Creative Alliance)

YOU CAN FOOTNOTE THAT ONE.

French • Type Revivals (Creative Alliance)

Wonder if G. Washington's

Technö—Outline • Type Revivals (C. Alliance)

Mother Warned Him About Wearing dirty underwear...

MetronomeGothic • A. Miller (Creative Alliance)

"George, Don't Wear Dirty Underwear"

Necrotic—Fluids • Vintage Type Library

Makes sense to me that she did, Although

Necrotic—Tissue • Vintage Type Library

there is no evidence to prove it.

TomFool—Highfalutin • Vintage Type Library

(Don't confuse me with the facts.)

TomFool—PlumLoco • Vintage Type Library

But it seems only natural that When

TomFool—Ransomer • Vintage Type Library

WASHINGTON WENT TO WAR,

Algerian • Title Wave Studios

His Mother would be concerned.

Chisel • Title Wave Studios

WHAT IF WASHINGTON WAS IN A

Chromatic • Title Wave Studios

BIG BATTLE (BEING THE HERO-KIND

Delphian Open Titling • Title Wave Studios

of guy he was) and he Got Shot,

Embie • Title Wave Studios

AND THE MEDICS CAME

and They Saw That Washington

DID NOT LISTEN TO HIS MOTHER.

There, beneath his pristine

GENERAL'S UNIFORM THEY WOULD

Be Stunned to Find That Washington,

George Washington, father of His Country, Was Wearing

DIRTY UNDERWEAR. WHAT A SCANDAL!

WELL, LUCKILY GEORGE

was Never wounded, and the medics

Never Had to come to His rescue,

and never had to cut off his pants.

So, we will never know for sure if Washington

DiD NOT WEAR DiRTY

UNDERWEAR. CAN YOU iMAgiNE

THE ELECTiON SCANDAL THAT

WOULD HAVE CAUSED?

THINK HOW THE OTHER PARTY WOULD

HAVE USED THIS AGAINST WASHINGTON.

But, we can assume that Washington's

Mother did the right thing, and so George

Washington Became Our First President.

WHAT IF DOGS HAD THEIR OWN NATION & CULTURE?

Arts And Crafts Tall • P22

If that were The Case, Dogs Would

Eaglefeather Bold • P22

have their own National Anthem.

Eaglefeather Bold Italic • P22

Here is a good National Anthem Just for Dogs:

Eaglefeather Italic • P22

While I lie here slee-ping, (chorus sings)

Clique Wedge • Aerotype

Getting rubbed on the ear, (band comes in)

Clique WedgeBold • Aerotype

I give thanks for my home (chorus again)

Clique Wedge Bold Oblique • Aerotype

And the People who live here...(trumpets)

Clique Wedge Oblique • Aerotype

Cats may have kitty litter...

Rebound • Aerotype

And beds made of velvet rags

Rebound Bold • Aerotype

But Only in the US...(trumpets)

Rebound Light • Aerotype

Do They Have Doggy Bags.

Rebound Outline • Aerotype

When the Dog's National Anthem

Rebound Outline Bold • Aerotype

is played, Dogs stand. Yes,

Rebound Outline Light • Aerotype

all Dogs stand when it is played.

Vector • Aerotype

You know, Dogs don't realize

Vector Bold • Aerotype

that there are different breeds.

Vector ExtraBold • Aerotype

To a dog, there are only

Vector Outline • Aerotype

three kinds of dogs.

Vector Outline Bold • Aerotype

1. There are bigger dogs.

Vector Outline Extra Bold • Aerotype

Bigger Dogs Get Respect.

Bossman—Dark • TypeArt

2. There are same size dogs.

Bossman—DarkOblique • TypeArt

Same Size Dogs Are Equals

Bossman—Light • TypeArt

No Matter What the Breed.

Bossman—LightOblique • TypeArt

3. And there are smaller dogs, who can be intimidated.

Fling a Ling—Bold • TypeArt

That's it. There are three kinds of dogs. No more.

Fling a Ling—BoldItalic • TypeArt

Ask any dog, and they will tell you: Size Doesn't Count.

No, size isn't important. All dogs want to be Lap Dogs.

I think that dogs fantasize about being Lap Dogs. Yes.

Even though dogs do not recognize different breeds,

Dogs DO have a major class

structure. There are two social

classes of dogs: outside dogs, and

the upper class of dogs, inside dogs.

Of course, it is true there are some "bi-side" dogs.

Those "bi-side" dogs are said to go both ways.

They are equally comfortable being inside or outside.

Outside Dogs Really Resent those Lucky Inside Dogs.

Especially When It's Cold, Rainy, or Snowy Outside.

Many People Take their Dog to Obedience School.

Post Industrial—MediumItalic • TypeArt

And When dogs are at Obedience School, they, like humans, have some pretty lame excuses.

Silverscreen—Bold • TypeArt

For example, when a dog doesn't have papers to turn in, they say "my human ate my homework."

Silverscreen—BoldItalic • TypeArt

Do You Know Why Dogs Howl? Most people have no idea that there has been research on this.

Silverscreen—Italic • TypeArt

Researchers have come up with three very good reasons why this is.

Silverscreen—Regular • TypeArt

Theory number 1: Howling is

Gonza • 2Rebels

how dogs clear their throats.

Gonza—Bold • 2Rebels

No. 2: Howling is a sound

Gonza—BoldOblique • 2Rebels

that, if translated from

Gonza—Oblique • 2Rebels

dog talk to human words,

GonzaPlus • 2Rebels

comes out as—I'm really bored.

GonzaPlus—Bold • 2Rebels

Theory Number Three on Howling:

GonzaPlus—BoldOblique • 2Rebels

Howling is a sign of DOG PMS.

GonzaPlus—Oblique • 2Rebels

Do You Know that Dogs Have Fantasies? Yes.

Coeval—Bold • 2Rebels

One Major Dog Fantasy Involves A Cook-Out.

Coeval—BoldItalic • 2Rebels

IN THIS FANTASY, THE GUY WHO LIVES IN THE HOUSE

Coeval—Expert • 2Rebels

IS COOKING SIX BIG STEAKS ON THE GRILL.

Coeval—ExpertBold • 2Rebels

THE GUY STARTS TELLING A JOKE AND HE FORGETS

Coeval—ExpertBoldItalic • 2Rebels

ABOUT THE STEAK COOKING AND SUDDENLY THE GUY

Coeval—ExpertItalic • 2Rebels

NOTICES THAT HE HAS BURNED THE STEAKS.

Coeval—ExpertMedium • 2Rebels

QUICKLY, HE MAKES A DECISION ON WHAT TO DO ABOUT IT.

Coeval—ExpertMediumItalic • 2Rebels

He knows that people won't eat the burned steaks,

Coeval—Italic • 2Rebels

but he knows exactly who WILL want them.

Coeval—Medium • 2Rebels

And the guy yells "C'mon Buster, get some steaks!"

Coeval—MediumItalic • 2Rebels

In the Dog Fantasy World, this Ranks Quite High.

Coeval—Regular • 2Rebels

if dogs were in charge of things,

Sofa—AB • 2Rebels

fleas would be as big as frogs and

those fleas would taste like hamburger.

and if dogs ran things, pizza would be

available in new flavors, but

the most popular one would be...

DIRTY SNEAKERS. THERE WOULD ALSO BE

HOME DELIVERY TO A DOG'S HOUSE.

IMAGINE HOW MUCH DOGS WOULD LIKE

PIZZA IF IT TASTED LIKE DIRTY SNEAKERS.

DO YOU REALIZE HOW MUCH MORE FUN

IT IS TO TAKE A DOG ON A CAR TRIP

THAN IT IS TO TAKE THE KIDS?

QUICK: WHY ARE DOGS MORE FUN IN A CAR?

THERE ARE THREE REASONS WHY DOGS

Malcom—ExpertSemiLight • 2Rebels

ARE MORE FUN IN A CAR THAN KIDS:

Malcom—ExpertSemiLightItalic • 2Rebels

1. Dogs Never Have Sticky Fingers

Malcom—Italic • 2Rebels

from Eating Candy. Never.

Malcom—Light • 2Rebels

2. Dogs don't want to stop every

Malcom—LightItalic • 2Rebels

time they see the Golden Arches.

Malcom—Medium • 2Rebels

And the third reason dogs are

Malcom—MediumItalic • 2Rebels

more fun is the most important.

Malcom—Regular • 2Rebels

Dogs never, ever, say to you

Malcom—SemiLight • 2Rebels

in a whiney voice, "Hey,

Malcom—SemiLightItalic • 2Rebels

WHEN WILL WE BE THERE?

Marker—Outline • 2Rebels

WHEN WILL WE BE THERE?"

Marker—Plain • 2Rebels

time and time again.

ElderSansSerif • 2Rebels

"WHEN WILL WE BE THERE?" NEVER,

Thais—Light • 2Rebels

NEVER DOES A DOG ASK THAT.

ThinMan • 2Rebels

No, Dogs just lie in the seat and sleep.

Voyou—Regular • 2Rebels

Every Dog I have owned has been a pleasure to travel with.

Akimbo—Bold • Treacyfaces

Yes, those dogs have found car travel to be a lot of fun.

Akimbo—Demibold • Treacyfaces

Not so for every kid I have had to travel with.

Akimbo—Extrabold • Treacyfaces

Kids can be a pain in the butt on long trips. Gotta eat.

Akimbo—Heavy • Treacyfaces

Gotta go to the bathroom. Gotta go to bathroom again.

Akimbo—Light • Treacyfaces

I can't wait any longer. Gotta go bathroom gotta

Akimbo—Medium • Treacyfaces

go now. Dogs don't do that. They seem to know

AkimboContrast—Bold • Treacyfaces

just what to do to pace themselves from

AkimboContrast—Demi • Treacyfaces

Rest Stop to Rest Stop. Dogs Seem to know how.

AkimboContrast—Extrabold • Treacyfaces

Dogs never say. "I gotta go to the bathroom. Now."

AkimboContrast—Heavy • Treacyfaces

Here is Another Dog Fantasy (read this and see

if you agree): The Inside Dog watches his people

as they leave the house. When they

are completely out of the driveway,

the Dog walks down the hall

to the Oasis. (The dog "Oasis" is

the bathroom.) The dog finds that someone has made blue Kool-Aid just for him. Imagine, blue water in the Oasis.

I mean, a dog finding fresh water at the Oasis, and finding fresh BLUE water at the Oasis, are wonderful occasions in the life of a dog. Yes.

I don't think there is a Comparable Surprise in the Human World. It takes a Dog to be able to have such a great surprise.

If dogs ran things, baths would

be optional. Do you understand?

Sometimes a dog wants to get

wet and sometimes he doesn't.

O
sans

Few people know that the

"sniffing" of other dogs is

actually governed by a very rigid

set of rules of etiquette entitled,

"Rules for Dogs Sniffing Each Other".

Knowing and abiding by these rules is

an integral part of a dog's self image.

Even stray and mongrel dogs are aware

that the Dog Sniffing Ceremony is very

old, and governed by strict protocol.

Did you ever see two dogs get into a fight

just after sniffing each other? It happens.

If One Dog doesn't follow the rules,

a dog fight just might come about.

Sniffing improperly is considered

rude in the Dog World. Improper

Sniffing Leads to Fights. Humans

have the handshake. Dogs sniff.

If dogs ran things, there would be

a Cat Fight every single night.

A Cat Fight Every Night ON HBO. Yes.

Here is another well-kept secret

from the World of Dogs. Very few

people know about this, so don't

you tell anyone. It's top dog secret.

Some very small dogs, are actually CATS!

Yes, some very small dogs are cats in drag.

Some Very Small Dogs are Cats in Drag.

Small Dogs are Cats in Drag.

Now you know it; maybe I've

said too much. I hope this

doesn't wind up on the cover

of the National Enquirer. It is,

after all, the kind of story one finds

on the cover of the National Enquirer.

If that were to happen, the dog who

told me would feel betrayed

because I was sworn to secrecy.

So, please keep this our little secret.

Are dogs conservationists? Maybe.

Ever watch a dog water the grass? Yes.

OR WATER A TREE?

I think we have all watched a dog water the grass, or water a tree—or even water a fire hydrant. Did we question what he was doing? NO.

Every fire hydrant has a sign only dogs

can see. Some font books are boring,

Like: Qwerty is the Meaning of Life.

Pretty boring. That's why this book is

full of new stuff. This is the Font Book I

always wanted. Why did I want to do it?

The Quick Brown Fox Jumped Over the

The Next Line was: Lazy Sleeping Dog.

One time I got a font book, and every line, more than 1200 of them ended with Lazy Sleeping Dog. I resented reading

about "Lazy Sleeping Dogs." That's why this book is

the way it is. I refuse to put out a book in which

EVERY line demeans an entire species. Dogs Aren't lazy.

I mean, who sleeps more, dogs or cats? If you are going

to hang the lazy word on a species, how about cats?

How Much Do Cats Sleep? A lot more Than Dogs. So why

is the "Lazy Sleeping Dog" used at all?

I know why. It's a thing that typing

teachers have typing students practice

typing because it has all the letters.

The Lazy Sleeping Dog line has all

the letters of the alphabet in it.

Is it any wonder that dogs can't type? Not at all.

Jocelyn—Light • ABCDesign (Creative Alliance)

It's no wonder at all dogs can't type.

Jocelyn—SemiBold • ABCDesign (C. Alliance)

Dogs will not type a sentence in

Ulissa • ABCDesign (Creative Alliance)

which their entire dog species

Ulissa—Bold • ABCDesign (Creative Alliance)

is demeaned and degraded.

Ulissa—BoldItalic • ABCDesign (C. Alliance)

No dog is going to type that sentence. Get it?

Ulissa—CondensedBold • ABCDesign (C.A.)

I mean would you want to type this sentence over and over?

Ulissa—CondensedBook • ABCDesign (C.A.)

"The Quick, Clever Dog bit the slothful, ugly human on his fat. . ."

Ulissa—CondensedLight • ABCDesign (C.A.)

No, you wouldn't want to type that sentence.

Ulissa—CondensedMedium • ABCDesign (C.A.)

If you HAD to type that sentence quickly,

Ulissa—Italic • ABCDesign (Creative Alliance)

over and over, you'd quit school.

UlissaRounded • ABCDesign (Creative Alliance)

That's what you would do.

UlissaRounded—Bold • ABCDesign (C.A.)

You would never type that line

UlissaRounded—BoldItalic • ABCDesign (C.A.)

quickly, time and time again.

UlissaRounded—Italic • ABCDesign (C.A.)

You would quit; you know you

Univers 65 Bold • Adobe (Creative Alliance)

would. So, is it any wonder

Univers 75 Black • Adobe (Creative Alliance)

that dogs can't type? Now

Univers 75 BlackOblique • Adobe (C. Alliance)

you know the reason. Yes,

Univers 65 BoldOblique • Adobe (C. Alliance)

generations of dogs have been denied

Univers 57 Condensed • Adobe (C. Alliance)

the opportunity to learn a new skill.

Univers 67 CondensedBold • Adobe (C. Alliance)

Dogs have not been permitted to

Univers 67 CondBoldObl • Adobe (C. Alliance)

take typing classes, and that's why.

Univers 47 CondensedLight • Adobe (C.A.)

A Bigoted Set of Typing Teachers have

Univers 47 CondLightObl • Adobe (C. Alliance)

driven millions of dogs away from

Univers 57 CondOblique • Adobe (C. Alliance)

Typing Classes, just because

Univers 45 Light • Adobe (Creative Alliance)

dogs are demeaned by the lessons.

Univers 45 LightOblique • Adobe (C. Alliance)

So next time you see a dog who

Univers 55 Oblique • Adobe (Creative Alliance)

can't type, try to be a little more

Univers 55 • Adobe (Creative Alliance)

understanding. It isn't his fault.

VAG Rounded Bold • Adobe (Creative Alliance)

When dogs apply for jobs, and

VAG Rounded Black • Adobe (Creative Alliance)

the job description says "computer

VAG Rounded Light • Adobe (Creative Alliance)

literate", the dog has to go away,

VAG Rounded Thin • Adobe (Creative Alliance)

because he never learned to type.

Rotis Sans Serif • Agfa (Creative Alliance)

Maybe someday this will **change.**

Rotis Sans Serif Bold • Agfa (Creative Alliance)

Will it take a generation of

Rotis Sans Serif ExBd • Agfa (Creative Alliance)

militant dogs to reverse this

Rotis Sans Serif Italic • Agfa (Creative Alliance)

oppression? Maybe dogs will someday

Rotis Sans Serif Light • Agfa (Creative Alliance)

all learn to type, but for now, please

Rotis Sans Serif Lt It • Agfa (Creative Alliance)

try to understand the dog's plight.

Rotis Semisans • Agfa (Creative Alliance)

If dogs ran things, leashes would

be just a little bit longer. In fact,

there wouldn't even be leashes. None.

Want to know a really bad dog nightmare?

Imagine a blind date, and the male

is a Chihuahua, a little guy. And

the Chihuahua goes to visit

the female, who is a big dog.

No, she is a BIG dog, like a

German Shepherd, or a St. Bernard.

Imagine that: male Chihuahua dog,

female St. Bernard. The poor

little guy would just be better off

if he went on home. Now.

No need to stay and embarrass

himself. Did you know that

dogs have Pick-Up Lines?

They do. Here's a good

pick-up line that is often

used by male dogs. Used

a lot. The dog says, "I've been

fixed. I swear." Female dogs have

pick-up lines as well. Here is

one of their great ones:

"Is that a bone in your pocket, or

are you just happy to see me?"

Quick answers are good for dogs.

Naniara Bold Italic • Bo Berndal (C. Alliance)

Quick answers are important

Naniara Heavy • Bo Berndal (Creative Alliance)

because if dogs don't act quickly, the

Naniara Light • Bo Berndal (Creative Alliance)

moment can pass quickly. Little Known

Naniara Light Italic • Bo Berndal (C. Alliance)

Facts About Dogs: singles bars are popular and there

AlpinGthNo1 • Creative Alliance

is a large national chain of Dogs Single Bars. Yes.

AlpinGthNo2 • Creative Alliance

The national chain of singles bars is called "HEAT".

AlpinGthNo3 • Creative Alliance

Don't believe me? Ask any female

GlobeGothicBd • Creative Alliance

dog—or any male dog. "Heat" is

GlobeGothicDm • Creative Alliance

very popular. Few people know about the

GlobeGothicLt • Creative Alliance

location of dog singles bars, but

GlobeGothicUl • Creative Alliance

you can often see dogs in line

Heldustry • Creative Alliance

Just waiting to get in. Really.

Heldustry—italic • Creative Alliance

Here's something else you

didn't know about your pooch.

Your faithful friend watches TV.

When your dog is lying in the TV

room, the dog is watching TV,

even if you don't know it. Dogs watch

some TV shows quite a lot. Do you

know just how many dogs are on TV?

More than cats! Whenever a good

dog sees another dog on television,

the television-watching dog

thinks, "Hey that's one of

my own. I could do that."

Quietly, the dog is very proud,

Congress Sans Extra Bold • Club Type (C.A.)

and at the same time, quite

Congress Sans Extra Bold Italic • Club Type (C.A.)

envious. Yes, the dog is quite envious.

Congress Sans Italic • Club Type (C. Alliance)

Dogs are just as prone to Envy as

Congress Sans Light • Club Type (C. Alliance)

people. The dog watching TV wishes

Congress Sans Light Italic • Club Type (C.A.)

HE were the star. All Dogs ſhare the

Eaglefeather Formal Bold • David Siegel (C.A.)

wish to be famous. ſo, it is Quite Natural

Eaglefeather Formal Bold Italic • D. Siegel (C.A.)

for dogs to fantasize about being TV ſtars.

Eaglefeather Formal Light • David Siegel (C.A.)

ſure, Lassie is Famous. And so is Rin Tin Tin.

Eaglefeather Formal Light It • D. Siegel (C.A.)

Envy is only Natural for Dogs with an ego.

Eaglefeather Formal Regular • D. Siegel (C.A.)

And yes, dogs have an ego, make no mistake.

Eaglefeather Formal Regular It • D. Siegel (C.A.)

Dogs want to be on TV just as much as anyone.

Eaglefeather Informal Bold • David Siegel (C.A.)

Dogs want fame just as much as anyone.

Eaglefeather Informal Bold It • D. Siegel (C.A.)

Can you imagine YOUR dog being on TV?

Eaglefeather Informal Light • David Siegel (C.A.)

Or how about your dog being in the movies?

Eaglefeather Informal Light It • D. Siegel (C.A.)

Maybe your dog would want to be on packages.

Eaglefeather Informal Reg It • D. Siegel (C.A.)

Surely your dog would like his picture used on

Eaglefeather Informal Regular • D. Siegel (C.A.)

PACKAGING TO SELL VARIOUS DOG PRODUCTS.

Eaglefeather Small Caps Bold • D. Siegel (C.A.)

BETTER STILL, IMAGINE YOUR DOG ON

Eaglefeather Small Caps Light • D. Siegel (C.A.)

MT. RUSHMORE. CAN YOU PICTURE YOUR

Eaglefeather Small Caps Regular • D. Siegel (C.A.)

dog's face on Mt. Rushmore? Just

BernhardGothicSG—Book • Fonthaus (C.A.)

imagine: Buster on Mt. Rushmore.

BernhardGothicSG—BookItalic • Fonthaus (C.A.)

Dogs everywhere would quickly

BernhardGothicSG—Heavy • Fonthaus (C.A.)

have their very own travel destination.

BernhardGothicSG—HeavyItalic • Fonthaus (C.A.)

There would be dog tour buses going

BernhardGothicSG—Light • Fonthaus (C.A.)

there—seasonal at first, then year-round.

BernhardGothicSG—LightItalic • Fonthaus (C.A.)

Just picture that: a big Greyhound Bus

(of course, Greyhound) with 44 Dogs on Vacation.

Forty-Four Dogs going to Mt. Rushmore.

When they got there, they would

see four presidents and one

famous dog. Surely this will

happen someday. Answer quick:

who do you think will be

the president to have the

courage to add a dog's face

to Mt. Rushmore? Which president would

add a dog to Mount Rushmore?

I would. But I'm not running for president.

Did you ever see a dog "running" while he slept?

CaponeLight • Fonthaus (Creative Alliance)

Sometimes, when this is happening, the dog is making "fear" noises.

CaponeLightCondensed • Fonthaus (C. Alliance)

Did you ever wonder what the dog is dreaming when this happens?

CaponeMediumCondensed • Fonthaus (C.A.)

Well, after long and careful research

PacificClipperBd • Fonthaus (Creative Alliance)

Dog Scientists know the Answer to this.

PacificClipperBk • Fonthaus (Creative Alliance)

The dog is having a nightmare,

PacificClipperDm • Fonthaus (Creative Alliance)

and it is about a "sniffing" scene

PacificClipperLt • Fonthaus (Creative Alliance)

gone bad. The dog having the dream

PacificClipperMd • Fonthaus (Creative Alliance)

is remembering the time he

Grotesk HeavyItalic • Title Wave Studios

was unforgivably rude to a little puppy. Rude!

Standard—CondObl • Fonthaus (C. Alliance)

In fact, the dreaming dog was very arrogant around the little pup.

Standard—MedCond • Fonthaus (C. Alliance)

And in the dog's dream, the little dog is back, as a huge dog.

Standard—MedCondObl • Fonthaus (C.A.)

Now the pup is BIG!

Standard—XBldExt • Fonthaus (C. Alliance)

In the dream,

THE **BIG** DOG QUIETLY

SNIFFS THE SLEEPING DOG.

HE SNIFFS THE SLEEPING DOG.

THE SLEEPING DOG IS BEING SNIFFED

AND QUICKLY, THE BIG DOG KNOWS

HE THINKS, "I REMEMBER."

The big dog thinks "I remember this guy."

Yes, the big dog remembers

just how arrogant the sleeping

dog once was to the big dog

And Now, Quickly, the big dog has

one thing on his mind, Revenge.

Standard—XBoldExtObl • Fonthaus (C.A.)

BriemScriptSC+OSF—Black • G. Se Briem (C.A.)

BriemScriptSC+OSF—Bold • G. Se Briem (C.A.)

BriemScriptSC+OSF—Book • G. Se Briem (C.A.)

BriemScriptSC+OSF—Light • G. Se Briem (C.A.)

BriemScriptSC+OSF—Medium • G. Se Briem (C.A.)

BriemScriptSC+OSF—UltraBold • G. Se Briem (C.A.)

AvantGardeCd—Book • ITC (Creative Alliance)

AvantGardeCd—Demi • ITC (Creative Alliance)

AvantGardeMd • ITC (Creative Alliance)

AvantGardeMd—Bold • ITC (Creative Alliance)

AvantGardeExtLt • ITC (Creative Alliance)

AvantGardeExtLt—Oblique • ITC (C. Alliance)

sans

Yes, the Big Dog has Revenge in Mind

And as you see the sleeping dog

run, t that very point in his dream,

he is running away from the dog

and he is thinking about how sorry

he is that he was mean to

the puppy a long time ago.

He is very sorry that he was

mean to the puppy who grew up and

became a huge dog. And now, the

sleeping dog is running away as fast as he can.

And as he Quickly runs away, he whimpers.

And now you know the inside story.

Speaking of Dog Psychology, do

Bauhaus—DemiBold • ITC (Creative Alliance)

you know why Dogs Chase Cats?

Bauhaus—Light • ITC (Creative Alliance)

It's actually a game. The dog

BauhausMd • ITC (Creative Alliance)

is pretending to be Sheriff,

BauhausMd—Bold • ITC (Creative Alliance)

And the cat is speeding.

BenguiatGot—Bold • ITC (Creative Alliance)

So the Dog Sheriff is Quickly chasing

BenguiatGot—BoldItalic • ITC (C. Alliance)

The Dog Sheriff is Quickly Chasing the

BenguiatGot—Book • ITC (Creative Alliance)

The Cat is Speeding Away from the

BenguiatGot—BookItalic • ITC (C. Alliance)

And the Dog is in Hot Pursuit of the Cat

BenguiatGotMd • ITC (Creative Alliance)

Sometimes, when dogs dream, a cat is

BenguiatGotMd—Heavy • ITC (C. Alliance)

The Cat is often part of dog dreams,

BenguiatGotMd—HeavyItalic • ITC (C.A.)

But most of the time when the dog is

BenguiatGotMd—Italic • ITC (C. Alliance)

The dog runs and whimpers,

Charlotte Sans Bold • ITC (Creative Alliance)

241

It's because the dog is being chased.

Charlotte Sans Book • ITC (Creative Alliance)

If dogs could type, they would write letters.

Charlotte Sans Book Italic • ITC (C. Alliance)

Dogs would write letters to

Charlotte Sans Medium • ITC (Creative Alliance)

TENNIS BALL MANUFACTURERS.

Charlotte Sans Small Caps • ITC (C. Alliance)

They Would Get Letters From Dogs.

Conduit Bold • ITC (Creative Alliance)

Here's what the dog letters to tennis ball

Conduit Bold Italic • ITC (Creative Alliance)

Dear Tennis Ball People: I have a Question for

Conduit Light • ITC (Creative Alliance)

My Question for You is this: Why do you make

Conduit Light Italic • ITC (Creative Alliance)

Why do you Make Tennis Balls taste Like fuzz

Conduit Medium • ITC (Creative Alliance)

Why do Tennis Balls Taste Like Green Fuzz?

Conduit Medium Italic • ITC (Creative Alliance)

Don't get me wrong. Tennis Balls

Crillee Bold Italic • ITC (Creative Alliance)

Balls that taste like green fuzz

Crillee Extra Bold Italic • ITC (C. Alliance)

Green Fuzz Isn't Bad, especially with

Crillee Italic • ITC (Creative Alliance)

Green Fuzz is OK, especially with dog

Crillee Italic Inline Shad • ITC (C. Alliance)

Quickly Mix Dog Saliva with the fuzz,

Flora • ITC (Creative Alliance)

And It actually Tastes Quite Good.

Flora—Bold • ITC (Creative Alliance)

But, if you realize that Tennis Balls are MORE

FranklinGotCd—Book • ITC (Creative Alliance)

Tennis Balls are more that just Tennis Balls.

FranklinGotCd—BookItalic • ITC (C. Alliance)

Tennis Balls Should Be Called Dog Balls.

FranklinGotCd—Demi • ITC (Creative Alliance)

Maybe that's a bad Idea. Anyway, Dogs like

FranklinGotCd—DemiItalic • ITC (C. Alliance)

Anyway, dogs love tennis balls. And a large

FranklinGotCdMd • ITC (Creative Alliance)

A Large number of tennis Balls Quietly

FranklinGotCdMd—Italic • ITC (C. Alliance)

TENNIS BALLS QUIETLY BECOME DOG TOYS.

FranklinGotCdMdSC • ITC (Creative Alliance)

SO WITH THAT IN MIND HOW ABOUT OTHER FLAVORS

FranklinGotCdSC—Book • ITC (C. Alliance)

How About Other Flavors for Tennis Balls? Think

FranklinGotCmp—Book • ITC (C. Alliance)

Think About that idea. Flavored Tennis Balls for dogs

FranklinGotCmp—BookItalic • ITC (C. Alliance)

Just for starters, you could have hamburger flavor.

FranklinGotCmp—Demi • ITC (C. Alliance)

I know lots of dogs would like Hamburger tennis

FranklinGotCmp—DemiItalic • ITC (C. Alliance)

Hamburger Flavored Tennis Balls would

FranklinGot—Book • ITC (Creative Alliance)

They would Sell Very Well. I think So.

FranklinGot—BookItalic • ITC (C. Alliance)

You could even have varieties of

FranklinGot—Demi • ITC (Creative Alliance)

Flavor varieties could be well done,

FranklinGot—DemiItalic • ITC (C. Alliance)

And Medium Rare, and Rare. And raw.

FranklinGotMd • ITC (Creative Alliance)

And the Hamburger Flavor is Just

FranklinGotMd—Heavy • ITC (C. Alliance)

It's just the beginning. Consider

FranklinGotMd—HeavyItalic • ITC (C. Alliance)

Other Flavors of Tennis Balls might be

FranklinGotMd—Italic• ITC (Creative Alliance)

Have you Ever Thought About Road-Kill Possum Flavor Tennis Balls?

FranklinGotXCmp—Book • ITC (C. Alliance)

If you haven't thought about it, you really should. Road kill possum

FranklinGotXCmp—Demi • ITC (C. Alliance)

Road Kill Possum Flavor is Very Good.

GoudySans—Bold • ITC (Creative Alliance)

Although I'm Quite Sure You Haven't

GoudySans—BoldItalic • ITC (Creative Alliance)

I'm Quite Sure You Haven't Tried that flavor.

GoudySans—Book • ITC (Creative Alliance)

Take it from Me, it would Be Good. Very good.

GoudySans—BookItalic • ITC (C. Alliance)

One thing I've never understood about

GoudySansMd • ITC (Creative Alliance)

People are hard to understand.

GoudySansMd—Black • ITC (Creative Alliance)

Question: How Good is Road Kill Food?

GoudySansMd—BlackItalic • ITC (C. Alliance)

It's Easy: Road Kill is Good Stuff. Ask a dog.

GoudySansMd—Italic • ITC (Creative Alliance)

PEOPLE EAT BEEF AND CHICKEN: THEY'RE MEATS.

GoudySansMdSC • ITC (Creative Alliance)

SO WHY DO YOU GET SO UPSET WHEN YOUR DOG

GoudySansSC—Book • ITC (Creative Alliance)

When your dog finds some road kill,

HighlanderBold • ITC (Creative Alliance)

What's the big deal, anyway? I don't

HighlanderBoldItalic • ITC (Creative Alliance)

I just don't know why people get so upset

HighlanderBook • ITC (Creative Alliance)

Just because your dog gets food "to go".

HighlanderBookItalic • ITC (Creative Alliance)

ANOTHER THING DOGS DON'T UNDERSTAND

HighlanderBookSC • ITC (Creative Alliance)

Dogs don't understand people directions.

HighlanderMedium • ITC (Creative Alliance)

Directions given by people are silly.

HighlanderMedItalic • ITC (Creative Alliance)

FOR EXAMPLE, THIS IS TYPICAL PEOPLE TALK:

HighlanderMediumSC • ITC (Creative Alliance)

Go three blocks, there's a red light.

Humana Sans Bold • ITC (Creative Alliance)

Hang a right at the light. Go 2 blocks.

Humana Sans Bold Italic • ITC (C. Alliance)

Turn left on Rhodes Avenue. Got it so far?

Humana Sans Light • ITC (Creative Alliance)

Next, go down that road till the gas station.

Humana Sans Light Italic • ITC (C. Alliance)

When you reach the gas station, go left.

Humana Sans Medium • ITC (Creative Alliance)

Now, look for the 2nd house on the left.

Humana Sans Medium Italic • ITC (C. Alliance)

The Porch Light Will be On for You.

Kabel—Book • ITC (Creative Alliance)

Dogs couldn't follow those directions.

Kabel—Demi • ITC (Creative Alliance)

Dogs don't understand that language.

KabelMd • ITC (Creative Alliance)

Here's how a dog gives directions.

KabelMd—Bold • ITC (Creative Alliance)

Go down that path to the cat smell,

KabelUltra • ITC (Creative Alliance)

Follow the cat smell until you see the

LegacySanBold • ITC (Creative Alliance)

Quietly go until you see the robin's nest tree.

LegacySanBoldItalic • ITC (Creative Alliance)

That's where you Want to Turn Right.

LegacySanBook • ITC (Creative Alliance)

Quietly go past the "Junkyard Dog" Place.

LegacySanBookItalic • ITC (Creative Alliance)

Go Quietly, but Go Fast. Really Fast.

LegacySanBookSC • ITC (Creative Alliance)

Then look for the dog with the spot.

LegacySanMedium • ITC (Creative Alliance)

The Quiet Nice spot on his eye. Black Spot.

LegacySanMediumIta • ITC (Creative Alliance)

Go Quietly or he'll bark at you. A lot.

LegacySanMediumSC • ITC (Creative Alliance)

Quickly come to the house next door

LegacySanUltra • ITC (Creative Alliance)

That's where I live, Next Door to Spot

OfficinaSanBlack • ITC (Creative Alliance)

That's my house. I live...INSIDE.

OfficinaSanBlackItalic • ITC (Creative Alliance)

HERE'S ANOTHER DREAM THAT DOGS HAVE.

OfficinaSanBlackSC • ITC (Creative Alliance)

Sometimes when a dog is running in

OfficinaSanBold • ITC (Creative Alliance)

THE DOG IS RUNNING IN THE DREAM, AND IT

OfficinaSanBoldSC • ITC (Creative Alliance)

It's not because of a Quick Big dog

OfficinaSanBoldItalic • ITC (Creative Alliance)

It's the famous "dog catcher" dream.

OfficinaSanBook • ITC (Creative Alliance)

This is a recurring dream for a lot of dogs.

OfficinaSanBookItalic • ITC (Creative Alliance)

IN THIS DREAM, THE DOG IS BEING PURSUED

OfficinaSanBookSC • ITC (Creative Alliance)

The dog is being pursued by the Evil

OfficinaSanExtraBold • ITC (Creative Alliance)

The Evil Dogcatcher is Chasing the dog

OfficinaSanExtraBoldItalic • ITC (C. Alliance)

THE DOG CATCHER HAS THIS HUGE NET AND

OfficinaSanExtraBoldSC • ITC (C. Alliance)

the dog catcher is apparently getting

OfficinaSanMedium • ITC (Creative Alliance)

The dog catcher is getting closer, closer...

OfficinaSanMediumItalic • ITC (C. Alliance)

BUT IN THIS DREAM, JUST AS THE DOG CATCHER

OfficinaSanMediumSC • ITC (Creative Alliance)

Just as the dog catcher Quickly jumps

QuaySans—Black • ITC (Creative Alliance)

The guy Quickly jumps at the dog,

QuaySans—BlackItalic • ITC (Creative Alliance)

And as he flings his net toward the dog,

QuaySans—Book • ITC (Creative Alliance)

At that very moment, the dog turns on the

QuaySans—BookItalic • ITC (Creative Alliance)

dog Quickly turns on the burners, and

QuaySansMd • ITC (Creative Alliance)

as the dog catcher Quickly Falls flat

QuaySansMd—Italic • ITC (Creative Alliance)

THE DOG CATCHER FALLS FLAT ON HIS FACE,

QuaySansMdSC • ITC (Creative Alliance)

AND HE HITS HARD ON THE STREET. BUMP!

QuaySansSC • ITC (Creative Alliance)

And as the dog Quickly Speeds

Stone Sans—Bold • ITC (Creative Alliance)

The dog Quickly Speeds Away, and

Stone Sans—BoldItalic • ITC (Creative Alliance)

As he Quickly goes out of sight, the

Stone Sans—Medium • ITC (Creative Alliance)

quiet dog catcher says "@%#*!"*

Stone Sans—MediumItalic • ITC (C. Alliance)

Did you ever see a dog smile?

Stone Sans—Semi • ITC (Creative Alliance)

Take a Good Look at

Blair Bold • ITC/Fontek (Creative Alliance)

Take a good look at the

Blair Light • ITC/Fontek (Creative Alliance)

Look At the Dreaming

Blair Medium • ITC/Fontek (Creative Alliance)

Quickly Look at the Dreaming Dog, and You

Claude Sans Bold Italic • ITC/Fontek (C.A.)

And You Will see the Quick Dog Smiling. It's easy.

Claude Sans Italic • ITC/Fontek (C. Alliance)

Yes, dogs smile. Even While they Dream.

Dyadis Bold • ITC/Fontek (Creative Alliance)

What a wonderful end to the Dogcatcher

Dyadis Bold Italic • ITC/Fontek (C. Alliance)

A Wonderful End to the Dog Catcher

Dyadis Bold SC • ITC/Fontek (Creative Alliance)

The Smiling Dog, at the End of the Dream.

Dyadis Book • ITC/Fontek (Creative Alliance)

While the Dogcatcher Quietly Goes Away.

Dyadis Book Italic • ITC/Fontek (C. Alliance)

When the Dog Wakes Up, He's Very Happy.

Dyadis Book SC • ITC/Fontek (C. Alliance)

Especially if he's an Inside Dog. Very Happy.

Dyadis Medium • ITC/Fontek (C. Alliance)

He may even go right Back to Sleep. Maybe.

Dyadis Medium Italic • ITC/Fontek (C. Alliance)

IF DOGS RAN THINGS, THERE WOULD BE A LOT OF

Dyadis Medium SC • ITC/Fontek (C. Alliance)

Many Things Would be different, just a little

Equinox • ITC/Fontek (Creative Alliance)

For a Quick example, if dogs ran

ErasBold • ITC/Fontek (Creative Alliance)

If Dogs Ran Things, Vacuum

ErasBold—Ultra • ITC/Fontek (C. Alliance)

Cleaners Would NOT be allowed

ErasBook • ITC/Fontek (Creative Alliance)

Vacuum Cleaners Could Not get

ErasBook—Demi • ITC/Fontek (C. Alliance)

Could Not Get Close to Food on the

Eras—Light • ITC/Fontek (Creative Alliance)

Food on the Floor is for Dogs Only.

Eras—Medium • ITC/Fontek (Creative Alliance)

FDO (For Dogs Only) signs would be up.

Lennox Bold • ITC/Fontek (Creative Alliance)

Those Signs Would be Everywhere. And Rightly So.

Lennox Book • ITC/Fontek (Creative Alliance)

Just Consider How Much Love Dogs Bring to life.

Lennox Medium • ITC/Fontek (C. Alliance)

Q. When was the ast time you argued with a dog?

Luna • ITC/Fontek (Creative Alliance)

Quick: Tell me the Answer. Never. Right?

Luna Bold • ITC/Fontek (Creative Alliance)

Dogs don't argue with you. They just give love.

Tannhauser • ITC/Fontek (Creative Alliance)

And if dogs ran things, there would

Tempus Sans • ITC/Fontek (Creative Alliance)

No Plate would EVER be put in the dish

Tempus Sans Italic • ITC/Fontek (C. Alliance)

THE DISHWASHER WOULD BE THE LAST

Tempus Sans SC • ITC/Fontek (C. Alliance)

NOTHING WOULD GO INTO THE DISH

Tempus Sans SC Italic • ITC/Fontek (C. Alliance)

Nothing Would Go into the Dishwasher until a Dog had licked

Wade Sans Light • ITC/Fontek (C. Alliance)

Dogs Must Lick All Plates Clean.

Bliss—Bold • Jeremy Tankard (Creative Alliance)

Only Then Would Plates Quickly Go to

Bliss—BoldItalic • Jeremy Tankard (C. Alliance)

After the Dog Had Cleaned, Quickly

Bliss—ExtraBold • Jeremy Tankard (C. Alliance)

Dogs Quickly clean all Plates Before the

Bliss—ExtraBoldItalic • Jeremy Tankard (C.A.)

The Dog Must release the Plate for

Bliss—Heavy • Jeremy Tankard (C. Alliance)

The Dog must lick the plate clean first.

Bliss—HeavyItalic • Jeremy Tankard (C.A.)

Only then can it go to the Quiet Dishwasher.

Bliss—Italic • Jeremy Tankard (C. Alliance)

Another thought about Dog Obedience...

Dog Obedience School thought: If people

If people turn in "dog-eared" papers,

Then do dogs turn in "people-eared"

Do dogs turn in "people-eared" papers?

I HAVE OFTEN WONDERED THAT QUESTION.

ANOTHER QUESTION? REMEMBER THE MT.

REMEMBER THE MT. RUSHMORE QUESTION?

ANOTHER QUESTION: ONCE DOGS GET A

ONCE A DOG QUICKLY GETS ON MOUNT

Q. ONCE DOGS ARE ON MT. RUSHMORE,

THEN WHY SHOULD THEY QUIT? NEXT STEP IS

THE NEXT STEP IS TO QUIETLY GO FOR THE

THE NEXT STEP IS GO FOR THE SPHINX.

BlissCaps—LightItalic • Jeremy Tankard (C.A.)

THAT EGYPTIAN THING LOOKS LIKE A CAT.

BlissCaps—Medium • Jeremy Tankard (C.A.)

Q. WHAT IS THAT ALL ABOUT? A CAT? No.

BlissCaps—MediumItalic • J. Tankard (C.A.)

WOULDN'T A DOG LOOK MUCH BETTER THERE?

BlissCaps—Regular • Jeremy Tankard (C.A.)

A QUICK EASY DECISION. DOG WINS.

Donatello Regular • Letterperfect (C. Alliance)

Anybody Can See the Answer. Dog over Cat.

Hardwood • Letterperfect (Creative Alliance)

Quickly change the cat Sphinx

Imperfect Bold • M. Strassburger/T-26 (C.A.)

And turn it into the Dog Sphinx. Yes.

Imperfect Bold Oblique • M. Strassburger/T-26 (C.A.)

Can anyone give you a single reason NOT

Imperfect Oblique • M. Strassburger/T-26 (C.A.)

Is there a reason NOT to do this? Not at all.

Imperfect Regular • M. Strassburger/T-26 (C.A.)

Just Picture a Quiet Dog on the Sphinx.

Abadi • Monotype (Creative Alliance)

Quick. Name a famous Cat. Ha. There.

Abadi Bold • Monotype (Creative Alliance)

So, it's time to Quietly change the cat.

Abadi Bold Italic • Monotype (C. Alliance)

Did you ever notice that dogs don't like coffee?

Abadi Cn • Monotype (Creative Alliance)

Did You Ever Wonder Why they don't like it?

Abadi Cn Bold • Monotype (Creative Alliance)

First reason: coffee keeps dogs awake.

Abadi Cn ExBold • Monotype (C. Alliance)

Coffee Keeps Dogs Awake During the Day. No good.

Abadi Cn Light • Monotype (Creative Alliance)

Dogs need Quiet Sleep Day Sleep.

Abadi Ex Bold • Monotype (Creative Alliance)

Another reason dogs don't like coffee

Abadi Ex Bold It • Monotype (Creative Alliance)

Dogs don't do spoons very well. Not at all.

Abadi Ex Light • Monotype (Creative Alliance)

And the final reason that dogs don't like

Abadi Ex Light It • Monotype (C. Alliance)

Dogs don't like coffee mainly because

Abadi Italic • Monotype (Creative Alliance)

water from the "oasis" is better.

Abadi Light • Monotype (Creative Alliance)

Q. How many colleges have dog mascots?

Abadi Light It • Monotype (Creative Alliance)

How many can YOU Name? Now.

Arial Monospaced • Monotype (C. Alliance)

How About the U. of Georgia?

Arial Monospaced Bold • Monotype (C.A.)

The University of Georgia,

Arial Monospaced BoldObliq • Monotype (C.A.)

They are the Bulldogs. Next,

Arial Monospaced Oblique • Monotype (C.A.)

there's Southern Illinois University

Arial • Monotype (Creative Alliance)

Southern Illinois University.

Arial Bold • Monotype (Creative Alliance)

Who is the Mascot for the SIU team?

Arial Bold Italic • Monotype (Creative Alliance)

Yes, it is a dog. The Salukis.

Arial Black • Monotype (Creative Alliance)

And there is the Mantz St. team.

Arial Black Italic • Monotype (C. Alliance)

Good Old Mantz St. They chose to recognize

Arial Condensed • Monotype (Creative Alliance)

Their enlightened management chose

Arial Condensed Bold • Monotype (C. Alliance)

They chose the noble Mongrel as their

Arial Cn Ex Bold • Monotype (Creative Alliance)

The Mongrel is the mascot of Mantz St. True.

Arial Cn Light • Monotype (Creative Alliance)

You Can Look it Up. Yes, you can.

Arial Ex Bold • Monotype (Creative Alliance)

And then there are the mythical

Arial Ex Bold Italic • Monotype (C. Alliance)

There are the Mythical Mascots .

Who are these mythical mascots?

For one, the Lake Wobegon team.

The Lake Wobegon Whippets.

Just Ask Garrison Keillor

If you don't believe me, ask Garrison Keillor.

You will Find that the Whippers Are

The Whippets Are the Mascot for Lake

Is a Whippet a Dog? You Bet. Look it up.

Or just listen to the Prairie Home Co

Just listen to Prairie Home Compa

Prairie Home Companion—NPR

Every Saturday Night at 6:00 pm est.

Did You ever Wonder Just Why Male

Arial SF • Monotype (Creative Alliance)

Why Male dogs don't Wear Boxer

Arial SF Bold • Monotype (Creative Alliance)

Male dogs don't wear boxer shorts?

Arial SF Bold It • Monotype (Creative Alliance)

Did you ever wonder why this is true?

Arial SF Italic • Monotype (Creative Alliance)

There are three reasons why this is true.

Blueprint • Monotype (Creative Alliance)

Reason Number One: They don't match

Blueprint Bold • Monotype (Creative Alliance)

They don't Match the Coat. Quickly...

Blueprint Bold Italic • Monotype (C. Alliance)

Reason Number 2: Where would the tail go?

Blueprint Italic • Monotype (Creative Alliance)

And Quietly, Reason Number 3:

Century Gothic • Monotype (Creative Alliance)

Boxer Shorts Would Interfere greatly

Century Gothic Bold • Monotype (C. Alliance)

would greatly interfere with sniffing.

Century Gothic Bold It • Monotype (C. Alliance)

Shorts Would Get in the Way as

Century Gothic Italic • Monotype (C. Alliance)

QUIT THE SNIFFING SHORTS WOULD SAY

Gill Sans BoldSC • Monotype (Creative Alliance)

You Quickly see Just how Important

Quickly see how important sniffing really

Quit sniffing? Never. So, no shorts are worn.

If dogs ran things, farmers would change

Farm Crops Would be Different

Quickly, Farmers Would Grow

Quickly, Farmers Would Have a new

Quietly, New Crops Would Be Grown.

Quickly, a crop called Table Scraps

Quickly, dogs could buy Table Scraps.

Quietly, Every Grocery Store Would Change.

Quality Table Scraps Would Be Sold.

High Quality Dog Food Would Be Available.

The Quintessence of Good Dog Food

GillSans Bold • Monotype (Creative Alliance)

Dog Food Would Have a Paradigm Shift.

GillSans BoldCondensed • Monotype (C.A.)

Quickly, Table Scraps Would Be a Dog

GillSans BoldItalic • Monotype (C. Alliance)

Dog Gourmet Foods Would be on Store Shelves Quickly.

GillSans Condensed • Monotype (C. Alliance)

Table Scraps Would Be a Big Hit.

GillSans ExtraBold • Monotype (C. Alliance)

High Quality Table Scraps Would Be Eaten.

GillSans Italic • Monotype (Creative Alliance)

Quickly, The Inside Dogs Would Change

GillSans Light • Monotype (Creative Alliance)

They would Quietly Change their Food habits,

GillSans LightItalic • Monotype (C. Alliance)

Yes to Table Scraps. Fresh.

GillSans UltraBold • Monotype (C. Alliance)

Yes, if dogs ran things the world would

GillSans UltraBdCondensed • Monotype (C.A.)

The world Would be a lot different.

Grotesque • Monotype (Creative Alliance)

And Farmers Would cater to dogs.

Grotesque Bold • Monotype (Creative Alliance)

Someday, this may happen.

Grotesque Bd Ex • Monotype (Creative Alliance)

Few people know that secret dog slang

Few people know that secret dog slang exists.

But it is very true. Here is one example.

Here is one example, "Dog Days".

People have one meaning for it, dogs another.

To dogs, the meaning of this phrase is

The meaning to dogs is: a traditional summertime group activity.

This traditional activity

This summertime activity is

This summertime activity has

The activity has another

This has a different name for dogs.

It's called "the sniffing festival".

Dogs have active fantasy lives.

Mahsuri Sans ExtraBold • Monotype (C.A.)

Another dog fantasy involves "fetch".

Mahsuri Sans • Monotype (Creative Alliance)

Dogs are often told to "fetch" a stick.

Mahsuri Sans Italic • Monotype (C. Alliance)

Well, in this fantasy, the kid next door

Mahsuri Sans Light • Monotype (C. Alliance)

The kid next door thinks he is very clever.

Mahsuri Sans LightItalic • Monotype (C.A.)

So he gets a big stick and throws it as

Mahsuri Sans Regular • Monotype (C. Alliance)

He throws it just as far as he can.

News Gothic • Monotype (Creative Alliance)

And when the kid says "fetch"

News Gothic Bold • Monotype (C. Alliance)

The dog turns to the kid and with

News Gothic Bold Italic • Monotype (C.A.)

a smile on the dog's face, he looks at the

News Gothic Cn • Monotype (Creative Alliance)

He looks at the kid from next door, and

News Gothic Cn Bd • Monotype (C. Alliance)

with a smile on his face, the dog

News Gothic Italic • Monotype (C. Alliance)

The dog says, "Fetch it yourself, kid."

Ocean Sans Bold • Monotype (Creative Alliance)

IF DOGS RAN THINGS, MONEY WOULD BE

Ocean Sans Bold SC • Monotype (C. Alliance)

The currency would be changed. A lot.

Ocean Sans BoldItalic • Monotype (C. Alliance)

IF DOGS RAN THINGS, BUSTER'S PICTURE

Ocean Sans BoldItalic SC • Monotype (C.A.)

Buster's Pictur e Would be on pa per

Ocean Sans Book • Monotype (C. Alliance)

BUSTER WOULD BE ON PAPER MONEY, AND

Ocean Sans Book SC • Monotype (C. Alliance)

the Cur rency Would Chang e Quic kly.

Ocean Sans BookItalic • Monotype (C. Alliance)

THE CURRENCY WOULD CHANGE FROM DOLLARS.

Ocean Sans BookItalic SC • Monotype (C.A.)

Dollars ($) would be replaced by Bones.

Ocean Sans ExtraBold • Monotype (C. Alliance)

YES, BONES (B) WOULD REPLACE $.

Ocean Sans ExtraBold SC • Monotype (C.A.)

Just imagine Buster's photo on the B10.

Ocean Sans ExtraBoldItalic • Monotype (C.A.)

AND ON THE B100 AS WELL. AND ON B20.

Ocean Sans ExBoldItalic SC • Monotype (C.A.)

Yes, if Dogs Ran Things, Life would Change.

Ocean Sans Light • Monotype (C. Alliance)

THAT MIGHT NOT BE A BAD IDEA, I THINK.

Ocean Sans Light SC • Monotype (C. Alliance)

Ever Wonder What Dogs Think About Each

Ocean Sans LightItalic • Monotype (C. Alliance)

WHAT DO DOGS THINK ABOUT EACH OTHER?

Ocean Sans LightItalic SC • Monotype (C.A.)

Like, what do big dogs think about small

Ocean Sans SemiBold • Monotype (C. Alliance)

WHAT BIG DOGS THINK ABOUT SMALL DOGS:

Ocean Sans SemiBold SC • Monotype (C.A.)

They think, "Why can't I find an outfit

Ocean Sans SemiBoldItalic • Monotype (C.A.)

FIND AN OUTFIT LIKE THAT IN MY SIZE?"

Ocean Sans SemiBoldItalic SC • Monotype (C.A.)

And what do small dogs think about

Sassoon Infant • Monotype (Creative Alliance)

Small dogs think about big dogs?

Sassoon Infant Bold • Monotype (C. Alliance)

They think, "Maybe If I started

Sassoon Primary • Monotype (Creative Alliance)

working out and lifting weights..."

Sassoon Primary Bold • Monotype (C. Alliance)

Fact is, everyone wants to be someone

Sassoon San Slope • Monotype (C. Alliance)

Everyone wants to be someone else

Sassoon San Slope Bold • Monotype (C.A.)

Even in the wonderful world of dogs.

Sassoon San Slope Medium • Monotype (C.A.)

The dyslexic dog got into big trouble.

Sassoon Sans • Monotype (Creative Alliance)

The dyslexic dog was punished bad.

Sassoon Sans Bold • Monotype (C. Alliance)

He went into a place that simply said

Sassoon Sans Medium • Monotype (C. Alliance)

The dog saw the sign, "no gods allowed".

Strayhorn Bold • Monotype (Creative Alliance)

Did you know that dog obedience school

Strayhorn Bold Italic • Monotype (C. Alliance)

Dog Obedience School has grades,

Strayhorn Extra Bold • Monotype (C. Alliance)

Not to mention dog Report Cards.

Strayhorn Extra Bold Italic • Monotype (C.A.)

What kind of things do they grade dogs on?

Strayhorn Italic • Monotype (Creative Alliance)

Well, "Roll Over" is one line on the cards.

Strayhorn Light • Monotype (Creative Alliance)

And another one is "Sit on Command".

Strayhorn Light Italic • Monotype (C. Alliance)

AND "STAY" IS PRETTY IMPORTANT, THEY SAY.

Strayhorn LightSC • Monotype (C. Alliance)

As is "Sit Up and Beg". Ask any dog.

Strayhorn Regular • Monotype (C. Alliance)

THE ABILITY TO SIT UP AND BEG MEANS FOOD.

Strayhorn RegularSC • Monotype (C. Alliance)

Of course, Fetch is an important topic.

And, just like grade school report cards use

Grade School report Cards once had Conduct ,

similarly for dogs, there is a "sniffing" line.

A very negative thing at dog school is when

The instructor write "sniffs improperly".

That is a very negative thing for a

Dogs can be ostracized for sniffing.

Improper sniffing can have a long-term effect.

The dog who sniffs improperly is often shunned.

Make one mistake and you re branded.

One mistake, they brand you for life."

That's the vital importance of sniffing.

If dogs ran things, Frisbee would be a major

Frisbee would be a major league

Yes, a major league sport.

And the best dogs would make a lot

Stars Would Make a Lot of Bones (B).

There is a lot more dog slang that

Most people don't know about Dog Slang.

Q. *What does the phrase "dog fashion" mean?*

Quick Answer: In the dog world, it means to be

It means to be nattily attired and well groomed.

And "dog fashion" is a requirement to take

To Take Part Successfully in the Heat Festival

AND THAT'S A VERY IMPORTANT PART OF DOG LIFE.

Here's just One More Reason Why Dogs are

Banjoman • Paul Veres (Creative Alliance)

Quick reason why dogs are Better than cats.

BanjomanBold • Paul Veres (Creative Alliance)

Cats bring you unwanted "presents". Yuck.

BanjomanLight • Paul Veres (Creative Alliance)

Q. Why don't they just bury that stuff once it

BanjomanText • Paul Veres (Creative Alliance)

Just bury those things once they're through?

BanjomanTextBold • Paul Veres (C. Alliance)

What are cats thinking about anyway? I mean

BanjomanTextLight • Paul Veres (C. Alliance)

Cats Bring Quirky Presents. Dogs Bring Balls.

Corvallis Sans • Philip Bouwsma (C. Alliance)

And Dogs Bring You Sticks. Quickly. When you

Corvallis Sans Oblique • Philip Bouwsma (C.A.)

When you come home, the dog

Mariposa Sans Black • Philip Bouwsma (C.A.)

The Dog Quickly brings stuff for you

Mariposa Sans Bold • Philip Bouwsma (C.A.)

The dog stuff is fun stuff. Play with me.

Mariposa Sans Book • Philip Bouwsma (C.A.)

And Cats Bring Those Freshly Killed Stuff.

Mariposa Sans Book Italic • P. Bouwsma (C.A.)

Geez. Give it a decent burial, will ya?

Mariposa Sans Medium • Philip Bouwsma (C.A.)

Dogs seem to like "ball" sports.

Bernhardt Bold • Photolettering (C. Alliance)

Dogs love to chase and fetch balls.

Bernhardt Light • Photolettering (C. Alliance)

Throw a baseball; Quickly the dog

Bernhardt Medium • Photolettering (C.A.)

Throw a tennis ball, watch the

BraziliaSeven • Photolettering (C. Alliance)

Even a basketball; just watch.

BraziliaThree • Photolettering (C. Alliance)

Lots of dogs love soccer balls.

Futura Maxi Bold • Photolettering (C. Alliance)

Same with volleyballs. They go

Futura Maxi Book • Photolettering (C. Alliance)

And many dogs like footballs.

FuturaMaxiDe • Photolettering (C. Alliance)

So, did you think that dogs like all

Grotesk Italic • Title Wave Studios

Well, dogs don't like ALL balls. Not by any stretch.

WesterveldtLt • Photolettering (C. Alliance)

Nope. Dogs don't like bowling balls.

Alinea Sans Bold • Thierry Puyfoulhoux (C.A.)

Want to know why dogs don't like

Alinea Sans Bold Italic • T. Puyfoulhoux (C.A.)

Why Dogs don't like bowling balls:

Alinea Sans Medium • T. Puyfoulhoux (C.A.)

There's no way to get a bowling ball

Can't get a bowling ball in your

Bowling ball in a dog's mouth? No way.

Another reason: The ball comes

The ball comes back to you. Shame.

Everyone knows that's dog work. Really.

A third reason why dogs don't like

Dogs don't like bowling balls because

Every one of those "pins" used to be

All those pins used to be trees.

And we all know dogs need trees.

Did you ever wonder why dogs

Wonder just why dogs chase cars?

Just why do dogs chase cars?

Some think it's a deep Freudian thing.

The dog is thinking "Is my Mother in

Is My mother in That Car?" Dog says.

Another Possible Motivation for Chasing

According to Dog Legend, there are Five dogs

AN OLD LEGEND TELLS OF FIVE FEMALE DOGS

Five Female Dogs Are in the Car. In the

They are in the back seat of the car.

And the Quaint old Legend Has It that

If the Dog catches the car...never mind.

Fact is that dogs never catch cars. It won't

And the third possible reason why dogs

Dog may chase cars because of

The Revenge Motive Says that

The Dog is Thinking "A car like that

hit my best friend." Revenge time.

Do you know that there is a No Dogs

A No Dogs policy is in effect at Wimbledon.

At Wimbledon, dogs simply aren't allowed.

THE REASON IS FAIRLY SIMPLE. TRUTH IS THAT

The Best Tennis Players in the World Have

They Have not learned how to play with

They don't know how to play with a ball

a Ball That is loaded with Dog Saliva.

So, there are no dogs at Wimbledon.

272

There are no famous dog singers.

Did you ever wonder why that is?

First: dogs have a very limited octave range.

#2: Without pockets, dogs find it difficult

Dogs Find it Very Difficult to Buy CDs. True.

The best composers don't under

THE BEST COMPOSERS DON'T UNDERSTAND

THEY DON'T UNDERSTAND DOG LANGUAGE.

THERE ARE ALSO THINGS DOGS

THINGS DOGS DON'T UNDERSTAND

Dogs don't understand why people show teeth

But they show teeth when they're happy?

That doesn't make sense to a dog. Not at all.

Dogs wonder why happy people don't just wag

Why don't Happy People Just Wag Their Tail?

Another Thing Dogs Don't Understand.

Why do some people take out their teeth

At Night, and Put their Teeth in a Glass?

They put their teeth in a glass of water.

Then, they don't even drink the water. Confusing for a dog.

Some dogs have a very rigid schedule. For example,

An active dog will eat at 8:00, walk to the tree at 9.

At noon, he has to bark at the mailman.

Then, at 6:00, it's time to eat again.

At 7:00, it's time to walk to the tree once again. Pee-time.

Then, at 8:00 it's bed time. Nice schedule—active dog.

For the Retired Dog, the Schedule is Just the Same. Almost.

Function Cond Oblique • Title Wave Studios

With one big exception. Just one.

Function Heavy • Title Wave Studios

For the Retired dog, he doesn't bark

Function HeavyOblique • Title Wave Studios

He doesn't bark at the mailman. In his case,

Function Light • Title Wave Studios

The mailman disturbs his nap. Everyday.

Function LightOblique • Title Wave Studios

Otherwise, the schedule of the two dogs is

Function Oblique • Title Wave Studios

THE SCHEDULE FOR THE TWO DOGS IS EXACTLY

Function Sm Caps • Title Wave Studios

THE SCHEDULE IS EXACTLY THE SAME. NICE.

Function Sm Caps Light • Title Wave Studios

If dogs could Type, here's a Letter They

Goudy Sans • Title Wave Studios

Here's a letter Dogs Might Write:

Goudy Sans Bold • Title Wave Studios

A Question for the People Who Make

Goudy Sans BoldItalic • Title Wave Studios

Question for Hot Dog Manufacturers. Don't

Goudy Sans Italic • Title Wave Studios

Don't Get me Wrong. Dogs love Hot

Lanston Koch • Title Wave Studios

Dogs love Hot Dogs. We Really Do.

But couldn't you call them something

Couldn't You Call Them Something Else?

Why give people any crazy ideas?

How about calling them Hot Cats?

I think that's a much better idea.

Things dogs think about while they nap:

Why has a dog never won the Nobel Prize?

Seems like "Species Discrimination" to

DOGS ARE PRETTY SPECIAL PEOPLE. YET, NOT ONE

NOT ONE HAS EVER WON THE NOBEL PRIZE. WHY?

Know why dogs love classical music?

Because violins use Cat Gut for strings.

Things dogs think are really stupid:

Cats playing with yarn is really stupid.

IN FACT, CATS ARE REALLY STUPID. REALLY!

GREAT DOG MOMENTS: THE PEOPLE

The People Forget to Buy Dog Food

And they don't want to go to the store,

So they decide to give the dog some

Yes. It's Table Scraps Time. YES!

Dogs have Profane Words. They Really Do. Promise.

To most dogs, BATH is a four-letter word.

The Dog in the bath says "Damn B**H!"

sans

Why dogs don't celebrate holidays. Never ever.

They're miffed that rabbits have Easter and

And worse than that, Cats have Halloween. What

And what do dogs have for a holiday? Nothing. Nada.

A dog loves watching the people go out for a few hours,

and then finding the lid off the

garbage can. Party Time! If dogs

ran things, rolling in the floor to scratch

your back would be an Olympic event.

Did you ever wonder why dogs have

such fast mood changes? The dog is

TERRITORIAL, BARKING AND THE BIG DOG

 COMES. OOPS. SORRY I BARKED.

Does Anybody Have Pink Flamingos?

Regeneration X • Synfonts

Not the movie; the plastic yard birds.

Regeneration X—Bold • Synfonts

Question: Why do people buy them?

Central Station • flashfonts

AƆEFGKLLONPTORSTHVWY AEFGHJKRSTV

Central StationExpert • flashfonts

The type above is purposely shown.

Central StationBold • flashfonts

There are too many nice letters.

StraightLight • flashfonts

Anyway, what is it with pink flamingos?

StraightMed • flashfonts

That sounds a little like a Seinfeld opening.

Clique Serif • Aerotype

So, what is there about these pink

Clique Serif Black • Aerotype

I seem to see them everywhere. Why?

Clique Serif Black Oblique • Aerotype

Why do people put them in their front yard?

Clique Serif Bold • Aerotype

I don't know the answer. I may never know.

Clique Serif Bold Oblique • Aerotype

That's enough time on the topic. Move on.

Clique Serif Oblique • Aerotype

Q. Why is it called a greasy spoon?

Do you know the answer to that?

If the spoons were really greasy,

no one would Quietly eat there, I think.

So, maybe the spoons there aren't really greasy.

Anyway, Greasy Spoon Restaurants seem to be

They all Seem to Be Old and Established. So

THAT MUST MEAN THAT THEY'VE BEEN

THEY HAVE BEEN AROUND FOR AWHILE.

THE SO-CALLED GREASY SPOONS HAVE

THEY HAVE QUIETLY SURVIVED. SO,

O
serif

THEY MUST HAVE CUSTOMERS.

THAT MEANS THEY CAN'T BE SO BAD.

Remember Pinky Lee? From 1950s TV?

He had two Co-Stars. Who were they?

Does this suddenly seem like a Trivia

IS THIS SUDDENLY A TRIVIA CONTEST?

IT MIGHT BE. EXCEPT THERE IS NO PRIZE.

SO WHO WERE HIS TWO CO-STARS?

VIVIAN BLAINE WAS THE FIRST. WHO

Was was the Second? Good Question.

Martha Stewart is the answer. When I

Whenever I think of Pinky Lee, I always

SEE HIM IN BLACK & WHITE. NEVER

IT'S NEVER IN COLOR. WONDER WHY?

DON'T ASK ME WHY I THINK OF PINKY

BECAUSE I DON'T KNOW. IT'S A 50S THING.

Do You Remember Sky King? No?

Want A Clue? Try Saturday Morning TV.

Does That Help? Maybe not. Early 50s

Sky King was a pilot. He had a twin-engine

Sky King Had a Twin-Engine Plane.

What was the name of the Aircraft? Do you

Do you remember? No? It was the Songbird. Yes.

His niece was Penny. Well...

At least, she was supposed to be

She was supposed to be his niece.

Back in the 50s, we never even

We never even thought about it.

O
serif

Now, things have changed so much.

Garaline—Bold • 2Rebels

Today, if Sky King were still on TV, we all

Garaline—BoldItalic • 2Rebels

WE ALL WOULD SAY "YEAH, SURE. NIECE. RIGHT."

Garaline—Expert • 2Rebels

SATURDAY MORNING TV WAS FULL OF GOOD CLEAN

Garaline—ExpertItalic • 2Rebels

Good Clean entertainment. Like Big Top. It was

Garaline—Italic • 2Rebels

It was a Circus Show. Ed McMahon was the

Garaline—Regular • 2Rebels

Ed McMahon was the Clown on Big Top. Look it

Pilgrim • 2Rebels

And there was a show called Captain Midnight.

Pilgrim—Bold • 2Rebels

And the Sponsor was a drink called Ovaltine.

Pilgrim—Italic • 2Rebels

Remember the ventriloquist program, that had

Pilgrim—ItalicBold • 2Rebels

Paul Winchell and Jerry Mahoney. And another one

Pilgrim—ItalicLight • 2Rebels

Another one with Jimmy Nelson and Danny O'Day.

Pilgrim—Light • 2Rebels

And there was a dog named Farfel. Sponsored by

TableManners—Proper • 2Rebels

The Sponsor was Nestle's. Farfel was a chocolate

TableManners—ProperItalic • 2Rebels

Of course, he was a puppet. But a good one. Very

Troiminut—Italic • 2Rebels

There was Capt. Gallant of the Foreign Legion

Troiminut—Regular • 2Rebels

Starring Buster Crabbe, plus his

Ardent—Extrabold • Treacyfaces

Plus His Very Own Son, Cuffy Crabbe.

Ardent—ExtraboldItalic • Treacyfaces

And, there was a guy named Fuzzy Knight.

Ardent—Italic • Treacyfaces

And this great program, Space Patrol.

Ardent—Regular • Treacyfaces

Best of all, there was Mr. Wizard.

Armada—Bold • Treacyfaces

Besides teaching kids Science,

Armada—Extrabold • Treacyfaces

In addition to the Science he taught

Armada—Light • Treacyfaces

Each week, he reminded kids about

Armada—LightItalic • Treacyfaces

Mr. Wizard told them about food &

Armada—Medium • Treacyfaces

He talked about Food and Nutrition.

Armada—MediumItalic • Treacyfaces

Things that every kid still remembers

Like How to Start Off the Day with a Good

Begin Every Day with a Good Breakfast,

And that Breakfast Consisted of Fruit, Cereal,

Milk, Bread and Butter, plus other foods, for

Plus Other Foods for Variety. I guess that meant

Eggs, Or Maybe Jelly, or Something Like That.

I'm sure he didn't mean to have Pepsi for breakfast.

Mr. Wizard Always Showed Kids Science Experiments.

Every Week, he would demonstrate what he called

The Magic and Mystery of Science in Everyday Living.

Kids everywhere loved Mr. Wizard.

His real name was Don Herbert, &

VOIDEASTNORTHPASSSOUTH

WHAT do all things above mean?

Buy the Font and then you'll know.

Did you know that every font in this book

Every font in this book is for sale online.

That's a huge change from the old days.

Hey, have you ever seen fonts this great?

No. Never. This is the greatest font

This is the very best font collection.

Ever. Without Question. And you can

AND YOU CAN HAVE ALL THE FONTS

Tf THIS IS AN ALTERNATIVE FONT. Tf

Every Font Collection Should Have

Has there ever been anyone half as good

CaslonDisplay—Light • Treacyfaces

as Johnny Carson as a talk show host?

CaslonDisplay—Medium • Treacyfaces

The answer is probably not. No way.

CaslonTen—Bold • Treacyfaces

How many other people could talk

CaslonTen—Extrabold • Treacyfaces

How many others could talk with people

CaslonTen—Light • Treacyfaces

Johnny could ask just the right question.

CaslonTen—Medium • Treacyfaces

He has a great ability to talk with regular

CaslonDisplay—Light—italic • Treacyfaces

He could talk with regular people,

CaslonDisplay—Medium—italic • Treacyfaces

and he could talk with the big stars,

CaslonThree—Bold • Treacyfaces

and nobody did it better. Nobody.

CaslonThree—BoldItalic • Treacyfaces

Just look at all the competition he had.

Habitat—Bold • Treacyfaces

Early on, he had Joey Bishop and Merv.

Habitat—BoldItalic • Treacyfaces

Not to mention Dick Cavett—good guy

Habitat—Book • Treacyfaces

Few people remember that Pat Sajak was

Habitat—BookItalic • Treacyfaces

Pat Sajak was a Johnny competitor.

Habitat—Demibold • Treacyfaces

So was Chevy Chase. For a week or so.

Habitat—DemiItalic • Treacyfaces

And Joan Rivers, for a short time, as well.

Habitat—Italic • Treacyfaces

There was the CBS Late Movie,

Habitat—Regular • Treacyfaces

and Nightline, with Ted Koppel.

HabitatBFlat—Book • Treacyfaces

Nightline actually started as a special report

HabitatCond—Bold • Treacyfaces

A special report each night on the Iranian hostage

HabitatCond—BoldItalic • Treacyfaces

Nightline actually started as a Nightly Report

HabitatCond—Italic • Treacyfaces

A nightly report on American Hostages in

HabitatCond—Regular • Treacyfaces

A report on Hostages in Iran.

HabitatExpanded—Bold • Treacyfaces

O *serif*

That's how the Nightline Show began.

Wembley—Light • Treacyfaces

And it's still on today. Good Show. Still.

Wembley—LightOblique • Treacyfaces

Johnny Carson has a wonderful ability to

Margate—Black • Treacyfaces

Johnny could hold a show together like no one.

Margate—Bold • Treacyfaces

He could do it like no one else. Before or since.

Margate—Demibold • Treacyfaces

The Mighty Carson Art Players Was a Hit.

Margate—Extrabold • Treacyfaces

Not to Mention the "Tea Time Movie" bits

Margate—Heavy • Treacyfaces

And Carol Wayne, the Tea Time Movie Girl. Great stuff.

Margate—Light • Treacyfaces

And Johnny was tops at finding new Comedy.

Margate—Medium • Treacyfaces

New comedians often got their big break

Polaris—Bold • Treacyfaces

The big break often came on the show.

Polaris—Extrabold • Treacyfaces

People like Steve Martin first got the

Polaris—Light • Treacyfaces

Steve Martin made his first big hit

Polaris—LightItalic • Treacyfaces

So did Jay Leno. And David Letterman.

Polaris—Medium • Treacyfaces

Leno and Letterman are OK. But

Polaris—MediumItalic • Treacyfaces

But compared to Johnny, they are

Poynder—Bold • Treacyfaces

They are in a different league. No doubt

Poynder—Book • Treacyfaces

What was the greatest sitcom of all

Poynder—Demi • Treacyfaces

The greatest sitcom of all time? Ask me,

Poynder—Light • Treacyfaces

There are some great ones out there.

Poynder—Medium • Treacyfaces

Some Quickly Would Say MTM.

QueenDido—Extrabold • Treacyfaces

Mary Tyler Moore was a breakthrough

Siena—Bold • Treacyfaces

A breakthrough show, no doubt.

Siena—Extrabold • Treacyfaces

The characters all had their own Quirks.

Siena—Light • Treacyfaces

Ted Baxter was perhaps the most Quirky. Way

Siena—LightItalic • Treacyfaces

He was the Quintessential Egotistical News

Siena—Medium • Treacyfaces

He was the prototype for the dumb news

Siena—MediumItalic • Treacyfaces

The dumb news guy who looked good

Trantino—Bold • Treacyfaces

The dumb guy who looked good on TV,

But who wasn't particularly smart. OK?

Ted Baxter was such a funny character.

And Lou Grant, the tough, lovable, news

The tough lovable News Editor. Lou

The Lou Grant character made TV

The character made TV history. How?

Lou Grant was a spinoff, but not in

It wasn't in the Usual Sense. Lou Grant

Lou Grant went from being a comedy

Lou Grant was a character in a sitcom, and

Lou Grant moved to a one-hour drama.

And the Show was quite a big hit. Good show.

Ever wonder what happens to lost luggage?

Jeunesse—Medium • ABCDesign (C. Alliance)

When the airline loses your luggage, where

JeunesseSlab • ABCDesign (Creative Alliance)

does the lost luggage actually go?

JeunesseSlab—Italic • ABCDesign (C. Alliance)

This doesn't refer to luggage

Americana • Adobe (Creative Alliance)

that is temporarily lost.

Americana—Bold • Adobe (Creative Alliance)

Some Luggage is lost Forever. Gone.

Utopia • Adobe (Creative Alliance)

Where does that go? I mean it's GONE.

Utopia Italic • Adobe (Creative Alliance)

When luggage never comes back,

Utopia Semibold • Adobe (Creative Alliance)

exactly what happens to the luggage?

Utopia SemiboldItalic • Adobe (C. Alliance)

It can't stay on a tarmac somewhere. No.

Rotis Semi Serif • Agfa (Creative Alliance)

Does it wind up being taken home by

Rotis Semi Serif Bold • Agfa (Creative Alliance)

Is it taken home by people who cannot

Rotis Serif • Agfa (Creative Alliance)

People who can't wear the stuff, cause

Rotis Serif Bold • Agfa (Creative Alliance)

Say a guy is a size 48 Long, and his

Luggage is Missing. Gone forever.

Sometime, somewhere, the luggage

The luggage turns up, and someone has

Someone has the luggage, and the stuff

Someone gets all the stuff that was inside.

What if that guy is a size 38 Short?

What can he do with all the clothes?

They don't fit, obviously. And they cost too

They cost too much to have altered.

So what happens to all that stuff?

Quickly, it loses its value, I think.

Does it go to a flea market somewhere?

O
serif

Mary Tyler Moore never lost her

MTM never lost her luggage on

Never lost it on her tv show.

"Mar" was everybody's sweetheart.

She single-handedly made Mustangs even more

She Quickly Made Mustangs even more

Mustangs became even more

Quickly, Mustangs were more popular.

Mary's friend, Rhoda, was the stereotypic

Rhoda was the prototype New Yorker.

O
serif

Brash, bold, and more. What an accent.

Mary and Rhoda lived in the same building

And their landlady was Phyllis Lindstrom.

Everyone remembers the MTM Show.

Carré Noir Light Italic • Albert Boton (C.A.)

Perhaps its most memorable show was

Carré Noir Medium • Albert Boton (C. Alliance)

In one show, Chuckles the Clown died.

Carré Noir Medium Italic • Albert Boton (C.A.)

IN THE SHOW, THE CLOWN WAS DRESSED IN A

Carré Noir SmallCaps Light • Albert Boton (C.A.)

He was Dressed in a Peanut Suit, and

Carré Noir SmallCaps Medium • A. Boton (C.A.)

He was crushed to death by a circus

Linex Sweet • Albert Boton (Creative Alliance)

A circus Elephant killed Chuckles

Linex Sweet Bold • Albert Boton (C. Alliance)

And at the funeral, Mary began to

Linex Sweet Italic • Albert Boton (C. Alliance)

Mary began to laugh at the funeral.

Linex Sweet Light • Albert Boton (C. Alliance)

And she couldn´t stop laughing.

Memo Bold • Albert Boton (Creative Alliance)

Then everyone began to laugh

Memo Bold Italic • Albert Boton (C. Alliance)

O
serif

And they couldn´t stop laughing. Not at

Memo Italic • Albert Boton (Creative Alliance)

That particular show won an Emmy.

Memo Light • Albert Boton (Creative Alliance)

Another great TV show was TAXI. The cast

The Cast Was Quality, among the top

Taxi´s cast was really outstanding.

Danny DiVito was Louie, the dispatcher.

Louie was devious, mean, and

He was a very funny character.

The favorite of many people was Jim.

Jim Ignatowski, the spaced-out taxi

IGGY WAS A MOST MEMORABLE CHARACTER.

He was involved in one scene that

One of Jim's scenes was voted the

FUNNIEST MOMENT IN SITCOM HISTORY

The funniest moment in sitcom history

The funniest moment in sitcom

Scherzo Bold • Albert Boton (Creative Alliance)

Jim had to take his driver's exam.

Scherzo Bold Italic • Albert Boton (C. Alliance)

And Alex went along to help, since

Scherzo Demi • Albert Boton (Creative Alliance)

Because Jim was not prepared at all.

Scherzo Demi Italic • Albert Boton (C. Alliance)

As Jim was taking his exam, he turned

Scherzo Italic • Albert Boton (Creative Alliance)

Jim turned to Alex and asked him:

Central • Aldo Novarese (Creative Alliance)

What does a flashing yellow light

Central Bold • Aldo Novarese (Creative Alliance)

What does a flashing yellow light mean?

Equilibre Gauche Bd Italic • A. Merlault (C.A.)

And Alex whispers to Jim—Slow Down

Equilibre Gauche Bold • Alexis Merlault (C.A.)

Jim Begins to talk Very Slowly. He says

Equilibre Gauche DemiBold • A. Merlault (C.A.)

"AWhaaaaaaaaat doesssssssss a flaaaa..."

Equilibre Gauche DmBd Italic • A. Merlault (C.A.)

O
serif

When he finally finishes the question

Equilibre Gauche ExBd Italic • A. Merlault (C.A.)

When Jim finishes the question, Alex

Equilibre Gauche ExtraBold • A. Merlault (C.A.)

Alex again tells him "Slow down." This

Equilibre Gauche Italic • Alexis Merlault (C.A.)

goes on for several minutes. Each time,

Equilibre Gauche Regular • A. Merlault (C.A.)

Each time Jim hears "slow down" he

Esquisse Bold • Alexis Merlault (C. Alliance)

Each time, he talks even slower. This goes

Esquisse DemiBold • Alexis Merlault (C.A.)

This goes on for 5 different segments.

Esquisse Light • Alexis Merlault (C. Alliance)

It was one of the funniest moments in TV

Esquisse Light Italic • Alexis Merlault (C.A.)

Tony Danza played a former professional boxer on

BernhardModernRoman • Creative Alliance

Danza played a former boxer on Taxi.

Buccardi • Bo Berndal (Creative Alliance)

Tony actually was a Former Boxer.

Buccardi Bold • Bo Berndal (Creative Alliance)

Strangely, he has had a long acting

Buccardi Bold Italic • Bo Berndal (C. Alliance)

career, even though he has always played

Buccardi Italic • Bo Berndal (Creative Alliance)

Tony Danza Has Always Played Himself.

Buccardi Schwash • Bo Berndal (C. Alliance)

HE IS A PERSONALITY, NOT AN ACTOR.

Buccardi SmallCaps • Bo Berndal (C. Alliance)

Is Seinfeld the greatest sitcom ever?

Some people would say that it is.

Talk About a Quality Cast. Just

look at the Quality of the people.

Start with Jason Alexander. He is

He is George Costanza, but he is also

He is also an actor. Jason actually did

He did Broadway, sang and danced,

and before Seinfeld, he was in a baseball

He was in a baseball movie, one of

He was in one of the best baseball movies

THE KEVIN COSTNER MOVIE, BULL DURHAM

Imagine: Costanza in Bull Durham.

How about Michael Richards?

He is the Ultimate Kramer. Sort of.

There is an actual Kramer in

The "real" Kramer lives in New

The "real" Kramer lives in New York, and

The real Kramer has a bus tour in which

The bus tour takes people to all the NYC

THE BUSES GO TO ALL THE NEW YORK

The Actual Locations Quickly

A Real Tour Showing Locations Where

Quietly, the tour goes to the place

The tour goes to the real restaurant where

The actual restaurant which is shown on the

O serif

THE ACTUAL RESTAURANT WHICH IS ON

Lacko SmallCaps • Bo Berndal (C. Alliance)

The restaurant shown on TV is really

Lacko—Regular • Bo Berndal (Creative Alliance)

Tom's Restaurant is at 112th Street

Magellan Bold • Bo Berndal (Creative Alliance)

Tom's is at 112th and Broadway, in NYC.

Magellan Italic • Bo Berndal (Creative Alliance)

*ADEFGKLMNPQRSTVWY*swash caps

Magellan Swash • Bo Berndal (Creative Alliance)

Quietly, groups go on the bus tour and

Magellan Regular • Bo Berndal (C. Alliance)

They see the Quality places where

Magellan SmallCaps • Bo Berndal (C. Alliance)

Places Where the Seinfeld Show Used

Promemoria • Bo Berndal (Creative Alliance)

Seinfeld Used these places for location

Promemoria Italic • Bo Berndal (C. Alliance)

SOME OF THE PLACES ARE FROM EPISODES

Promemoria SmallCaps • Bo Berndal (C.A.)

Some of them are from episodes like the

Sabellicus Italic • Bo Berndal (Creative Alliance)

Remember the "Soup Nazi" episode?

Sabellicus Regular • Bo Berndal (C. Alliance)

THE ONE WHERE THE SOUP GUY WOULD

Sabellicus SmallCaps • Bo Berndal (C. Alliance)

O
serif

The soup guy would not serve

Moorbacka Bold • Bo Berndal (C. Alliance)

The soup guy would not serve people.

Moorbacka Italic • Bo Berndal (C. Alliance)

If he didn't like you, he would not

Moorbacka Regular • Bo Berndal (C. Alliance)

HE WOULD NOT SELL TO YOU. NO WAY.

Moorbacka Small Caps • Bo Berndal (C. Alliance)

Well, there is an actual place like

Nordik Bold • Bo Berndal (Creative Alliance)

There is a real place like. The guy will not

Nordik Italic • Bo Berndal (Creative Alliance)

The guy won't serve just anybody. Not

Nordik Regular • Bo Berndal (Creative Alliance)

IT IS ON 55TH STREET, BETWEEN 7TH &

Nordik SmallCaps • Bo Berndal (C. Alliance)

Between 7th Avenue & 8th Avenue.

Pockettype Bold • Bo Berndal (C. Alliance)

And, I must tell you, the soup is outstanding

Pockettype Italic • Bo Berndal (C. Alliance)

The Soup is really delicious. Really.

PockettypeRegular • Bo Berndal (C. Alliance)

I DON'T EXPECT TO GET FREE SOUP FOR

Pockettype SmallCaps • Bo Berndal (C. Alliance)

ADEFGLMNPQRSTVWY swash caps

Pockettype Swash • Bo Berndal (C. Alliance)

O serif

Anyway, has there ever been a funnier

Q. Has there ever been a funnier

Has there ever been A Funnier Character

Q. Has there been a funnier character

Kramer is one of the Funniest Characters

Kramer could make you laugh just by

Just by entering a room, he

Kramer had about a thousand

He had about a thousand different entrances

Has anyone else ever made such entrances as Kramer?

Nobody ever did it as well as Kramer.

O
serif

We finally learned what his first name

Kramer's First Name was Cosmo. Yes.

And Consider Elaine. She was great.

Julia Louis-Dreyfus was on Saturday

She was on Saturday Night Live for

She was on SNL for a couple of years,

But you don't see a lot of clips that feature

The people at SNL under-utilized her talent

They didn't know what they had, and didn't

They didn't use her as well as they could have.

But Quickly, Seinfield Recycled Her.

Right Quick, She Was a Star. A Big

Elaine was the perfect example of

Elaine perfectly played the beautiful woman.

Elaine was beauty with flaws, BIG flaws.

She played the woman that every man

Schneidler—bold • Creative Alliance

Every man desired her, until he got to know

Schneidler—bold italic • Creative Alliance

Once Men Got to Knew Elaine, It was "Yikes!"

Schneidler—italic • Creative Alliance

Quickly, they Departed. Swift and

SignatureBl • Creative Alliance

Quirky Elaine; Beautiful and Impossible to

SignatureLt • Creative Alliance

She was so beautiful, but inept at

SouvenirGthDm • Creative Alliance

Q. Can anyone every forget the way

SouvenirGthDm—italic • Creative Alliance

Can you forget the Elaine "dance"? What a

SouvenirGthLt • Creative Alliance

What a Graceless Dancer she Was.

SouvenirGthLt—italic • Creative Alliance

And she was SO self-centered.

TriplettBlack • Creative Alliance

Everything was always about her.

TriplettLight • Creative Alliance

O serif

Elaine was a wonderful Character.

Column Bold • Club Type (Creative Alliance)

She was the perfect blend for the other actors.

Column Book • Club Type (Creative Alliance)

Jerry Seinfeld was the only non-actor in the Cast.

Column Book Italic • Club Type (C. Alliance)

Basically, Jerry Played Jerry Seinfeld.

Column Medium • Club Type (Creative Alliance)

ADEFGKLMNPQRSTUWY eff ffifflrst

Column Swash Book Italic • Club Type (C.A.)

The above line is swash characters. Nice stuff

Monkton • Club Type (Creative Alliance)

I never met a swash that I didn't like.

Monkton Bold • Club Type (Creative Alliance)

When the Seinfeld Show was in

Monkton Bold Italic • Club Type (C. Alliance)

When the Show was in Production, they

Monkton Book • Club Type (Creative Alliance)

a d e l m n r s t ff fi ffi A E F G H J K

Monkton Expert Book • Club Type (C. Alliance)

They Would Refer to Real Jerry and TV Jerry.

Monkton Italic • Club Type (Creative Alliance)

And when Seinfield Went off the Air,

Monkton Medium • Club Type (C. Alliance)

Thursday Nights Were Never the Same.

MonktonMedium Italic• Club Type (C. Alliance)

Hey, Seinfeld Gang, we all miss you. But you live

Poseidon • Club Type (Creative Alliance)

You will live forever in reruns.

Poseidon Bold • Club Type (Creative Alliance)

O serif

Lots of people love All in the Family.

Poseidon BoldItalic • Club Type (C. Alliance)

When the show went on the air, it was ground

Poseidon Italic • Club Type (Creative Alliance)

The Show Was Ground Breaking; Archie

Poseidon Medium • Club Type (Creative Alliance)

Bunker was a bigot, and he said things on

Poseidon MediumItalic • Club Type (C. Alliance)

Archie Said Things on the air

AccoladeBd • Cofino Sa (Creative Alliance)

Archie Seemed to Offend Nearly

AccoladeLt • Cofino Sa (Creative Alliance)

Archie Bunker Offended Everyone

AccoladeLt—italic • Cofino Sa (C. Alliance)

Edith Bunker was the wife; poor

AccoladeMd • Cofino Sa (Creative Alliance)

Rob Reiner played the son-in-law

Claridge • Cofino Sa (Creative Alliance)

Archie called him "Meathead".

Claridge—bold • Cofino Sa (Creative Alliance)

Meathead was Carl Reiner's son

ClaridgeBl • Cofino Sa (Creative Alliance)

O
serif

Meathead wound up doing well in

Claridge—italic • Cofino Sa (Creative Alliance)

Rob Reiner, now a famous director, was

Congress • Cofino Sa (Creative Alliance)

How About Laverne & Shirley? Remember

The two girls worked in Milwaukee at

They worked in a Milwaukee brewery.

Quick: Who Played Laverne? Do You Know?

Quick Answer: It was Penny Marshall.

Quirky Laverne always wore an "L" on her

Quirky Laverne wore "L" on her shirt

Quirky Shirley Didn't Wear an L. Surprise.

Quickly, Laverne & Shirley was a Top show

A Companion Show, Happy Days, was on at

Quickly, Happy Days Became the #1 show

And both shows had kids who later directed

Quickly, Ron Howard & Penny Marshall

Interesting footnote: Laverne & Shirley and

Throhand Reg Roman • D. Berlow/Font Bureau (C.A.)

Q. HAPPY DAYS AND LAVERNE & SHIRLEY

Throhand Reg Roman Exp • D. Berlow/Font Bureau (C.A.)

THE SHOWS WERE #1 AND #2

Engravure • Creative Alliance

The two shows were the top two shows on TV for the 77 & 78

CorvinusSkyline • Fonthaus (Creative Alliance)

Richie Cunningham was the star of Happy Days

Eden—Bold • Fonthaus (Creative Alliance)

Actually, Ron Howard was the star; he played Richie

Eden—Light • Fonthaus (Creative Alliance)

And Ron Howard used to be Opie on Andy Griffith.

Eden—Medium • Fonthaus (Creative Alliance)

Richie Cunningham Was the Star of the Show, but

EvaAntiquaHv • Fonthaus (Creative Alliance)

Fonzie was the character who made the huge splash.

EvaAntiquaLt • Fonthaus (Creative Alliance)

The Fonz was a national icon. He was

Kandal Black • Fonthaus (Creative Alliance)

Fonzie was a huge favorite among

Kandal Black Italic • Fonthaus (C. Alliance)

Who knew then: "Fonzie" was a Yale

Kandal Bold • Fonthaus (Creative Alliance)

And he was a Shakespearian actor.

Kandal Bold Italic • Fonthaus (Creative Alliance)

Remember the Bionic Woman, and the

And the Bionic Man, what was that about?

And the Six Million Dollar Man. And

The Six Million Dollar Woman was the

The Waltons was totally different from those

The Waltons was a highly popular TV program. It

The Waltons took America back to a simpler

The Waltons was simple, good pro

John Boy Walton was the star of the

Every night, the whole family would say

O serif

The Whole Family Would Say Good Night

Quietly, the whole family said "Good night,"

Q. Who always Said "Good Night Grandpa?"

Another "simple time" program

Latienne Bold • Fonthaus (Creative Alliance)

Little House on the Prairie Quickly

Latienne Bold Italic • Fonthaus (C. Alliance)

ADEFGKLMQR nice swash caps

Latienne Bold Italic Swash • Fonthaus (C.A.)

ADEFGKMRT more swash caps

Latienne Bold Swash • Fonthaus (C. Alliance)

The Love Boat ran for a Long, long time.

Latienne Italic • Fonthaus (Creative Alliance)

ADEFGKLMPQRST more swash caps

Latienne Italic Swash • Fonthaus (C. Alliance)

And the Love Boat Captain was from

Latienne Medium • Fonthaus (Creative Alliance)

The Love Boat Captain used to be a

Latienne Medium Italic • Fonthaus (C. Alliance)

ADFGKLMNPQR more swash caps

Latienne Medium Italic Swash • Fonthaus (C.A.)

THE CAPTAIN USED TO BE A NEWS WRITER

Latienne Medium SC • Fonthaus (C. Alliance)

ADEGLNPQRSTVY swash caps

Latienne Medium Swash • Fonthaus (C. Alliance)

O
serif

He played a news writer on The Mary

Latienne Roman • Fonthaus (Creative Alliance)

HE WAS A WRITER ON THE MARY TYLER

Latienne Roman SC • Fonthaus (C. Alliance)

ADEFGKMNPQR swash caps here

Latienne RomanSwash • Fonthaus (C. Alliance)

What if the characters on TV were real?

RioChico • Fonthaus (Creative Alliance)

For example, the Love Boat captain,

RioGrande • Fonthaus (Creative Alliance)

The Captain Was a News Writer at WJM

RioMedio • Fonthaus (Creative Alliance)

His name was Murray Slaughter

RioNegro • Fonthaus (Creative Alliance)

MURRAY QUIT WRITING AND BECAME

Schneidler Initials CS Regular • Fonthaus (C.A.)

Murray Slaughter quit writing news for WJM TV and

TorinoModern—Bold • Fonthaus (C. Alliance)

he went on to Become a Captain on the Love Boat.

TorinoModern—BoldItalic • Fonthaus (C.A.)

Just like Richie Cunningham's dad later was sheriff of

TorinoModern—Italic • Fonthaus (C. Alliance)

Mr. Cunningham became Sheriff of Cabot Cove, Maine.

TorinoModern—Roman • Fonthaus (C. Alliance)

CABOT COVE, A PLACE TO

Xavier—Black • Fonthaus (Creative Alliance)

Cabot Cove, good place to die

Xavier—Medium • Fonthaus (Creative Alliance)

good place to be murdered

Briem Mono • Gunnlauger Se Briem (C. Alliance)

If I were in Maine, I

Briem Mono Bold • Gunnlauger Se Briem (C.A.)

would never go to Cabot

Briem Mono Bold Oblique • G. Se Briem (C.A.)

If I were in Maine, I would never go to Cabot Cove.

Briem Mono Compressed • G. Se Briem (C.A.)

Every week, someone gets killed in Cabot Cove, ME.

Briem Mono Comp Bold • G. Se Briem (C.A.)

Poor Jessica Fletcher seems to be a death magnet.

Briem Mono Comp Bold Obl • G. Se Briem (C.A.)

And some of the people who were on other shows got

Briem Mono Comp Obl • G. Se Briem (C.A.)

People from other shows died,

Briem Mono Condensed • G. Se Briem (C.A.)

They went to Cabot Cove & died.

Briem Mono Cond Bold • G. Se Briem (C.A.)

Bobby Wheeler from Taxi went.

Briem Mono Cond Bold Obl • G. Se Briem (C.A.)

He went to Cabot Cove and died.

Briem Mono Condensed Obl • G. Se Briem (C.A.)

Bad idea. Stay away from

Briem Mono Obl • Gunnlauger Se Briem (C.A.)

Warning to everyone: don't go there!

Basilia • Haas (Creative Alliance)

Stay Away from Cabot Cove, Maine.

Basilia—bold • Haas (Creative Alliance)

I don't think Kermit the Frog ever

Basilia—bold italic • Haas (Creative Alliance)

Kermit never went to Cabot Cove.

Basilia—italic • Haas (Creative Alliance)

Big Bird Never Went there either.

Basilia Black • Haas (Creative Alliance)

Not a bad idea. Stay Away from

Basilia Black—italic • Haas (Creative Alliance)

Once Upon a Time, there were four

Basilia Medium • Haas (Creative Alliance)

There were four TV Networks. And

Basilia Medium—italic • Haas (C. Alliance)

Q. WHICH ONE WAS THE FOURTH?

Handle Oldstyle • Creative Alliance

Clue: It wasn't the Fox Network. Not yet.

Bailey Quad Bold • ITC (Creative Alliance)

Back in TV's Golden Age, there were four

BenguiatCd—Book • ITC (Creative Alliance)

There were four Networks Back Then.

BenguiatCd—BookItalic • ITC (C. Alliance)

The "Big Three" were ABC, NBC, & CBS.

BenguiatCdMd • ITC (Creative Alliance)

The Fourth network then was DuMont.

BenguiatCdMd—Italic • ITC (Creative Alliance)

IT DIDN'T LAST A LONG TIME, BUT IT

Handle Oldstyle—italic • Creative Alliance

Four Networks Back Then, and

Benguiat—BoldItalic • ITC (Creative Alliance)

In television history, there were 4

Benguiat—Book • ITC (Creative Alliance)

Four Programs Appeared on all 4

Benguiat—BookItalic • ITC (Creative Alliance)

These programs appeared on all four

BerkeleyOld—Bold • ITC (Creative Alliance)

All Four Networks Had These Programs.

BerkeleyOld—BoldItalic • ITC (C. Alliance)

On their Schedule at one time or another

BerkeleyOld—Book • ITC (Creative Alliance)

The Arthur Murray Dance Party was one.

BerkeleyOld—BookItalic • ITC (C. Alliance)

Another one was Down You Go, a game

BerkeleyOldMd • ITC (Creative Alliance)

The Original Amateur Hour was also

BerkeleyOldMd—Black • ITC (Creative Alliance)

Quick: What was the fourth program?

BerkeleyOldMd—BlackItalic • ITC (C. Alliance)

Q. What was the fourth program to be on

BerkeleyMd—Italic • ITC (Creative Alliance)

ADEFGKLMQSY nice swash font

Bodoni Sev Swash Bold Italic • ITC (C. Alliance)

ADEFGNPRTVW more swash stuff

Bodoni Sev Swash Book Italic • ITC (C. Alliance)

The show Pantomime Quiz also was on all

These Four Shows were on all four networks.

Many shows have appeared on three different

All these shows appeared on three different

THE SHOW BACHELOR FATHER WAS ON ALL THREE

Candid Camera was also on 3.

And Candid Camera has lasted

Candid Camera has been on TV,

on and off for more than 50 years.

FATHER KNOWS BEST ALSO WAS ON 3.

Father Knows Best starred Robert

Young was the star of Father Knows

That was a great show back in the 1950s.

The oldest daughter in the family was

BodoniTweBookItalic • ITC (Creative Alliance)

BETTY ANDERSON WAS THE OLDEST DAUGHTER

BodoniTweBookSC • ITC (Creative Alliance)

Betty Anderson was so beautiful. (rowr)

CaslonTwoTweFour—Bold • ITC (C. Alliance)

I worshipped Betty Anderson from a

CaslonTwoTweFour—BoldIta • ITC (C. Alliance)

Q. Ever Heard of Ethel & Albert? It was

CaslonTwoTweFour—Book • ITC (C. Alliance)

Ethel & Albert was on back in the 50s.

CaslonTwoTweFour—BolokIta • ITC (C. Alliance)

The Smother Brothers Comedy Hour

CaslonTwoTweFourMd • ITC (Creative Alliance)

Tom & Dick Smothers were also on 3

CaslonTwoTweFourMd—Black • ITC (C.A.)

The Smothers Brothers was on three

CaslonTwoTweFourMd—BlkItalic • ITC (C.A.)

Q. Which one was the "dumb one"?

CaslonTwoTweFourMd—Italic • ITC (C. Alliance)

A. Neither. Tom just played dumb. He is

Caxton Light Italic • ITC (Creative Alliance)

O
serif

Tom Smothers is Quietly Smart. True.

Caxton Roman Bold • ITC (Creative Alliance)

The Steve Allen Show was on three

Caxton RomanBook • ITC (Creative Alliance)

Steve Allen was one of the most talented

Caxton Roman Italic • ITC (Creative Alliance)

Steve was one of the most talented people

CenturyBookCd • ITC (Creative Alliance)

First of all, he was a great comedic

CenturyBookCd—Italic • ITC (Creative Alliance)

Did you know he was the first host

CenturyBookCd—Ultra • ITC (Creative Alliance)

Steve Allen was the first Tonight

CenturyBookCd—UltraItalic • ITC (C. Alliance)

First host of the Tonight Show NBC

CenturyBook • ITC (Creative Alliance)

Steve Allen was also a talented

CenturyBook—Italic • ITC (Creative Alliance)

A talented musician & composer

CenturyBook—Ultra • ITC (Creative Alliance)

Musician & Composer? Very

CenturyBook—UltraItalic • ITC (C. Alliance)

And, he wrote many, many books. Few

CenturyCd—Bold • ITC (Creative Alliance)

people have the talent of Steve Allen.

CenturyCd—BoldItalic • ITC (Creative Alliance)

"Hello, I'm Gordon Hathaway, I live in Manhattan"

CenturyCd—Light • ITC (Creative Alliance)

If you remember that line, you're a 50s guy.

CenturyCd—LightItalic • ITC (Creative Alliance)

The Golden Age of Television, 50s

Alfred Hitchcock Presents. What a

Century—BoldItalic • ITC (Creative Alliance)

What a great show. Each week, a full

Century—Light • ITC (Creative Alliance)

A full mystery unfolded, from the great

Century—LightItalic • ITC (Creative Alliance)

The great Hitchcock directed many

Cerigo—Bold • ITC (Creative Alliance)

Was Psycho his greatest movie direction?

Cerigo—BoldItalic • ITC (Creative Alliance)

Remember the Amazing Dunninger?

Cerigo—Book • ITC (Creative Alliance)

Not to mention the Amazing Randi. Smart.

The Danny Thomas Show was a classic.

Ernie Kovacs was a great comedian back

THE GALE STORM SHOW WAS A FAVORITE.

CerigoMdSC • ITC (Creative Alliance)

MY LITTLE MARGIE WAS A BIG HIT BACK

CerigoSC—Book • ITC (Creative Alliance)

ADEFGKLMNPQRST nice swash font

CerigoSwash—Book • ITC (Creative Alliance)

ADEFGKLMNPQRSTVWY swash font

CerigoSwash—BookItalic • ITC (C. Alliance)

The George Gobel Show was so funny.

Charlotte Bold • ITC (Creative Alliance)

"Well I'll be a Dirty Bird." That's what he

Charlotte Book • ITC (Creative Alliance)

Herb Shriner Was a dry comedian from

Charlotte Book Italic • ITC (Creative Alliance)

Herb Shriner was from Indiana. True.

Charlotte Medium • ITC (Creative Alliance)

JACK BENNY WAS ONE OF THE BEST EVER.

Charlotte Small Caps • ITC (Creative Alliance)

Joey Bishop had a number of TV

Charter Black • ITC (Creative Alliance)

Joey Bishop also had a late night

Joey Bishop had a talk show late at

Charter Bold • ITC (Creative Alliance)

Q. Do you know who his "sidekick"

Charter BoldItalic • ITC (Creative Alliance)

SURPRISE. IT WAS A YOUNG GUY NAMED

Charter BoldSC • ITC (Creative Alliance)

The "sidekick" was Regis Philbin. True.

Charter Regular • ITC (Creative Alliance)

Kukla, Fran & Ollie was a big TV show.

Charter RegularItalic • ITC (Creative Alliance)

LEAVE IT TO BEAVER WAS A BIG TV SHOW.

Charter RegularSC • ITC (Creative Alliance)

That was a huge hit show in the 1950s.

CheltenhamBookCd • ITC (Creative Alliance)

The Beav was a huge national sensation.

CheltenhamBookCd—Italic • ITC (C. Alliance)

The title probably wouldn't fly today.

CheltenhamBookCd—Ultra • ITC (C. Alliance)

The title sounds a little like a porn film.

CheltenhamBookCd—UltraItalic • ITC (C.A.)

The Liberace Show was a huge hit with

CheltenhamBook • ITC (Creative Alliance)

Little old ladies loved Liberace's show.

CheltenhamBook—Italic • ITC (C. Alliance)

Milton Berle was more than a star.

CheltenhamBook—Ultra • ITC (C. Alliance)

Uncle Miltie wasn't just a big star, he was

CheltenhamCd—Bold • ITC (Creative Alliance)

Milton Berle was Mister Television. His show

CheltenhamCd—BoldItalic • ITC (C. Alliance)

His show is credited with selling millions of TVs.

CheltenhamCd—Light • ITC (Creative Alliance)

O
serif

Millions of TV sets were sold by Uncle Miltie.

CheltenhamCd—LightItalic • ITC (C. Alliance)

Tuesday night belonged to Berle. It is

Cheltenham—Bold • ITC (Creative Alliance)

321

Milton Berle had this extremely huge

Cheltenham—BoldItalic • ITC (C. Alliance)

He had an enormous audience, and

Cheltenham—Light • ITC (Creative Alliance)

he always showed just enough to win.

Cheltenham—LightItalic • ITC (C. Alliance)

The Real McCoys was a hit show.

Esprit—Bold • ITC (Creative Alliance)

Walter Brennan was good as Grandpa.

Esprit—BoldItalic • ITC (Creative Alliance)

Grandpa McCoy was a huge movie star.

Esprit—Book • ITC (Creative Alliance)

He was so good, he won an Oscar way back

Esprit—BookItalic • ITC (Creative Alliance)

The Red Skelton Show was one of the

EspritMd • ITC (Creative Alliance)

Red Skelton was a great comedian.

EspritMd—Black • ITC (Creative Alliance)

He got a large audience every time.

EspritMd—BlackItalic • ITC (Creative Alliance)

Q. What were the names of the two seagulls

EspritMd—Italic • ITC (Creative Alliance)

THE NAMES OF HIS TWO SEAGULLS WERE

EspritMdSC • ITC (Creative Alliance)

HEATHCLIFFE AND GERTRUDE WERE HIS

EspritSC • ITC (Creative Alliance)

The two seagulls were part of his monologue.

FCaslon 12 • ITC (Creative Alliance)

Q. How did Red wear his hat? Upside down.

FCaslon 12 Italic • ITC (Creative Alliance)

Q. Who was Freddie the Freeloader? It

FCaslon 12 RomanSC • ITC (Creative Alliance)

Red Skelton Quickly became a huge star.

FCaslon 30 • ITC (Creative Alliance)

Tell me the Question, and I'll give you an

FCaslon 30 Italic • ITC (Creative Alliance)

The question is, what was Red's big hobby?

FCaslon 30 RomanSC • ITC (Creative Alliance)

Q. What was Red's other artistic hobby?

FCaslon 42 • ITC (Creative Alliance)

Red Skelton was Quite a Talented Artist. He

FCaslon 42 Italic • ITC (Creative Alliance)

ADEFGKLMNPQRSTUWY mo' swash

FCaslon 42 Italic Alternate • ITC (C. Alliance)

Red Skelton Quietly Painted Clowns.

FCaslon 42 RomanSC • ITC (Creative Alliance)

The Clown is the symbol of comedians.

FCaslon Poster • ITC (Creative Alliance)

Red was one of the best. His art was also

Fenice • ITC (Creative Alliance)

His art was also very high quality. Much

Fenice—Italic • ITC (Creative Alliance)

Bonanza. Huge hit. NBC. Sunday.

Fenice—Ultra • ITC (Creative Alliance)

The Ponderosa. Near Virginia City,

Fenice—UltraItalic • ITC (Creative Alliance)

but not in Virginia. Not even close. Nevada.

FeniceLight • ITC (Creative Alliance)

Ben Cartwright was the Father of the

FeniceLight—Bold • ITC (Creative Alliance)

There were three sons on the Ponderosa.

FeniceLight—BoldItalic • ITC (Creative Alliance)

Hoss Cartwright was played by Dan Blocker.

FeniceLight—Italic • ITC (Creative Alliance)

Little Joe was Michael Landon.

FrizQuaBold • ITC (Creative Alliance)

Adam Cartwright was the other son.

FrizQuaBoldItalic • ITC (Creative Alliance)

Q. Why did Hoss look older than his

FrizQuaRegular • ITC (Creative Alliance)

For a long time, I thought Hoss was the

FrizQuaRegularItalic • ITC (Creative Alliance)

I thought Hoss was the Father on

FrizQuaRegularSC • ITC (Creative Alliance)

Your Hit Parade was a big NBC hit.

GalliardBold • ITC (Creative Alliance)

Q. The Show was on what night? Saturday.

GalliardBold—Italic • ITC (Creative Alliance)

Your Hit Parade spotlighted the top

GalliardBold—Ultra • ITC (Creative Alliance)

The Quick Show had Top 10 songs

GalliardBold—UltraItalic • ITC (C. Alliance)

The Top Ten Songs Were On Each week.

Galliard • ITC (Creative Alliance)

Snooky Lanson was one of the singers.

Galliard—Black • ITC (Creative Alliance)

Quiet Giesele McKenzie was also on the

Galliard—BlackItalic • ITC (Creative Alliance)

Quiet Dorothy Collins was on the show, too.

Galliard—Italic • ITC (Creative Alliance)

Every Saturday night, people wondered which

GaramondCd—Book • ITC (Creative Alliance)

The Big Question: Which Song will be #1?

GaramondCd—BookItalic • ITC (C. Alliance)

Your Show of Shows was one of the best.

GaramondCd—Ultra • ITC (Creative Alliance)

One of the best shows was Your Show

GaramondCd—UltraItalic • ITC (C. Alliance)

Your Show of Shows was Great. Really.

Garamond—Book • ITC (Creative Alliance)

O serif

Q. Who were some of the writers on

Garamond—BookItalic • ITC (Creative Alliance)

Some writers on Your Show of

Garamond—Ultra • ITC (Creative Alliance)

Your Show of Shows had great

Garamond—UltraItalic • ITC (Creative Alliance)

Some Great Writers were there with Your Show

GaramondLitCd • ITC (Creative Alliance)

Your Show of Shows had Neil Simon.

GaramondLitCd—Bold • ITC (Creative Alliance)

Neil Simon's Brother, Doc, was also a

GaramondLitCd—BoldItalic • ITC (C. Alliance)

Doc Simon was also a writer for Your Show

GaramondLitCd—Italic • ITC (Creative Alliance)

Not to mention Carl Reiner, one of the

GaramondLit • ITC (Creative Alliance)

One of the Best writers ever, Carl

GaramondLit—Bold • ITC (Creative Alliance)

Q. Who is Carl Reiner's famous

GaramondLit—BoldItalic • ITC (C. Alliance)

Rob Reiner is the son of Carl Reiner.

GaramondLit—Italic • ITC (Creative Alliance)

And the young Woody Allen was

GiovanniBlack • ITC (Creative Alliance)

Woody Allen was a writer for Your Show

GiovanniBlack—Italic • ITC (Creative Alliance)

Woody Allen Wrote for Your Show of

Giovanni—Bold • ITC (Creative Alliance)

Steve Martin wrote for Smothers Brothers

Giovanni—BoldItalic • ITC (Creative Alliance)

In the 1950s, for some strange reason,

Giovanni—Book • ITC (Creative Alliance)

A huge number of hit TV shows were

Giovanni—BookItalic • ITC (Creative Alliance)

WESTERNS DOMINATED TV FOR MANY

GiovanniSC—Bold • ITC (Creative Alliance)

FOR A LONG TIME, WESTERNS WERE TV

GiovanniSC—Book • ITC (Creative Alliance)

YES, WESTERNS. WHY? ✳ ❖

Golden Cockerel Init Orn • ITC (C. Alliance)

QUICK: Tell me why westerns dominated TV

Golden Cockerel Italic • ITC (Creative Alliance)

Quietly, Westerns Took over TV's top 10.

Golden Cockerel Roman • ITC (C. Alliance)

GUNSMOKE WAS THE TOP SHOW.

Golden Cockerel Titling • ITC (Creative Alliance)

Gunsmoke was the top TV show for

Isbell—Bold • ITC (Creative Alliance)

Gunsmoke was the Top 10 Show for

Isbell—BoldItalic • ITC (Creative Alliance)

Matt Dillon, the Marshal, was the gun

Isbell—Book • ITC (Creative Alliance)

Marshal Dillon was the Law. THE law.

Isbell—BookItalic • ITC (Creative Alliance)

He had a sidekick named Chester.

Humana Serif Bold • ITC (Creative Alliance)

O
serif

Dennis Weaver was the sidekick. He

Humana Serif Bold Italic • ITC (C. Alliance)

Chester grew up and moved to Taos, where

Humana Serif Light • ITC (Creative Alliance)

After moving to Taos, Chester changed his

Humana Serif Light Italic • ITC (C. Alliance)

Chester changed his name: McCloud.

Humana Serif Medium • ITC (Creative Alliance)

McCloud moved from Taos to New York.

Humana Serif Medium Italic • ITC (C. Alliance)

At least on TV...yes he did. But later.

Italia—Bold • ITC (Creative Alliance)

On Gunsmoke, Miss Kitty Ran the bar.

Italia—Book • ITC (Creative Alliance)

I often wondered about Miss Kitty. I did

ItaliaMd • ITC (Creative Alliance)

Now that I know a little more about

Kallos Bold • ITC (Creative Alliance)

The history of the old west is interesting.

Kallos Bold Italic • ITC (Creative Alliance)

The history of the old west would suggest

Kallos Book • ITC (Creative Alliance)

Perhaps Miss Kitty wasn't a woman of virtue.

Kallos Book Italic • ITC (Creative Alliance)

Somehow, I think that Miss Kitty was

Kallos Medium • ITC (Creative Alliance)

Now that I consider it, I really believe that

Kallos Medium Italic • ITC (Creative Alliance)

Miss Kitty may have been running a

KorinnaBold • ITC (Creative Alliance)

Miss Kitty might have been a

KorinnaBold—Heavy • ITC (Creative Alliance)

May have run a house of ill repute

KorinnaBold—HeavyKursiv • ITC (C. Alliance)

Good for you Miss Kitty. Good job.

KorinnaBold—Kursiv • ITC (Creative Alliance)

Another big hit back then was Wagon

Korinna • ITC (Creative Alliance)

Wagon Train was a huge hit show.

Korinna—ExtraBold • ITC (Creative Alliance)

Ward Bond played the Wagon Master.

Korinna—ExtraBoldKursiv • ITC (C. Alliance)

Ward Bond Was the Wagon Master.

Korinna—Kursiv • ITC (Creative Alliance)

Was Ward Bond the Master of his

Leawood—Bold • ITC (Creative Alliance)

Was he the master of his domain?

Leawood—BoldItalic • ITC (Creative Alliance)

O
serif

That question would not have been on tv

Leawood—Book • ITC (Creative Alliance)

Never have been on TV back in the 50s.

Leawood—BookItalic • ITC (Creative Alliance)

Miss Kitty probably was the master

Miss Kitty was the master of her

She was the master of her domain.

Miss Kitty. I'll never see her the same

Miss Kitty, where were you when I needed

Q. Where were you when I needed you?

Have Gun Will Travel, another western

Q. Who was the star of Have Gun Will Travel?

A. RICHARD BOONE WAS THE STAR OF HAVE

His name on the Show was Paladin.

Q. What did his card say? Do you really know?

THE WORDS: HAVE GUN WILL TRAVEL

and: Wire Paladin San Francisco.

O
serif

The Rifleman was another big Western.

LubalinGraphCd—Book • ITC (C. Alliance)

The show starred Chuck Conners. Remember?

LubalinGraphCd—BookOblique • ITC (C.A.)

Remember him? He also played baseball.

LubalinGraphCd—Demi • ITC (C. Alliance)

Chuck Conners played for the LA Dodgers.

LubalinGraphCd—DemiOblique • ITC (C.A.)

As CASEY STENGEL WOULD SAY, YOU CAN LOOK

LubalinGraphCdSC—Book • ITC (C. Alliance)

"You can look it up," Casey would say.

LubalinGraph—Book • ITC (Creative Alliance)

The Lawman was another western.

LubalinGraph—BookOblique • ITC (C. Alliance)

Can't tell you much about that one.

LubalinGraph—Demi • ITC (Creative Alliance)

Never watched it. Don't remember

LubalinGraph—DemiOblique • ITC (C. Alliance)

Don't remember why I never watched it.

LubalinGraphMdCd • ITC (Creative Alliance)

One of my favorites was Maverick. Great.

LubalinGraphMdCd—Bold • ITC (C. Alliance)

O
serif

Great Show. Starred James Garner and

LubalinGraphMdCd—BoldOblique • ITC (C.A.)

Jack Kelley was also a star of the show.

LubalinGraphMdCd—Oblique • ITC (C.A.)

MAVERICK HAD A GREAT DEAL OF HUMOR.

LubalinGraphMdCdSC • ITC (Creative Alliance)

Quickly, because Garner Was There.

LubalinGraphMd • ITC (Creative Alliance)

Jack Kelley was good, but Garner

LubalinGraphMd—Bold • ITC (C. Alliance)

James Garner was the best one.

LubalinGraphMd—Bold Oblique • ITC (C.A.)

Rawhide was another western show.

LubalinGraphMd—Oblique • ITC (C. Alliance)

Can't tell you anything about it. Nada.

LubalinGraphXLit • ITC (Creative Alliance)

Wyatt Earp was a hit show. Big one.

LubalinGraphXLit—Oblique • ITC (C. Alliance)

Hugh O'Brien was the star. Big star.

MendozaRomBold • ITC (Creative Alliance)

Cheyenne was another big western show.

MendozaRomBoldItalic • ITC (Creative Alliance)

In 1960, four of the Top 6 TV shows

MendozaRomBook • ITC (Creative Alliance)

Four of the Top Six shows were westerns

MendozaRomBookItalic • ITC (C. Alliance)

HOW MANY WESTERNS ARE ON TV TODAY?

MendozaRomBold • ITC (Creative Alliance)

Westerns went away, and never came

MendozaRomBookSC • ITC (Creative Alliance)

Lassie was a huge Television Star. The show

THE LASSIE SHOW WAS ON FOR 17 YEARS.

Q. What gender was Lassie? A girl?

Nope. Lassie was always played by a

Lassie was always played by a male dog,

but Lassie never won an Emmy Award.

Remember Dragnet, with Jack Webb?

He was so cool. "My name's Friday.

I'm a cop. Let's go downtown." Go Joe!

Thursday nights at 9:30. That was when

The Dragnet music is still memorable.

After all these years, the music from

The Dragnet theme music is still very

Dum-De-DUM-Dum. Dum-de-DUM-dum-de

Novarese—BookItalic • ITC (Creative Alliance)

Can you hear it in your Mind Right now?

NovareseMd • ITC (Creative Alliance)

Ben Alexander played Joe Friday's partner.

NovareseMd—Italic • ITC (Creative Alliance)

He was Frank Smith on the show.

NovareseMd—Ultra • ITC (Creative Alliance)

ADEFGKLMNP aefghjkrstvwyz

Obelisk Bold • ITC (Creative Alliance)

Then later, Harry Morgan played the

Obelisk Light • ITC (Creative Alliance)

Harry Morgan played Officer Bill Gannon.

Obelisk Light Italic • ITC (Creative Alliance)

After Dragnet went off the air, he

Obelisk Medium • ITC (Creative Alliance)

BILL GANNON TURNED INTO COL. POTTER.

Obelisk SC Light • ITC (Creative Alliance)

Colonel Potter was on M*A*S*H.

OfficinaSerBlack • ITC (Creative Alliance)

Does anybody know that Dick Clark

OfficinaSerBlackItalic • ITC (Creative Alliance)

Dick Clark is no longer a teenager. Barely

OfficinaSerBold • ITC (Creative Alliance)

DICK CLARK IS BARELY OUT OF HIS TEENS.

OfficinaSerBoldSC • ITC (Creative Alliance)

How does he do it? Dick Clark looks about

OfficinaSerBoldItalic • ITC (Creative Alliance)

Dick Clark looks like he's about 16 or 22.

OfficinaSerBook • ITC (Creative Alliance)

Or some young age. He has more hair than

OfficinaSerBookItalic • ITC (Creative Alliance)

HE HAS MORE HAIR THAN A LOT OF HIGH SCHOOL

OfficinaSerBookSC • ITC (Creative Alliance)

Dick Clark has more hair than school

OfficinaSerExtraBold • ITC (Creative Alliance)

He was the original American Bandstand

OfficinaSerExtraBoldItalic • ITC (C. Alliance)

DICK CLARK WAS THE ORIGINAL BANDSTAND

OfficinaSerExtraBoldSC • ITC (Creative Alliance)

Lots of my friends watched Bandstand

OfficinaSerMedium • ITC (Creative Alliance)

Lots of my friends watched Bandstand for

OfficinaSerMediumItalic • ITC (C. Alliance)

THE GIRLS WATCHED BANDSTAND FOR THE

OfficinaSerMediumSC • ITC (Creative Alliance)

THE GUYS WATCHED BANDSTAND FOR THE

OfficinaSerBlackSC • ITC (Creative Alliance)

O
serif

Quietly, we ogled the hot, Philadelphia

Romic Light • ITC (Creative Alliance)

Yes I confess. We watched the Philly girls.

Romic Light Italic • ITC (Creative Alliance)

When they danced, we liked it when

We liked it when they had their backs to

We liked to watch them from behind.

Whenever I see MTV today, I realize just

I realize just how clean-cut we guys

With Bandstand, we had to use our

We used our imagination watching

With MTV, there's nothing left to imagine.

Bandstand, everyday after high school.

I give it an 85. The words are good,

but it's hard to dance to, Dick.

Mister Peepers was a hit show for

For several years, Mr. Peepers was a

Wally Cox was the star of Mr. Peepers.

Slimbach—Bold • ITC (Creative Alliance)

Yes, the same Wally Cox on Hollywood

Slimbach—BoldItalic • ITC (Creative Alliance)

Squares: "Wally Cox to block."

Slimbach—Book • ITC (Creative Alliance)

Marion Lorne was Mrs. Gurney. She

Slimbach—BookItalic • ITC (Creative Alliance)

Mr. Peepers taught at Jefferson High

SlimbachMd • ITC (Creative Alliance)

He was a shy science teacher there.

SlimbachMd—Black • ITC (Creative Alliance)

He was such a nice guy that every

SlimbachMd—BlackItalic • ITC (C. Alliance)

Everyone tried to mother him, and his

SlimbachMd—Italic • ITC (Creative Alliance)

STUDENTS ALL LIKED HIM. HIS BEST FRIEND

SlimbachMdSC • ITC (Creative Alliance)

MR. PEEPERS BEST FRIEND WAS HARVEY

SlimbachSC—Book • ITC (Creative Alliance)

Weskit was played by Tony

Stone Inf—Bold • ITC (Creative Alliance)

Randall played Harvey Weskit

Stone Inf—BoldItalic • ITC (Creative Alliance)

Mr. Peepers had a love interest in

Stone Inf—Medium • ITC (Creative Alliance)

His love interest was Nurse Nancy

Stone Inf—MediumItalic • ITC (C. Alliance)

Nancy Remington was his girl

Stone Inf—Semi • ITC (Creative Alliance)

Mr. Peepers and Nancy were married.

Stone Inf—SemiItalic • ITC (Creative Alliance)

THE WEDDING WAS AN EPISODE OF

Stone Inf SC—Medium • ITC (Creative Alliance)

THE WEDDING WAS A HUGE TV EVENT.

Stone Inf SC—Semi • ITC (Creative Alliance)

Jack Warden also had a part on

Stone Serif—Bold • ITC (Creative Alliance)

Mr. Peepers was a very good show.

Stone Serif—BoldItalic • ITC (Creative Alliance)

NBC was the first network to broadcast

Stone Serif—Medium • ITC (Creative Alliance)

the first regularly scheduled news show.

Stone Serif—MediumItalic • ITC (C. Alliance)

The show was The Esso Newsreel,

Stone Serif—Semi • ITC (Creative Alliance)

and later was The Esso Reporter. It

Stone Serif—SemiItalic • ITC (Creative Alliance)

THE NEWS SHOW WAS ON THREE TIMES

Stone Serif SC—Medium • ITC (C. Alliance)

IT APPEARED THREE TIMES A WEEK.

Stone Serif SC—Semi • ITC (Creative Alliance)

The show was on Monday, Thursday

Syndor Bold • ITC (Creative Alliance)

The show was also on Sundays, I guess

Syndor Bold Italic • ITC (Creative Alliance)

There must have been no news on the

Syndor Book • ITC (Creative Alliance)

On the Other Days, there Was Nothing Going

Syndor Book Italic • ITC (Creative Alliance)

Nothing was happening on the other

Syndor Medium • ITC (Creative Alliance)

That's hard to imagine now, in the CNN

Syndor Medium Italic • ITC (Creative Alliance)

THE CNN ERA MAKES THIS SEEM SO STRANGE

Syndor SC Book • ITC (Creative Alliance)

THE FIRST MAJOR NEWSMAN WAS ON THE

Syndor SC Medium • ITC (Creative Alliance)

The Camel News Caravan was the

TiepoloBlack • ITC (Creative Alliance)

NBC's nightly news program was

TiepoloBlack—Italic • ITC (Creative Alliance)

The News was called the Camel News.

Tiepolo—Bold • ITC (Creative Alliance)

The Camel News Caravan featured John

Tiepolo—BoldItalic • ITC (Creative Alliance)

John Cameron Swayze was the news

Tiepolo—Book • ITC (Creative Alliance)

John Cameron Swayze was the first big

Tiepolo—BookItalic • ITC (Creative Alliance)

YES, THIS IS THE SAME "TIMEX" GUY.

TiepoloSC—Bold • ITC (Creative Alliance)

HE'S THE ONE WHO WOULD SUBJECT A

TiepoloSC—Book • ITC (Creative Alliance)

A watch would be subjected to a beating

Tiffany—Light • ITC (Creative Alliance)

The watch would get beat to death,

Tiffany—LightItalic • ITC (Creative Alliance)

and he would pick it up and listen to

TiffanyMd • ITC (Creative Alliance)

He Would Pick Up the watch, and hear

TiffanyMd—Italic • ITC (Creative Alliance)

He would hold the watch to his ear

Tyfa Bold • ITC (Creative Alliance)

and then he would say, "It takes a...

Tyfa Bold Italic • ITC (Creative Alliance)

It takes a licking and keeps on ticking."

Tyfa Book • ITC (Creative Alliance)

It takes a licking and keeps on ticking.

Tyfa Book Italic • ITC (Creative Alliance)

That was John Cameron Swayze's

Tyfa Medium • ITC (Creative Alliance)

That was his famous line. Made lots of

Tyfa Medium Italic • ITC (Creative Alliance)

They got some unusual "tests" for

Usherwood—Bold • ITC (Creative Alliance)

The Timex watch got lots of different

Usherwood—BoldItalic • ITC (Creative Alliance)

The watch had different punishments.

Usherwood—Book • ITC (Creative Alliance)

The watch Quietly got punished all

Usherwood—BookItalic • ITC (C. Alliance)

The watch was punished on TV.

UsherwoodMd • ITC (Creative Alliance)

Quickly, they would strap a Timex

UsherwoodMd—Black • ITC (Creative Alliance)

A Timex Got Strapped to a whale

UsherwoodMd—BlackItalic • ITC (C. Alliance)

and the Whale Quickly Went under

UsherwoodMd—Italic • ITC (Creative Alliance)

The whale went underwater.

Veljovic—Bold • ITC (Creative Alliance)

And after the whale came back up,

Veljovic—BoldItalic • ITC (Creative Alliance)

they would get the watch, check it,

Veljovic—Book • ITC (Creative Alliance)

and it would always "take a licking"

Veljovic—BookItalic • ITC (Creative Alliance)

Those commercials made the bra

VeljovicMd • ITC (Creative Alliance)

Mr. Ed was a Quirky Show. It

Alan Young played Wilbur Post.

Wilbur owned a horse who could

Mr. Ed Was a Talking Horse. Really, he

Wilbur was the only one who could hear.

Nobody else could hear Mr. Ed Talk. Strange,

but it made for a good comedy. Or at least it

What if TV shows had "visitors" just like

Visitors, just like regular people do.

Wouldn't it be funny for Mr. Ed to visit

Mr. Ed would visit Gilligan's Island. What

THAT WOULD BE AN INTERESTING SHOW.

HORSES CAN SWIM, CAN'T THEY? YES.

Gilligan's Island will Likely live Forever, in Reruns.

Aquinas • ITC/Fontek (Creative Alliance)

Bob Denver Played Gilligan; I don't think we ever knew his first name. They all called him Gilligan.

Bordeaux Italic • ITC/Fontek (Creative Alliance)

One thing I always wondered: Why did they take so many clothes just for a "3-hour tour"? I don't

Bordeaux Roman • ITC/Fontek (C. Alliance)

The "ensemble" cast of Gilligan's Island was full of unique characters. Each was special.

Bordeaux Roman Bold • ITC/Fontek (C.A.)

Q. Which character did you like best?

Brighton Bold • ITC/Fontek (Creative Alliance)

The Quirky Gilligan was such an interesting guy.

Brighton Light • ITC/Fontek (Creative Alliance)

Quirky Gilligan could be the subject of several

Brighton Medium • ITC/Fontek (C. Alliance)

Gilligan Could Be the subject of Psych 101 and 102. He

Carlton • ITC/Fontek (Creative Alliance)

Gosh. This is one of my favorite type characters: "&"

Caslon Italic with Swashes • ITC/Fontek (C.A.)

That Quirky "&" above is a neat design.

Edwardian Medium • ITC/Fontek (C. Alliance)

Gilligan probably never knew much about fonts, but he had a 3-year run on

Heliotype • ITC/Fontek (Creative Alliance)

O
serif

Quirky Gilligan Was on Network TV for 3 years. .

Locarno Italic • ITC/Fontek (Creative Alliance)

I always liked Thurston Howell III, the rich guy. Jim

Locarno Light • ITC/Fontek (Creative Alliance)

Jim Backus played him so well.

Elysium Bold • ITC/Fontek (Creative Alliance)

In a previous life, Jim Backus was also

Elysium Book • ITC/Fontek (Creative Alliance)

Quirky Jim Backus was the Nearsighted Mr.

Elysium Book Italic • ITC/Fontek (C. Alliance)

Backus was the Nearsighted Mr.

Elysium Medium • ITC/Fontek (C. Alliance)

THE NEARSIGHTED MR. MAGOO. YES HE

Elysium Small Caps • ITC/Fontek (C. Alliance)

And before that, he was Judge

Figural Bold • ITC/Fontek (Creative Alliance)

He was Judge Bradley J. Stevens, on

Figural Book • ITC/Fontek (Creative Alliance)

the funny show, I Married Joan, Jim Backus

Figural Book Italic • ITC/Fontek (C. Alliance)

Jim Backus was Judge Bradley Stevens.

Figural Medium • ITC/Fontek (C. Alliance)

QUIRKY JOAN DAVIS WAS HIS CO-STAR

Figural Small Caps • ITC/Fontek (C. Alliance)

Quickly, Jim Backus went from Judge to

University Roman • ITC/Fontek (C. Alliance)

Quirky Backus was a judge, a cartoon

University Roman Bold • ITC/Fontek (C.A.)

And Quickly turned into Thurston Howell III.

University Roman Italic • ITC/Fontek (C.A.)

The Skipper was Alan Hale, Jr. He called

Gilgamesh Bold • ITC/Fontek (Creative Alliance)

The Skipper called Gilligan "Little Buddy".

Gilgamesh Book • ITC/Fontek (C. Alliance)

Do You Have any idea what the Skipper's

Gilgamesh Book Italic • ITC/Fontek (C. Alliance)

Do you know What the Skipper's Name

Gilgamesh Medium • ITC/Fontek (C. Alliance)

Do you know the name of the Skipper?

Gilgamesh Small Caps • ITC/Fontek (C. Alliance)

I Bet One Person in a Thousand won't.

Tempus • ITC/Fontek (Creative Alliance)

I'll Bet You don't Know This One.

Tempus Italic • ITC/Fontek (Creative Alliance)

OK. Here it is: Jonas Grumby was

Tempus SC • ITC/Fontek (Creative Alliance)

Jonas Grumby was the Skipper. Jonas

Tempus SC Italic • ITC/Fontek (C. Alliance)

That's a Name I have Never heard about

Loire • Jean Lochu (Creative Alliance)

Quickly, Gilligan Would Snooze on the Island.

Loire Italique • Jean Lochu (Creative Alliance)

ADEFGKLMNPQRSTUWY aseff

Loire Ornaments Italique • Jean Lochu (C.A.)

The above font has special Swash characters

Loire Pale • Jean Lochu (Creative Alliance)

O
serif

Gilligan Once Snoozed While a Gorilla was there.

Loire Pale Italique • Jean Lochu (C. Alliance)

GILLIGAN ONCE WORE A GORILLA SUIT.

Loire Petites Capitales • Jean Lochu (C. Alliance)

Q. How did they get a gorilla suit on the

Loire Sombre • Jean Lochu (Creative Alliance)

Quiz—How did they get the suit on the island?

Loire Sombre Italique • Jean Lochu (C. Alliance)

Was that gorilla suit on the boat?

Apolline Bold • Jean-François Porchez (C.A.)

What was the Gorilla suit doing on a

Apolline Bold Italic • Jean-François Porchez (C.A.)

QQ a fb & e ff fh fifj ffi fl ffl ftq r st t z

Apolline Alt Bold Italic • Jean-François Porchez (C.A.)

Perhaps Mr. Howell & his wife were a little

Apolline Italic • Jean-François Porchez (C.A.)

Perhaps the Quirky was more Kinky.

Apolline LF Bold • Jean-François Porchez (C.A.)

I wonder which one wore the gorilla suit.

Apolline LF Bold Italic • Jean-François Porchez (C.A.)

Q. Did he say "Will you wear the gorilla suit?"

Apolline LF Italic • Jean-François Porchez (C.A.)

Maybe it belonged to the Professor.

Apolline LF SemiBold • Jean-François Porchez (C.A.)

Q. Was he a biology professor? Did he

Apolline LF SemiBold Italic • J-F Porchez (C.A.)

Q. Did he study Primates? Did he wear

Apolline Regular • Jean-François Porchez (C.A.)

Did he wear the suit to study primates?

Apolline SemiBold • Jean-François Porchez (C.A.)

That might not be such a good idea, you

Apolline SemiBold Italic • J-François Porchez (C.A.)

What if the suit is a little too realistic looking?

Runa Serif Italic • Lennart Hansson (C. Alliance)

And what if a real male gorilla takes a liking

Runa Serif Light • Lennart Hansson (C. Alliance)

The real gorilla decides that mating season

Runa Serif Medium • Lennart Hansson (C.A.)

"MATING SEASON IS HERE," THE GORILLA SAYS.

Beata • Letterperfect (Creative Alliance)

QUIRKY GORILLA SMILES. THE

Cresci • Letterperfect (Creative Alliance)

Gorilla has seen Deliverance.

Visage Black • Letterperfect (Creative Alliance)

Quirky guy has seen Deliverance.

Visage Black Oblique • Letterperfect (C.A.)

Guy in the gorilla suit is suddenly in

Visage Bold • Letterperfect (Creative Alliance)

Guy in the suit shouldn't be there.

Visage Bold Oblique • Letterperfect (C. Alliance)

Gorillas don't like to be fooled. They also

Visage Book • Letterperfect (Creative Alliance)

They also don't like playing "hard to get"

Visage Book Oblique • Letterperfect (C.A.)

Quickly, you can see this is not a good idea

Visage Light • Letterperfect (Creative Alliance)

Better take along a possum suit. At least

Visage Light Oblique • Letterperfect (C. Alliance)

At least, you Can Outrun a Possum.

Visage Medium • Letterperfect (C. Alliance)

Q. Why is the proper term Opossum?

Visage Medium Oblique • Letterperfect (C.A.)

Quick—are O'Possums Irish animals?

Alisal • Matthew Carter (Creative Alliance)

Quiz answer: No they are not Irish.

Alisal Bold • Matthew Carter (Creative Alliance)

Quick Animals they are NOT. So, if you are

Alisal Italic • Matthew Carter (Creative Alliance)

IF YOU ARE GOING TO BE PURSUED,

Galba • Mecanorma (Creative Alliance)

If a Quirky animal follows you with

Renault • Mecanorma (Creative Alliance)

Quick Action in mind, you are

Renault Bd • Mecanorma (Creative Alliance)

You're better off if it is an O'Possum.

Sully Jonquieres • Mecanorma (C. Alliance)

Actually, Kermit the Frog looks Irish.

Sully Jonquieres Bd • Mecanorma (C. Alliance)

Kermit the Frog Always wore Green.

Shouldn't he be Kermit the O'Frog?

IT MAKES MORE SENSE THAN O'POSSUM.

How did we get from Gilligan's Island to

HOW DID KERMIT GET INTO THE GAME?

DID KERMIT THE FROG HAVE A CRUSH ON

DID ANYONE NOT HAVE A CRUSH ON MARY

Ann, from Gilligan's Island, lovely

Q. ANYONE KNOW HER LAST NAME?

Mary Ann Summers, that's who she was.

WHILE WE'RE ON NAMES, DOES ANYONE

O
serif

Does anyone know the Professor's name?

EVERYONE ALWAYS CALLED HIM "PROFESSOR"

I don't think I ever knew what his real

Albertus • Monotype (Creative Alliance)

Does anyone know what his real name was?

Albertus Italic • Monotype (Creative Alliance)

He was Prof. Roy Hinkley. Actually,

Albertus Light • Monotype (Creative Alliance)

he wasn't a real professor. Not at all.

Amasis • Monotype (Creative Alliance)

He was a high school science teacher.

Amasis Bold • Monotype (Creative Alliance)

Ginger was also a beautiful castaway.

Amasis Bold It • Monotype (Creative Alliance)

Do you know her last name? Do

Amasis Black • Monotype (Creative Alliance)

Quick? OK, she was Ginger Grant.

Amasis Black It • Monotype (Creative Alliance)

She was supposed to be a movie star. She

Amasis Italic • Monotype (Creative Alliance)

Funny. A TV star playing a movie star.

Amasis Light • Monotype (Creative Alliance)

"Hi, I'm not a movie star, but I play one on TV."

Amasis Light It • Monotype (Creative Alliance)

"Hi, I'm not a doctor, but I play one."

Amasis Medium • Monotype (Creative Alliance)

Is that a pick up line, or what? But if

Amasis Medium It • Monotype (C. Alliance)

But if you were on Gilligan's Island, you

wouldn't need a pick up line. They were

They were on the island from September '64

UNTIL THE SHOW WAS CANCELED IN 1967,

September of 1967, to be exact. 3 years.

When you're on an island for 3 years,

you don't need a Quick pick-up line.

Anyway, where do you go Quietly?

Where do you go out to dinner?

Quiz: Did Gilligan ever have a relationship with

Q. Did Gilligan ever have a girlfriend?

Q. Did Ginger or Mary Ann ever go

Did either one ever get involved with Gilligan?

O
serif

Apparently, only the Gorilla ever got…

Never mind. I'll Quit that story line.

You Know Mr. Howell's Wife's Name?

Quick Answer: It was Lovey. No Surprise

Everyone knows the name of the boat

THE QUIRKY BOAT WAS THE MINNOW. IT

Do you how many things you could learn

YOU LEARN A LOT OF STUFF WATCHING

Just From Watching Gilligan, you can

You can learn to make a radio from

You can make a radio from coconuts.

They made a radio from coconuts.

They did. It must be true. It was on TV.

Remember a show called "That's Life"?

It was on beginning September 1968.

The show starred Robert Morse and it was

The Show was Quite Unusual; it

was a full musical comedy each week.

It was also a serial. Each week's show built on

the Previous Week's Show. The theme

The Plot Followed the romance and

The romance and Married life of a young

The young couple's life was followed through

sketches, monologues, and typical

The standard musical comedy format was

The Musical COMEDY Format was

Each week, there was a special celebrity

Special celebrity guests were on each

Kermit the Frog was a guest on the show

Really, you can look it up. He was on

He was on the St. Patrick's Day

And he wore his green suit, but

in the credits, he was not listed as Kermit O'Frog.

Wally Cox was also a guest star. He was not in a show

He was NOT in a show about a football

He did not play the football

He wasn't a football player.

Q. Why would someone think he

Did Wally Cox ever play football?

For years, every time I heard the

phrase "Wally Cox to Block",

that made me think of a huddle.

Think of Wally Cox in a huddle,

and the Quarterback is giving directions

just the way it's done in Sandlot Football.

Little Wally Cox dressed out for the big

Think of Wally Cox in Football Pads, in the

Mr. Peepers wearing a helmet,

Q. Did you ever dream of Fonts at night?

AND ALL THESE QUIRKY LETTERS ARE THERE?

And Wally Cox is in the huddle, and the QB

The Quarterback said "Wally Cox to Block."

LOTS OF PEOPLE WON'T HAVE A CLUE WHAT

Bulmer SemiBoldSC • Monotype (C. Alliance)

They will never know what that means. Tough.

Bulmer Bold Display • Monotype (C. Alliance)

Some people are now and forever

Calvert—italic • Monotype (Creative Alliance)

Do you think Wally Cox ever played football?

Bulmer BoldItalic Display • Monotype (C.A.)

His body type seemed much more

Calvert Bold—italic • Monotype (C. Alliance)

Q. Why would he have wanted to play football?

Bulmer Italic Display • Monotype (C. Alliance)

He probably would've done better

Calvert Light—italic • Monotype (C. Alliance)

By the way, are you counting all these fonts?

Bulmer Regular Display • Monotype (C.A.)

YOU WANT TO MAKE SURE YOU GET YOUR $

Bulmer SemiBoldSC—italic • Monotype (C.A.)

Are You Counting all these Fonts?

Calisto • Monotype (Creative Alliance)

Remember when I said that we were a

Calisto Bold • Monotype (Creative Alliance)

When I said that we were 13 fonts shy of

Calisto Bold It • Monotype (Creative Alliance)

I Quietly Confessed that we didn't have all

Calisto Italic • Monotype (Creative Alliance)

I felt compelled to admit we didn't

We didn't really have 5,000 fonts.

I think that I told you we were 13 shy.

We Appeared to be 13 fonts shy of a

Q. How many fonts do we actually

Is this Really the Book of 5,000 Fonts?

Q. How many fonts are in this

If you are counting, you should be

You should be at about 4,000-and-some.

Did I tell you that I have a short attention

A very short attention span. Is it really ADD?

Q. Is this Attention Deficit Disorder?

If I were a kid, would they put me on

If I were a kid, I'd be put on ritalin, and

Centaur • Monotype (Creative Alliance)

Then I would grow up to be normal, and I

Centaur Bold • Monotype (Creative Alliance)

Q. Would I ever do books like this if I was normal?

Centaur Bold It • Monotype (Creative Alliance)

Probably Not. Quick observation, but probably True.

Centaur Italic • Monotype (Creative Alliance)

ADEGLMNQRSTVY aegkrsttvw z Swash

Centaur Swash • Monotype (Creative Alliance)

They tell the story of the comedian

Century Bold • Monotype (Creative Alliance)

The comedian went to see a psych

Century Bold It • Monotype (Creative Alliance)

The word "shrink" is shorter than

Century Ep • Monotype (Creative Alliance)

The comedian went to a shrink. *He did*

Century Ep It • Monotype (Creative Alliance)

and the shrink cured him. But he wasn't

Century OS • Monotype (Creative Alliance)

The comedian was cured, but he

Century OS Bold • Monotype (Creative Alliance)

The comedian was no longer funny.

Century OS Bd It • Monotype (Creative Alliance)

No longer funny. Just normal. What a fate!

Century OS It • Monotype (Creative Alliance)

I just had a flashback. There is this

There is a office building that

The office building houses a

A creative organization is in the office.

The office actually has a strait jacket

The strait jacket is on a wall, and

The strait jacket is behind glass,

kind of the way they do fire hoses.

The sign at the bottom of the glass case

The sign says "Break in case of Emergency".

Quirky, but true. This is a true story. Really.

"You can look it up," as Casey used to

This Quirky truth is found in my office.

O serif

Yes, there is a strait jacket on the wall of

Columbus • Monotype (Creative Alliance)

My office building has a strait jacket

Columbus Bold • Monotype (Creative Alliance)

Q. Has it ever been used? Do you really want

Columbus Bd It • Monotype (Creative Alliance)

Do you Really Want The Question Answered?

Columbus Italic • Monotype (Creative Alliance)

Some would advise me to take the 5th,

Columbus Sm Bd • Monotype (Creative Alliance)

as in "I refuse to Answer on the Grounds that…"

Columbus Sm Bd It • Monotype (C. Alliance)

The Answer May tend to Incriminate Me.

Dante Bold • Monotype (Creative Alliance)

Do you think that some day I may be in the

Dante BoldItalic • Monotype (Creative Alliance)

What if I'm in the position of having to testify

Dante Italic • Monotype (Creative Alliance)

Answer Questions Under Oath, Swearing…

Dante Medium • Monotype (Creative Alliance)

Swearing to God to Tell the Truth, and all that,

Dante MediumItalic • Monotype (C. Alliance)

and then someone ambushes me with the

Dante Regular • Monotype (Creative Alliance)

SOMEONE SAYS TO ME: "IS IT TRUE THAT…"

Clarendon—smallcaps • Monotype (C. Alliance)

DO YOU have a strait jacket on your

Is there a strait jacket on your

Strange things run through the

Would the mere ownership of a

Would simply owning a strait

Would owning a strait jacket be

Would Simple Ownership be Enough

OK. So I bought a strait jacket for the

I bought it for the office. It's a

It was a joke, get it? No one really

It's just a fun thing, get it through

WILL THAT BE THE FINAL

WILL THAT BE ENOUGH?

Will this be one more example of the sad

Ellington • Monotype (Creative Alliance)

The sad story of "Make one mistake,

Ellington Bold • Monotype (Creative Alliance)

and they Brand you for Life." So Sad.

Ellington BoldItalic • Monotype (C. Alliance)

Ever wonder why I never ran for public

Ellington ExtraBold • Monotype (C. Alliance)

Imagine what the press would do with

Ellington ExtraBoldItalic • Monotype (C.A.)

The press would have a feeding frenzy with

Ellington Italic • Monotype (Creative Alliance)

The Strait Jacket Would be good for a week's

Ellington Light • Monotype (Creative Alliance)

Larry King Live would have a full week of stories

Ellington LightItalic • Monotype (C. Alliance)

Who is this crazy guy running for office?

Glouces Bd • Monotype (Creative Alliance)

He has a strait jacket in his office, and it says

Glouces Cn Bd • Monotype (Creative Alliance)

"Emergency Use Only"

Glouces Et Bd • Monotype (Creative Alliance)

And then someone would find my records from my tailor,

Glouces Ex Cn Bd • Monotype (C. Alliance)

and, horrors, they discover that my suit size

Glouces Old Style • Monotype (C. Alliance)

Q. Why is your suit size the same as

Footlight Bold • Monotype (Creative Alliance)

Why is your suit size the same as the

Footlight BoldItalic • Monotype (C. Alliance)

Next question: was the strait jacket

Footlight ExtraBold • Monotype (C. Alliance)

Was it custom tailored for you, sir?

Footlight ExtraBoldItal • Monotype (C. Alliance)

Hello, sir. I'm with the National Enquirer.

Footlight Italic • Monotype (Creative Alliance)

The National Enquirer Would like to do

Footlight Light • Monotype (Creative Alliance)

We'd like to get a photo of you in the

Footlight LightItalic • Monotype (C. Alliance)

A PHOTO OF YOU IN YOUR CUSTOM TAILORED

Glouces Old Style—smallcaps • Monotype (C.A.)

Quick photo of you snoozing in your custom

Fournier Italic • Monotype (Creative Alliance)

About that time, the Fund Raising would pretty

Fournier Italic Tall Caps • Monotype (C.A.)

Contribution to my Senatorial Campaign

Fournier Regular • Monotype (Creative Alliance)

THE MONEY WOULD PRETTY WELL STOP ABOUT…

Fournier Regular SC • Monotype (C. Alliance)

About that time, the money would dry up. No,

Fournier Regular Tall Caps • Monotype (C.A.)

That's just one reason that I can't run for

This would be a good time to let my

The Mind Quickly Wanders to Another

No, Sir. I do not have the Same Tailor as Kermit.

Quiz Kermit, not me. I don't even own a green suit

ADEFGK MNPQ ase ſgghgjkſtsſtʋfrgyzy

ADEFGKLMNPQRSTV nice swashes.

I once owned a Green Plaid suit though. Really.

DPQRTafflfghffkrs vwyz nice swashes.

The green plaid suit was sold to me by a

LiQURQuWEefffehthfflrso mo' swashes.

The green Plaid suit was sold by a friend.

LiQURQuWEefffehfflrsstyz swashes.

O
serif

I didn't wear it a whole lot. Not after I heard one

Gill Facia Italic Display • Monotype (C. Alliance)

particular comment that

Goudy Ex Bold—italic • Monotype (C. Alliance)

Q. Why didn't I wear the suit a lot?

Goudy Catalogue • Monotype (Creative Alliance)

I Quietly stopped after I heard a comment

Goudy Catalogue Italic • Monotype (C. Alliance)

Someone Quietly said something behind my

Goudy Modern • Monotype (Creative Alliance)

Yes, words were spoken behind my back.

Goudy Modern Bold • Monotype (C. Alliance)

"Golly, gee," someone said, "lookit the…"

Goudy Modern BoldItalic • Monotype (C.A.)

No one Gave Me Any Compliments on the

Goudy Modern Italic • Monotype (C. Alliance)

Not at all. I got scorn, and lots of it.

Goudy Bold • Monotype (Creative Alliance)

Q. What kind of scorn did I get? Lots of

Goudy Bold Italic • Monotype (C. Alliance)

Lots of scorn. I was shunned.

Goudy Ex Bold • Monotype (Creative Alliance)

But the worst thing was the one

Goudy Old Style • Monotype (Creative Alliance)

"Good gosh," I said. "Quit picking At My…"

Goudy Old Style Italic • Monotype (C. Alliance)

What did someone say about the green

OK. It was called my Stevie Wonder

It was called my "Stevie Wonder Suit",

because the story was that Stevie Wonder

Stevie Wonder got the suit as a gift, and

he refused to wear the suit, the green plaid.

There is absolutely no truth to that story.

Which story? That I bought a Green

I bought a Green Plaid Suit, or the Story that

Stevie Wonder had the suit, and would

Stevie Wonder Quietly Gave it Away. That's

That is The Qwazy Story that Went Around. But it

NEVER HAPPENED. THE STEVIE WONDER PART

O
serif

The Stevie Wonder Part Never

Imprint • Monotype (Creative Alliance)

It never happened. None of it, not

Imprint Bold • Monotype (Creative Alliance)

Nobody ever called it a Stevie

Imprint Bold It • Monotype (Creative Alliance)

Nobody called it a Stevie Wonder Suit.

Imprint Italic • Monotype (Creative Alliance)

It was a very nice suit, except for

Ionic • Monotype (Creative Alliance)

except for the green and the plaid.

Ionic Bold • Monotype (Creative Alliance)

Except for the Green and the Plaid,

Ionic Italic • Monotype (Creative Alliance)

Except for the Green and the Plaid it was

Italian Old Style • Monotype (Creative Alliance)

It was a very nice suit. Nice 100% wool.

Italian Old Style Bold • Monotype (C. Alliance)

100% Wool. Yes, some unsuspecting sheep

Italian Old Style Bd It • Monotype (C. Alliance)

Some unsuspecting Sheep Somewhere gave

Italian Old Style Italic • Monotype (C. Alliance)

The sheep gave a full year's wool for the

Janson • Monotype (Creative Alliance)

At least it wasn't leather. Whoever gives

Janson Bold • Monotype (Creative Alliance)

Whoever gives Leather, Quietly Gives ALL.

I bet the sheep would have been embarrassed if it

If the Sheep had seen where his wool went,

The sheep would have been pretty

The sheep would have been depressed. Green Plaid

Wonder if sheep have social classes?

The Sheep Who give their wool for Navy Pin Stripes

THOSE SHEEP WOULD BE THE HIGHEST CLASS.

AND THE SHEEP WHO GIVE THEIR WOOL FOR

Those whose wool winds up as green plaid,

Green Plaid Sheep are pretty much outcasts. For a

For awhile, anyway. Wait til next year.

Next year, the Green Plaid sheep may

O
serif

Do Animals Have social classes? Of course.

Modern Condensed • Monotype (C. Alliance)

Remember just how much outside dogs resent

Modern CondensedItalic • Monotype (C.A.)

Outside Dogs Resent Inside Dogs.

Modern Extended • Monotype (C. Alliance)

Well, Green Plaid Suit Sheep are shunned.

Modern ExtendedItalic • Monotype (C. Alliance)

Green Plaid sheep are low class

Modern Wide • Monotype (Creative Alliance)

and the Gray Flannel Sheep are

Modern WideItalic • Monotype (C. Alliance)

Those sheep are really high status.

New Clarendon • Monotype (Creative Alliance)

But, unlike some societies, each

New Clarendon Bd • Monotype (C. Alliance)

year, the whole sheep social structure

News Plantin • Monotype (Creative Alliance)

The whole social structure of sheep

News Plantin Bd • Monotype (Creative Alliance)

Each year, a whole new social order

News Plantin Bd It • Monotype (C. Alliance)

A whole new social order Emerges. True.

News Plantin It • Monotype (Creative Alliance)

I bet the Green Plaid Sheep Had a

Nimrod • Monotype (Creative Alliance)

It was a Long Year, waiting for

Waiting for the chance to be a

The Chance to Be a Grey Flannel

Talk About social Climbing. Going from Green

Going from Green Plaid to Grey Flannel in one

In One short Year, the Whole Social Strata

HEY, FONT COUNTER: WHAT NUMBER ARE

What Number Are You On NOW? Do

Don't Lost Count, or you'll have to

You will have to go back to page one and

Start All over Again, and if you really

If you really want to be totally

To be totally accurate, you Must count

You must count the fonts not just

Perrywood BoldItalicExp • Monotype (C.A.)

Not just once, but twice. Or maybe 3 times.

Perrywood Condensed • Monotype (C. Alliance)

There's a pretty good chance you

Perrywood Ex Bd • Monotype (C. Alliance)

will probably count a different

Perrywood Ex Bd It • Monotype (C. Alliance)

You Will Get a Different Total

Perrywood Expanded • Monotype (C. Alliance)

Each time you count, you will get a

Perrywood ExtraBoldCon • Monotype (C.A.)

If you get a different count

Perrywood ExtraBoldExp • Monotype (C.A.)

If each count is different, what does

Perrywood ExtraBoldItaCon • Monotype (C.A.)

Exactly What does that Mean?

Perrywood ExtraBoldItaExp • Monotype (C.A.)

For one thing, it's a Red Flag About your

Perrywood It • Monotype (Creative Alliance)

Yes, It's a Red Flag About Your Counting Skill

Perrywood ItalicCondensed • Monotype (C.A.)

What number are you on now?! 3877?

Perrywood ItalicExpanded • Monotype (C.A.)

Oops, did that number make you lose count? Ha!

Perrywood LightCondensed • Monotype (C.A.)

Well, just in case you had planned

Perrywood LightExpanded • Monotype (C.A.)

If you planned to count them all and then tell me,

Perrywood LightItalicCon • Monotype (C.A.)

"Hey, there are fewer than 5,000 fonts in…"

Perrywood LightItalicExp • Monotype (C.A.)

If you planned to tell me that there are less

Perrywood Light • Monotype (Creative Alliance)

If you planned to tell me that some fonts are

Perrywood Light It • Monotype (C. Alliance)

The case of the Missing Fonts, by Earle

Perrywood SemiBoldCon • Monotype (C.A.)

By Earle Stanley Gardner. Or

Perrywood SemiBoldExp • Monotype (C.A.)

If there are any fonts Missing, I suggest

Perrywood SemiBoldItaCon • Monotype (C.A.)

Before you cast any aspersions,

Perrywood SemiBoldItaExp • Monotype (C.A.)

and before you write any notes about

Perrywood Sm Bd • Monotype (C. Alliance)

Don't write any notes about Missing Fonts

Perrywood Sm Bd It • Monotype (C. Alliance)

Before the Missing Fonts are Blamed on Me,

Poliphilus Regular • Monotype (C. Alliance)

JUST CHECK TO SEE IF THE FONTS MAYBE HAVE

Poliphilus RegularSC • Monotype (C.A.)

Were any of those Fonts last Seen at

Photina • Monotype (Creative Alliance)

Yes. Missing Fonts Last Seen at Cabot

Photina Bold • Monotype (Creative Alliance)

Q. WERE THE MISSING FONTS IN MAINE?

Poliphilus RegularSC—bold • Monotype (C.A.)

Q. Were the Missing Fonts in Cabot

Photina BoldItalic • Monotype (C. Alliance)

Were the Missing Fonts in Cabot Cove, by

Photina Italic • Monotype (Creative Alliance)

WHERE FONTS GO TO DIE, THAT WOULD BE

Photina Regular SC • Monotype (C. Alliance)

Quickly, the National Enquirer would

Photina SemiBold • Monotype (C. Alliance)

The Quality Reporters of the National

Photina SemiBoldItalic • Monotype (C. Alliance)

They would Quickly be hot on

Photina UltraBold • Monotype (C. Alliance)

The Story of the Missing Fonts

Photina UltraBoldItalic • Monotype (C. Alliance)

Fast Headlines: Missing Fonts!

Plantin • Monotype (Creative Alliance)

O
serif

Every Super Market Shopper in

Plantin Bold • Monotype (Creative Alliance)

Every Supermarket Shopper in America

Plantin BoldCondensed • Monotype (C. Alliance)

Every Supermarket Shopper in the

Q. Where are the Missing Fonts? Once the

Once the Question is Asked Publicly,

Seven Congressmen Would Quickly Deny

They Would Deny Any Knowledge of

"The fonts were just close friends,"

That's the story for the press.

And Questions Would Continue to Fly.

Truth now emerges. There are no

There are no missing Fonts. Not on

O
serif

No Missing Fonts. Not at all. In fact,

In fact, there are more than 5,000

Yes. YES. There are MORE than 5,000 fonts

There are More Than 5,000 Fonts in

Rockwell BoldItalic • Monotype (C. Alliance)

More than 5,000 Fonts in This Book. Now. I've said

Rockwell Condensed • Monotype (C. Alliance)

I said it, and I'm glad. Yes.

Rockwell Extra Bold • Monotype (C. Alliance)

This Book is a Bigger Bargain Than

Rockwell Italic • Monotype (Creative Alliance)

The book has given you more than

Rockwell Light • Monotype (Creative Alliance)

You got more than you bargained for.

Rockwell LightItalic • Monotype (C. Alliance)

You actually got more than you paid for.

Sabon • Monotype (Creative Alliance)

You Quietly Expected 5,000 Fonts,

Sabon Italic • Monotype (Creative Alliance)

AND QUICKLY, WE DELIVERED 5,000 AND

Sabon RegularSC • Monotype (Creative Alliance)

Q. 5,000 *and how many more? Well,*

Sabon SemiBoldItalic • Monotype (C. Alliance)

I Wish Pee Wee Herman Were here to

Sabon Sm Bd • Monotype (Creative Alliance)

HE WOULD ANSWER THAT QUESTION WITH THIS

Spartan Four • Monotype (Creative Alliance)

"THAT'S FOR ME TO KNOW, AND YOU TO..."

Spartan Four Bd • Monotype (Creative Alliance)

MINE TO KNOW, YOURS TO FIND OUT. THERE.

SO, IF YOU WANT TO PAY LITTLE MORE

IF YOU WANT TO PAY A LITTLE

WHY DOES THIS PAGE LOOK LIKE A

DO YOU SUDDENLY FEEL LIKE

THIS IS LIKE TAKING AN EYE

ARE WE TAKING AN EYE EXAM?

I AN NOT AN OPTHOLMOLOGIST, BUT I PLAY ONE

BUT I AM PLAYING ONE IN THIS FONT BOOK.

CAN YOU READ THIS LINE? COVER YOUR

COVER YOUR LEFT EYE. CAN YOU READ THE

CAN YOU READ THIS? WHICH LINE

IS THIS LINE CLEARER? OR THAT LINE?

O
serif

This concludes your visit to the eye doctor.

Please Pay at the desk as you leave. Q. Which desk?

You can't see that big desk over there? You DO need

IF YOU CAN'T SEE THAT DESK THERE, YOU NEED

You Really Need glasses; watch out for

Watch out for that desk over there. It's in

How come there are no door-to-door eye docs?

Say an eye doctor goes house to house and knocks

He Quietly Knocks on doors, and when someone

When someone comes to the door,

He holds up an eye chart and says,

serif

"Would You Like to Have your eyes..."

"Want Your Eyes Checked Today?" He

Does this really seem silly? Or is it really

Times NR • Monotype (Creative Alliance)

This just might be a really good idea.

Times NR Bd • Monotype (Creative Alliance)

Or, it could be a Quirky and Stupid one.

Times NR Bd It • Monotype (Creative Alliance)

The Hard Part is Knowing Which…

Times NR Ex Bd • Monotype (Creative Alliance)

Q. Which one it is: Really Silly. Or

Times NR It • Monotype (Creative Alliance)

This might be a really smart idea.

Times NR Md • Monotype (Creative Alliance)

There are many things that have a long

Times NR Md It • Monotype (Creative Alliance)

Many occupations have a long

Times NR Sm Bd • Monotype (Creative Alliance)

A long tradition of selling door-to-door

Times NR Sm Bd It • Monotype (C. Alliance)

The Fuller Brush Man sold door

Times NR Seven • Monotype (Creative Alliance)

So do Vacuum Cleaner People.

Times NR Seven Bd • Monotype (C. Alliance)

And Quietly, Encyclopedia Salesmen

Times NR Seven Bd It • Monotype (C. Alliance)

Oh, Encyclopedia Salesman Quietly

Times NR Seven It • Monotype (C. Alliance)

Encyclopedia Salesmen are

Encyclopedia sales died when

CDs and the Internet were

When the internet and Encyclopedia CDs

The 30-volume set of Encyclopedias

They pretty much died. Did they go to

Did all the encyclopedias go to Cabot

Q. Do Encyclopedias go to Cabot Cove to Die?

Just Like Clue: The Killer was New Tech

Q. WHO KILLED THE ENCYCLOPEDIAS?

New Tech, in Cyberspace, with a Gigabyte.

And they dumped the body in the bay at Cabot

They dumped the body at Cabot Cove, ME

Avon Ladies sell door-to-door. So do

Walbaum Md It • Monotype (Creative Alliance)

Tupperware ladies do the same.

StratfordBd • Pacella (Creative Alliance)

Well, they actually sell party-to-party.

Corvallis • Philip Bouwsma (Creative Alliance)

A smart marketing guy would see a lot of things

Corvallis Oblique • Philip Bouwsma (C. Alliance)

Lots of stuff can be sold door-to

Mariposa Black • Philip Bouwsma (C. Alliance)

What things could be sold door-to

Mariposa Bold • Philip Bouwsma (C. Alliance)

Get creative, and find some new niche.

Mariposa Book • Philip Bouwsma (C. Alliance)

Take Firemen. Why should they sit around

Mariposa Book Italic • Philip Bouwsma (C.A.)

Why sit around and wait for the phone

Mariposa Medium • Philip Bouwsma (C.A.)

Why wait for the phone to ring? Why not go door-to-door?

TowerCd • Photolettering (Creative Alliance)

KNOCK, AND WHEN SOMEONE

Pietra • Creative Alliance

Q. THEN WHAT? WHEN SOMEONE

Pontif • Creative Alliance

When someone comes to the door, simply

Missive • S. Farrell/T-26 (Creative Alliance)

You just say, "Do you have any fires you need put out?"

I know, it seems a little out there, at first,

but think about it, and you realize that

Maybe once a week, you will get there

You will get there at the Exact Moment

You arrive at the exact moment when a fire

A fire has just started, and you just got

Q. IS THAT GOOD TIMING, OR WHAT? THIS

MIGHT A GOOD BUSINESS. WANNA BUY

WANNA BUY A FRANCHISE?

IF THINGS GET SLOW, YOU

O serif

could always ask more than one question when you go

When you go to the door, you could always ask more

Ask more than one question at the door.

Truesdell • Steve Matteson (Creative Alliance)

Start with asking if they need any fires put

Truesdell—Bold • Steve Matteson (C. Alliance)

And Kindly Ask Quickly if they have Ghosts.

Truesdell—BoldItalic • Steve Matteson (C.A.)

"What Kind of Ghosts?" You Inquire. And

Truesdell—Italic • Steve Matteson (C. Alliance)

ÆDEFG•• M •P •R •Tfffiffi ae••h•••stThv•••

TruesdellAlternate—Italic • S. Matteson (C.A.)

•••••••••••••st•fffiffi NICE LIGATURES HERE

TruesdellAlternate—Roman • S. Matteson (C.A.)

Remember the movie Ghostbusters? Hey, the

Arepo • Sumner Stone (Creative Alliance)

They had a good business going there,

Arepo Bold • Sumner Stone (Creative Alliance)

So, you Quickly start with Fire Services, Expand

Arepo Italic • Sumner Stone (Creative Alliance)

ADEFGKLMNPQRSTVW ae fine swashes

Arepo Italic Swash • Sumner Stone (C. Alliance)

You expand to Ghost Busting, then see

Silica—Black • Sumner Stone (Creative Alliance)

what other services you can ask about

Silica—Bold • Sumner Stone (Creative Alliance)

Ask about any other services they might

Silica—Semibold • Sumner Stone (C. Alliance)

Here is a great business idea. Really

Eco101Roman •The Economist (C. Alliance)

Q. What is this great idea? Well,

Eco102Italic •The Economist (Creative Alliance)

You just bought this Quality Book.

Eco201Demi •The Economist (Creative Alliance)

You already have this book, and it

Eco202DemiItalic •The Economist (C. Alliance)

You can Quietly Make This Book a

Eco301Bold •The Economist (Creative Alliance)

Q. How Does This Book become a

Eco302 BoldItalic •The Economist (C. Alliance)

CAN THIS BOOK BECOME A PROFIT

Eco401Scaps •The Economist (Creative Alliance)

This book is a Profit Center? No Way.

Cicero •Thierry Puyfoulhoux (Creative Alliance)

You have one of the finest font

Cicero Bold •Thierry Puyfoulhoux (C. Alliance)

You have one of the finest font sources

Cicero Bold Italic •Thierry Puyfoulhoux (C.A.)

One of the finest font books known to

Cicero Italic •Thierry Puyfoulhoux (C. Alliance)

This is one big font book. Right? So

Cicero Medium •Thierry Puyfoulhoux (C.A.)

take this book with you door-to-door

Cicero Medium Italic •T. Puyfoulhoux (C.A.)

Take the book with you door-to

Alinea Incise Bold •Thierry Puyfoulhoux (C.A.)

And if they don't need any fires put

Alinea Incise Bold Italic •T. Puyfoulhoux (C.A.)

If they don't have any fires, or have

Alinea Incise Medium •T. Puyfoulhoux (C.A.)

And if they don't have any Ghosts,

Alinea Incise Medium Italic •T. Puyfoulhoux (C.A.)

They you bring out this font book,

Alinea Incise Regular •T. Puyfoulhoux (C.A.)

and you clear your throat, stand a

Alinea Incise Regular Italic •T. Puyfoulhoux (C.A.)

STAND A LITTLE TALLER, AND THEN

PlantagenetSC—Roman—italic •Tiro Type. (C.A.)

AND THEN YOU QUIZ THEM,

PlantagenetTT—Roman—italic •Tiro Type. (C.A.)

"Do You Need Any Fonts Identified?"

PlantagenetCND—Roman—italic •Tiro Type. (C.A.)

Now before you laugh, just think about it.

PlantagenetCND—Roman •Tiro Typeworks (C.A.)

HOW MANY PEOPLE DON'T EVEN KNOW

PlantagenetSC—Roman •Tiro Typeworks (C.A.)

ADEFGKLMNPQRSTUWY

PlantagenetSW—Italic •Tiro Typeworks (C.A.)

HOW MANY DON'T KNOW SWASH

PlantagenetTT—Roman •Tiro Typeworks (C.A.)

HOW MANY PEOPLE DO NOT KNOW

Aeneas—Dark • Tiro Typeworks (C. Alliance)

RIGHT. THEY DO NOT KNOW SWASH.

Aeneas—Light • Tiro Typeworks (C. Alliance)

NOT KNOWING SWASH IS BAD. VERY

Aeneas—Regular • Tiro Typeworks (C. Alliance)

Not Knowing SQUAT is bad enough, but

Manticore Bold • Tiro Typeworks (C. Alliance)

in some social Circles, Not knowing Swash is

Manticore Italic • Tiro Typeworks (C. Alliance)

Not Knowing Swash is Socially Unacceptable.

Manticore Regular • Tiro Typeworks (C.A.)

IMAGINE THE SCORN HEAPED UPON THOSE

Manticore SmallCaps • Tiro Typeworks (C.A.)

THE FONT-CHALLENGED FACE AN

Manticore Titling • Tiro Typeworks (C. Alliance)

They, frankly, face an uncertain future.

Egyptian 505 • Visual Graphics Corp (C. Alliance)

Would YOU hire someone who can't tell

Egyptian 505 Light • Visual Graphics Corp (C.A.)

Anyone who can't tell a ligature from

Egyptian 505 Medium • Visual Graphics Corp (C.A.)

He can't tell a ligature from his ascend

AdroitLt • Typespectra (Creative Alliance)

Doesn't know his ascender from a

AdroitMd • Typespectra (Creative Alliance)

Doesn't know his ascender from a hole

From a hole in the ground. There I said

The font-challenged. We all know some

We all know someone who can't tell

Can't Tell Bodoni from Helvetica. No

And worse, some people misread it,

and they call it Bidini. Wrong! It's

Quickly help these people. Help the font

Help the Font-Challenged. Go door-to

Quietly Go Door-to-Door and Ask the

O
serif

Ask the Question, "Need Any Fonts?

Need any fonts Identified Today?" You

You will be surprised how many people

You will be surprised how many

Millions of Americans are Font Illiterate.

Yes, Font illiteracy Strikes 99 % of

Only one American out of 100 is Font Lit

Q. "Is it Font Illiteracy, doctor?" "Yes..."

"Yes, I'm afraid our tests showed that

you don't know Copperplate from..."

Don't know Copperplate from Caslon!

Q. "Is it Serious, Doctor? I'm so afraid."

"It is serious, but there is hope. A small..."

Q. "I'll do anything doctor. Just tell me what."

"There are only two possibilities: One is,

the next time someone comes to your front

Next time someone comes to your front...

Galena Bold • Typorium (Creative Alliance)

Next time someone comes to your front door,

Galena Bold Italic • Typorium (Creative Alliance)

Next time someone comes to your front door, and asks

Galena Condensed • Typorium (C. Alliance)

'Do You Need Any Fonts Identified Today?' invite

Galena Condensed Black • Typorium (C.A.)

him in immediately, and do not fear, just

Galena Condensed Black Italic • Typorium (C.A.)

open up and say 'I'm font illiterate. Please help.'

Galena Condensed Bold • Typorium (C. Alliance)

And when the door-to-door font person tells you the

Galena Condensed Bold Italic • Typorium (C.A.)

When you finally learn the names of some common fonts,

Galena Condensed Italic • Typorium (C. Alliance)

Just note that that fine volunteer was carrying

Galena Italic • Typorium (Creative Alliance)

THAT FINE VOLUNTEER WAS CARRYING THIS

Galena Small Caps • Typorium (Creative Alliance)

Yes, THAT CARING PERSON HAD THIS very

Galena Small Caps Bold • Typorium (C. Alliance)

This very Book was in the Font

Stancia • Typorium (Creative Alliance)

This book is The Cure." This is True.

Stancia Lyrica • Typorium (Creative Alliance)

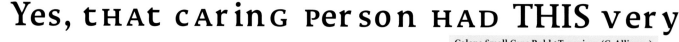

If you are by chance looking at

Stancia Lyrica—Black • Typorium (C. Alliance)

Quiz: Are you looking at this book

Stancia Lyrica—BlackItalic • Typorium (C.A.)

And secretly peeking at the small

Stancia Lyrica—Bold • Typorium (C. Alliance)

Q. Are you Peeking at the Fine Print

Stancia Lyrica—BoldItalic • Typorium (C.A.)

Checking to see the name of the Font?

Stancia Lyrica—Italic • Typorium (C. Alliance)

Do you have to do this for at least

Stancia—Black • Typorium (Creative Alliance)

If you do this at least twice per page

Stancia—BlackItalic • Typorium (C. Alliance)

Then you suffer from Font Illiteracy

Stancia—Bold • Typorium (Creative Alliance)

There is no shame to this. Just solve it.

Stancia—BoldItalic • Typorium (C. Alliance)

Buy this book. Get a plain brown bag.

Stancia—Italic • Typorium (Creative Alliance)

Quietly, get a plain brown bag, so even

CualaCaslon • Vintage Type Library

So Even your Best Friends Don't Know that

CualaCaslon—Italic • Vintage Type Library

No One Should Know You Have this Book.

PabstOldstyle • Vintage Type Library

Now, Take This Book to the Cashier. Buy

fiffiflſſ st ſi tt *Ti The Qu* ſ fiffiſiflſt ſi tt ſ

fiffi ſl ſſ st ſi tt *Ti The* *Qu*ſ fiffi ſi ſl st ſi tt

Buy the book, Take it Home and Read

ADGHJKMNOPQR nice swashes!

Yes, buy this book, take it home and read.

Read it in the Privacy of Your Own home

Even your Closest Friends Need not Know.

Nobody will know that you are a font illit

Font illiteracy Can Be Overcome. Now.

You Can Study This Book, Read it Every

Read it Every Night. Memorize Fonts.

You Will Soon Be Able To Speak

Speak the Language of Typography.

You will soon learn that thin hairline

This Hairline is not about baldness, it's

Thin Hairline is a Typographic Term

You will soon go to Parties, and,

Quickly, You Will Become a Font Name

Font Name Droppers are big Hits at Parties—

If those Parties Include Designers, Art Directors and

Creative People Will Perk Up When They

When They Hear You Say "Goudy Bold"

Or when you see a TV show title

And Quickly, You Identify the type face.

Suddenly, you become a Cult Hero Among

The Designer Crowd Will Admire you.

Bergamo • Title Wave Studios

You will be the hero of small children.

Bergamo Bold • Title Wave Studios

Small Children with Crayons Will ask

Bergamo BoldItalic • Title Wave Studios

Yes, young aspiring Art Directors will ask for

Bergamo Italic • Title Wave Studios

"PLEASE, MAY I HAVE YOUR AUTOGRAPH?"

Bergamo Sm Caps • Title Wave Studios

AND YOU WILL NOT WRITE YOUR NAME

Bergamo Sm Caps Bold • Title Wave Studios

You will Never Again Write Your Name in Cursive.

Caslon Antique • Title Wave Studios

No, you will print it, with Swashes. Maybe

Century Old Style • Title Wave Studios

Or maybe, you will print your name in

Century Old Style Bold • Title Wave Studios

Cheltenham Italic, or maybe you will even

Century Old Style Italic • Title Wave Studios

MAYBE YOU WILL USE LARGE & SMALL CAPS.

Century Old Style SC • Title Wave Studios

Nonetheless, You will be a Type Mogul.

Cheltenham • Title Wave Studios

All because you bought this book,

Cheltenham Bold • Title Wave Studios

and you Took the Time to become a

Cheltenham BoldItalic • Title Wave Studios

Yes, You Became a Typographic Genius. It can

Cheltenham Cond • Title Wave Studios

It can happen to you. While others will

Cheltenham Cond Bold • Title Wave Studios

Other People Will Watch Jeopardy, or maybe

Cheltenham Cond BoldItalic • Title Wave Studios

Or Maybe Watch Ben Stein's Money on Comedy

Cheltenham Cond Italic • Title Wave Studios

And while these people are good at answering trivia

Cheltenham Cond Light • Title Wave Studios

Others May Be Able to Answer Trivial Questions.

Cheltenham Cond LightItalic • Title Wave Studios

Hey, here's a Trivial Fact: Did You Know

Cheltenham Italic • Title Wave Studios

at Silver Spring High School one year,

Cheltenham Light • Title Wave Studios

there were two guys who were next-door

Cheltenham LightItalic • Title Wave Studios

Two guys were next-door neighbors and

Jenson Recut • Title Wave Studios

O
serif

One of them was Carl Bernstein, the

Jenson Recut Bold • Title Wave Studios

Q. Was this the Carl Bernstein of Watergate fame?

Jenson Recut Italic • Title Wave Studios

Yes, this was the same C. Bernstein,

As in Woodward & Bernstein.

Same Guy. And his next door

Bernstein lived next door to Ben

Yes, He & Ben Stein were neighbors. True.

One was a junior, the other a Senior.

And there were two other "I will be…"

"I will be famous someday" people were in the school.

A girl named Goldie Hawn was a sophomore. Yes.

And in the Freshman Class, there was a

Connie Chung was a Freshman

Imagine, all those people grew up

They all became Famous Later On.

Quietly, in high school, they were just

English Serif Bold • Title Wave Studios

They were Just Regular Kids, not Famous.

English Serif BoldItalic • Title Wave Studios

ALSO, DID YOU KNOW THAT AL GORE AND

English Serif SC • Title Wave Studios

GORE AND TOMMY LEE JONES WERE

English Serif SC Bold • Title Wave Studios

Gore and Tommy Lee Jones Were college

Flanders • Title Wave Studios

They Were College Roommates. Yes.

Flanders Bold • Title Wave Studios

At Harvard, of all places. Imagine that.

Flanders BoldItalic • Title Wave Studios

Anyway, that's the kind of trivia that

Flanders Italic • Title Wave Studios

Your friends Will Know Stuff Like that,

Savoy • Title Wave Studios

But Only YOU Will Know Fonts Stuff.

Savoy Bold • Title Wave Studios

Quickly, You Will Become the Font Guy,

Savoy Italic • Title Wave Studios

OR FONT PERSON, TO BE LESS SEXIST. OK?

Savoy Sm Caps • Title Wave Studios

DON'T WRITE ME NOTES, I UNDERSTAND.

Savoy Sm Caps Bole • Title Wave Studios

Quickly, I do understand. My two

My two Daughters Use "guys" to

Guys can also mean women, they say.

Anyway, You Will Become The Font Guru.

You Will Be able to Say "See the 18º..."

"That Font has an 18-degree Italic..."

People Will Marvel at Your Knowledge.

Some May be Awe-Stricken by your

Your Knowledge Will Surprise All.

And, just by buying this book and

ONCE YOU BECOME FONT LITERATE, YOU WILL

Quietly, You Will Forever Avoid Having

Quickly, you Will Become a Font Person.

O
serif

And You Will Never Ever Have to Go

Quickly, You will Avoid The Social Stigma of

You will Never, Ever, Have to Go To

Imagine The Shame of Going to a

Meeting of Font Illiterates Anonymous.

The Shame* of Meeting *Your New Help

The Shame of Going Before the Group and

saying to The Strangers There, "Hi, I'm Dave."

"Hi, I'm David and I'm a Font Illiterate.'

The Shame, Oh, The High Degree of Shame.

Quietly, People Admit They Don't Know Squat.

O
serif

Quit Pretending! Do you Know Squat?

Quit Acting. Font Illiteracy is Rampant. It

Font Illiteracy is Shameful. But there

New Baskerville • Title Wave Studios

Yes, Buy This Book. No Longer will

New Baskerville Bold • Title Wave Studios

You Can Hang Out With Top Designers.

New Baskerville BoldItalic • Title Wave Studios

Quickly, You Will be Part of The in-group.

New Baskerville Italic • Title Wave Studios

Quickly, Art Directors Will embrace

New Baskerville SemiBold • Title Wave Studios

You Will Be Embraced by Art Directors.

New Baskerville SemiBoldItalic • T. Wave Studios

Designers Will Have Great Respect for

Gareth • Title Wave Studios

Once you Can Say "Sans Serif, Italic"

Gareth Bold • Title Wave Studios

Quietly, You Gain Respect. Type is the

Gareth BoldItalic • Title Wave Studios

Queens Will Knight You. Typography is

Gareth Italic • Title Wave Studios

Typographic Wisdom Will Be Yours,

Glytus • Title Wave Studios

All Because you Bought This Book.

Glytus Bold • Title Wave Studios

Attractive People Will Seek you Out

Glytus BoldItalic • Title Wave Studios

And Think How Proud Your Parents

Your Parents Will Be Proud of Your Typo

Your Typographic Knowledge Will Be the

Quickly, your Mother's friends Will All

Every friend Will Share Your Success in

Your Command of Typography Knowledge

They will Talk About Your Childhood, and

How other Children Were Learning A-B-C,

And you were actually identifying

While other kids just knew letters, A-B-C,

You Would Quickly Name the Font, that will

THAT WILL BE THE STORY, EVEN IF IT'S NOT

EVEN IF IT'S NOT TRUE, THE STORY WILL

The Story Will be Told at Family

At Family Reunions, Your Name

Your Name Will become legendary.

Uncles Will Say, "I used to buy that kid..."

Yes, he will tell about buying crayons,

and Small Children Will Want to be

They Will Want to be Just Like You.

The Typographer. You. Fame.

It's hard to imagine that now, as you

As you flip through this book, to see

Reading a line here, another there, and

IT'S HARD TO IMAGINE THAT YOU COULD

ALL THESE GOOD THINGS MIGHT JUST

These Good Things Just Could

It Could All Happen to YOU, *just*

because You Bought This book.

This Book Will Become The Whole

This will become the Whole Reason For Your

Your Success Will Center On This Book,

and Someday, When you're Getting a Major

You get a Major Award for Design,

and Art Directors are applauding,

And when the ovation is over, you will

you will Give Your Acceptance Speech.

O serif

And Quietly, You will Tell The Assembly

about the Quiet Day you Got This Book,

and how your life is now divided

You divide your Life into Two

Your life has two parts: Before &

Before you Bought This Book, and

AFTER YOU BOUGHT THIS BOOK.

YES, YOU ARE FACING A TURNING POINT.

This Could Be The Turning Point in

Your Career is at a Crossroads now.

Buy this book, become a Typograph

Become a Typographic Genius,

and Fame, Fortune, and Happiness

O *serif*

Or, take the other path, and the scene

The Whole Scene Changes. Don't buy

Don't Buy This Book. Remain a Typograp

IF YOU REMAIN A TYPOGRAPHIC ILLITERATE,

the Future is Very Bleak Indeed, but

the Choice is Yours. This Book is

This Book is the Key to Everything you ever wanted.

Take this to the Cashier. Now. Before it's too late.

O
serif

I

I

I

All the fonts shown in this book are available for purchase. Information on each company is shown below. For your convenience, each company is color-coded to match the identification shown in the fonts section of this book.

2 Rebels

2 Rebels
6300 Parc Avenue
Suite 420
Montréal, Quebec
Canada H2V 4H8
t: 888.538.9550
    514.278.9550 (Montréal)
www.2rebels.com

Aerotype

Aerotype
501 West Glenoaks Blvd #523
Glendale, CA 91202
t: 800.865.2718
    818.841.7120
f: 818.843.7153
e: catalog@aerotype.com
www.aerotype.com.

Comicraft

Comicraft
Active Images
430 Colorado Avenue, Suite 301
Santa Monica, CA 90401
t: 310.458.9094
f: 310.451.9761
e: rita@comicbookfonts.com
www.comicbookfonts.com

Creative Alliance

Agfa Monotype Corporation
200 Ballardvale Street
Wilmington, MA 01887
t: 800.424.8973
www.studio.agfamonotype.com

International Typeface Corporation
200 Ballardvale Street
Wilmington, MA 01887
t: 866.823.5828
www.itcfonts.com

flashfonts

flashfonts.com
261 South Orange Drive
Los Angeles, CA 90036
t: 323.kix.0700
www.flashfonts.com

Fonthead Design

Fonthead Design
3210 S Landsdowne Drive
Wilmington, DE 19810
t: 302.479.7922
f: 302.479.7923
e: sales@fonthead.com
www.fonthead.com

P22

P22 Type Foundry
P.O. Box 770
Buffalo, NY 14213-0770
t: 716.885.4490
e: p22@p22.com
www.p22.com

Synfonts

Synstelien Designs
2216 Cedar Forks Trace
Marietta, GA 30062
t: 888.842.3065
    402.968.0147
www.synfonts.com

Title Wave Studios

Title Wave Studios
2787 Sandy Drive
Camano Island, WA 98282
f: 360.387.3486
e: info@fontsite.com
www.fontsite.com

Treacyfaces

Treacyfaces, Inc.
P.O. Box 26036
West Haven, CT 06516-8036
www.treacyfaces.com

Typeart

TypeArt Foundry Inc.
t: 800.BUY.TYPE
    604.602.0331
www.typeart.com

Vintage Type Library

Vintage Type
t: 800.656.5426
e: info@vintagetype.com
www.vintagetype.com

I

Free Fonts

All the following were actively offering free fonts as of the publication date:
www.007fonts.com
http://fonts.tom7.com
www.fontpool.com
www.coolarchive.com
www.fontsnthings.com
www.chank.com
www.sunwalk.com